About Island Press

Since 1984, the nonprofit organization Island Press has been stim-
ulating, shaping, and communicating ideas that are essential for
solving environmental problems worldwide. With more than 1,000
titles in print and some 30 new releases each year, we are the
nation's leading publisher on environmental issues. We identify innovative thinkers and emerging trends in the environmental
field. We work with world-renowned experts and authors to
develop cross-disciplinary solutions to environmental challenges.

Island Press designs and executes educational campaigns, in
conjunction with our authors, to communicate their critical mes-
sages in print, in person, and online using the latest technologies,
innovative programs, and the media. Our goal is to reach targeted
audiences—scientists, policy makers, environmental advocates,
urban planners, the media, and concerned citizens—with information that can be used to create the framework for long-term
ecological health and human well-being.

Island Press gratefully acknowledges major support from The
Bobolink Foundation, Caldera Foundation, The Curtis and Edith
Munson Foundation, The Forrest C. and Frances H. Lattner Foundation,
The JPB Foundation, The Kresge Foundation, The Summit Charitable
Foundation, Inc., and many other generous organizations and indi-
viduals.

The opinions expressed in this book are those of the author(s)
and do not necessarily reflect the views of our supporters.

THE BLUE REVOLUTION

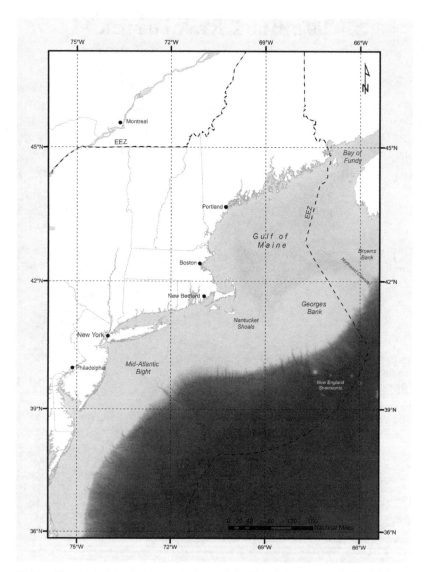

Fishing Grounds off the Northeastern Coast of the United States. The Gulf of Maine, Georges Bank, Nantucket Shoals, and the Mid-Atlantic Bight are major fishing grounds off the US Northeast coast. The light gray shade in this ocean map denotes the continental shelf of the United States. The dotted line denotes the US exclusive economic zone, 200 miles off the coast, and also marks the division between Canadian and US waters in Georges Bank and the Gulf of Maine. Copyright Michelle Bachman.

The Blue Revolution

Hunting, Harvesting, and Farming Seafood in the Information Age

Nicholas P. Sullivan

Barton

Many Thanks for your contributions and support on this book — at well at your great seafood advocacy.

with regard,

N P Sullivan

ISLANDPRESS | Washington | Covelo

Library of Congress Control Number: 2021943376

All Island Press books are printed on environmentally responsible materials.

Manufactured in the United States of America
10 9 8 7 6 5 4 3 2 1

Keywords: Island Press, 3D farming, aquaculture, bivalves, blue carbon, bluefin
tuna, BlueTech, bycatch, carbon buffer, cod, Community Supported Fisheries
(CSFs), dam removals, farmed fish, finfish, fish quotas, forage fish, Georges Bank,
groundfish, Gulf of Maine, Innovasea, Integrated Multi-Trophic Aquaculture
(IMTA), IUU fishing, kelp, Magnuson-Stevens Act, mariculture, Marine
Protected Areas (MPAs), Maximum Sustainable Yield (MSY), mussels, New
Bedford, New England Fisheries Management Council, NOAA Fisheries, ocean
acidification, Ocean Clusters, ocean farming, ocean warming, overfishing, oysters,
phytoplankton, Recirculating Aquaculture Systems (RAS), restorative farming,
river herring, salmon, shellfish, sustainable fishing, underutilized fish, wild fish

For my wife, Deborah Kovacs,
who swims with the fishes,
for her love, support, encouragement, and advice.

Contents

Preface

The Blue Revolution, Version 2.0

This book is about the transformation of commercial fishing—from maximizing volume to maximizing value, from wild hunting to controlled harvesting and farming. It's about sensible stakeholders staring at a "tragedy of the commons" that has depleted a global, natural resource—and collaborating to preserve the resource and its ocean habitat. Commercial fishing, long a traditional throwback industry, is moving in fits and starts into the postindustrial age—propelled by the Fourth Industrial Revolution of big data, sensors, machine learning, and artificial intelligence. The fish in our stores and on our plates are increasingly the product of smart decisions about ecosystems, environment, waste, efficiency, transparency, and quality.

The Blue Revolution of the 1980s, which followed the agricultural Green Revolution that started in the 1960s, was largely an Asian phenomenon that focused on doubling production of farmed freshwater fish, such as carp and tilapia. Over the last two decades, the Blue Revolution has spread around the world and moved into a new phase—increasingly focused on marine species and increasingly dependent on digital tools and new technologies for both wild-capture and farmed seafood. This transformation of seafood production represents a dramatic pullback from the relentless industrial hunting of fish that started after World War II and peaked in the 1990s, and the industrial farming of fish that began in earnest in the 1990s.

This book's subject matter is global, but the framing lens is New England, where American commercial fishing started in the precolonial era, as arguably the country's first industry. For centuries, the legendary hunting grounds of Georges Bank and the Gulf of Maine—the nutrient-rich waters fueled by the interaction between the cold, south-flowing Labrador Current and the warm, north-flowing Gulf Stream—have made commercial fishing an integral part of New England's socioeconomic fabric. In terms of seafood value, Maine ranks second in the nation, largely thanks to lobsters, and Massachusetts third, largely thanks to scallops (Alaska is first, thanks to wild salmon and pollock). New England is also home to the top-value (New Bedford) and oldest (Gloucester) American ports, the oldest fish pier (Boston), and numerous world-class, ocean-research institutes and universities that are collaborating with fishermen and fish farmers to modernize the industry.

New England is a good case study for the rise, fall, and rebirth of an ancient industry. Focusing on a historic fishing region that is driving or adopting new models shines a light on ways to maintain healthy and sustainable wild-capture and mariculture (marine aquaculture) industries. That has relevance for every other fishing nation and region. And, as the world's top importer of fish, the United States has leverage to change the way the world's top-traded food is produced and distributed.

I have been following this industry since I was in college in the 1970s, when I watched and wrote about Russian factory ships from the shores of Cape Cod. I was taken by the fact that fishermen in Chatham on Cape Cod had formed a cooperative to combat the Russian incursion, while fishermen in New Bedford kept to their individualistic, free-market ways. That foreign plunder of the hallowed Georges Bank fishing grounds—first fished by the Basques in AD 1000—led to the introduction of the 200-mile territorial limit in 1976.

Since the 1980s, I have lived near New Bedford. I have watched as government subsidies in the 1980s enabled American fishermen to buy bigger boats and ravage the fish stock as the Russians had been doing a decade before—which led to the slow but steady collapse of cod stocks in the northwest Atlantic Ocean. I saw the shutdown of the Atlantic sea-scallop industry in the 1990s and its rebirth in 2000—thanks to collaboration between fishermen, scientists, and regulators. Scallopers morphed from hunters into harvesters, rotating beds like land farmers to protect the resource. As a result, scalloping has blossomed into a nearly $600 million fishery.

Thanks to strong US fishery management, there are now more groundfish (bottom-feeding fish) in the Greater Atlantic Region (ranging from Cape Hatteras to the maritime boundary between the United States and Canada) than there were 20 or 30 years ago. After a 50-year oscillating wave of crisis and response, this recent fishing rebound seems different. The demise of the Atlantic cod (in part a function of an unanticipated *acceleration* of warming in the Gulf of Maine) was a real wakeup call for scientists, regulators, and fishermen. Now, with sensors, underwater cameras, robotics, satellite imagery, and advanced data-analytic tools, all stakeholders are refining their view of the marine ecosystem. The Global Fishing Watch website, for example, allows a near-real-time view and location of most large fishing boats on the oceans at any time, a breakthrough in transparency.

In the late 1970s, I wrote a proposal for a book called *Fish Tales*, which was more about fishermen than fish as food. I saw fishermen as nineteenth-century Americans, rugged individualists who were anti-union and anti-government, and who didn't take subsidies like dirt and dairy farmers did. They lived in another world. They were cowboys of the sea.

I never finished that book. I went into the magazine world, writing and editing stories about business, technology, and, eventually, development economics. And that, some 40 years later, brought me back to fishing. Food security is, of course, a pillar of development economics, and in many parts of the world fish is the main source of protein. More than 3 billion people now get 20 percent of their protein from fish (second only to milk as a protein source); that number is 26 percent in developing countries, according to the United Nations' Food and Agriculture Organization. Fish is lean protein that also provides essential vitamins and minerals—and omega-3 fatty acids. As the world population edges toward 10 billion and more people eat more fish, demand for fish will continue to increase. Between 1990 and 2018, global fish consumption rose by 122 percent.

Given the stress on wild-fish stocks in the ocean, where are the fish going to come from? The short answer is from farmed fish, which already account for more than half the fish eaten globally. But wild fish, at roughly half of today's production, are still a big part of the answer, especially as wild hunting morphs into sustainable harvesting. That's happening in the United States and a significant swath of the rest of the world.

As for farmed fish, there are clear ecological and environmental benefits compared to meat production—what I call "fish for a small planet" after the best-selling *Diet for a Small Planet* (Frances Moore Lappé) in the 1970s. Fish production uses less space (a water farm is a three-dimensional farm), almost no land or water (ocean water suffices and land-based fish farms recirculate most of the water they use), and fish have a far superior food-conversion ratio compared to land animals (given the physiology of fish and their ability to efficiently convert feed into energy and protein).

Most reporting about commercial fishing laments the decline of wild fish due to overfishing and the negative side effects of fish farming. That reflects, and contributes to, the largely negative public perception of both wild and farmed fish—a perception seemingly fixed 20 or more years ago when environmental nongovernmental organizations filed numerous lawsuits against the fishing industry and its regulators to bring an end to overfishing and protect against accidental bycatch. There is no denying the ongoing major problems afflicting global fisheries: illegal, unreported, unregulated fishing; degradation of mangrove swamps and the sea-floor; and use of drift nets (outlawed by the United Nations in 1992) that collect everything from sea birds to turtles to sharks to tunas and octopi. And there is too much waste; nearly 60 percent of most landed fish goes unused or is converted to low-value pet food and fertilizer.

Those are the issues that attract public attention, as they should. What is less often reported and thus less well known is the twenty-first-century transformation of the country's original industry—transformation from unsustainable to sustainable, from sustainable to restorative, from industrial to postindustrial. A growing "fishie" movement parallels the decades-old locavore "foodie" movement. New entrepreneurs and investors are developing ways to create more value from fish beyond the food product, which helps lessen fishing pressure and provides new business opportunities in coastal communities.

Global fisheries aren't done yet. They are slowly joining the Fourth Industrial Revolution, giving more than a ray of hope for the last commercially hunted wild food. Illegal fishing, climate change, and conservation are certainly major worries. But the good news is that mariculture has significantly reduced its negative side effects as it has scaled. On the wild side, marine extinctions are negligible to date and fish stocks have shown that they will rebound quickly if protected.

That is the story I want to tell, and I do so by telling the stories of people who are changing this ancient industry.

Notes on the Book

Structure. The book is split more or less evenly between wild-capture fisheries and mariculture—with a shorter concluding section on the global challenges of illegal fishing, conservation, and climate change.

Endnotes. I use endnotes to source third-party material from newspapers, magazines, books, and websites. The exception is quotes from people (more than 100) I interviewed. If there is no endnote, the quote is from a direct interview with me.

The term "fishermen." I generally default to the Slow Fish USA (an outgrowth of the international Slow Food organization) approach: "In the US context, 'fishermen' is an inclusive and gender-neutral term for us, and the one used most commonly among women in our network who fish. It's meant to refer to those who might also use the terms fish harvesters, fisherwomen, fishermisses, fishers, and intertidal gatherers, as well as those practicing restorative aquaculture on a sustainable scale."

I have mostly followed this practice, as most wild-capture fishermen are male. That is less true in mariculture, which is attracting women scientists and entrepreneurs, and artisanal fisheries are dominated by women, so I sometimes use the gender-neutral term "fishers."

The art. Each chapter opens with a fish print created by Stephanie Mason. A graduate of the Rhode Island School of Design, Mason was a textile designer in New York and Boston before she moved to Gloucester, Massachusetts, and became intrigued by the nineteenth-century Japanese folk art of Gyotaku, the painting and rubbing of fish to preserve a record of the size of the species. Each print includes a Japanese "hanko" (or "chop") as a signature.

"The process starts by painting a dead fish, placing paper directly onto it, then gently rubbing to produce a unique and beautiful art form," says Mason. "Throughout this journey, I have documented many species that are now under strict fishing regulations." Most of the fish she paints are caught off the coast of New England.

PART I

Wild-Capture Fisheries

When people hear about overfishing, they may think fish are disappearing. Some stocks are certainly in distress, but overfishing is not the only reason. Fish go through sometimes inexplicable spawning cycles, and climate change is changing habitats. In countries with strong regulatory regimes, like the United States, fish are generally sustainably harvested, meaning stocks will continue to yield if fishermen stick to their catch quotas.

Globally, the proportion of fish stocks that are within "biologically sustainable levels" was roughly 66 percent in 2017; in terms of landings, a more important metric, roughly 79 percent of marine fish landings were from biologically sustainable stocks, according to the Food and Agriculture Organization of the United Nations. Of course, these numbers usually don't include the huge artisanal, small boat catch in many parts of the world.

Seafood is the world's top traded food commodity, and the United States is the largest importer in the world. The quip is that Boston's Logan Airport is the top fishing port in the country—because Americans export most of what they catch and import most of what they eat. But an emerging "local-catch" and community-supported fishery movement may be breaking that global supply chain and introducing consumers to hitherto underutilized but plentiful species. In addition, more fishermen are selling both fresh and flash-frozen fish direct to consumers. And entrepreneurs and "innovation clusters" are devising new ways to hunt and farm more efficiently, and to get more value from landed fish, which increases profits for fishermen and lessens fishing pressure.

ATLANTIC COD

Chapter 1

Sacred Cod,
Sustainable Scallops

*It is the same old story. The buffalo is gone; the whale is disappearing;
the seal fishery is threatened with destruction. Fish need protection.*
—Edwin W. Gould, Maine's fishery commissioner, 1892

"I am a pirate," Carlos Rafael once told a group of federal regulators at a New England Fisheries Management Council meeting. "It's your job to catch me."[1] And they did.

Rafael, aka the "Codfather" for his ruthless command of the docks, was one of the most successful fishermen on the East Coast. Originally from the island of Flores in the Azores, Rafael owned more than forty boats, both scallopers and groundfishing trawlers, in New Bedford, the top-value fishing port in the United States for the last 20 years. Most boats were painted green and emblazoned with his trademark "CR"; many had Greek names like Poseidon, Hercules, and Hera; some had Portuguese names like Acores and Ilha do Corvo (an Azorean island). In 2015, he employed 285 fishermen and paid them salaries of $12 million. He paid out another $4 million to local businesses for repairs, equipment, and supplies.[2] Rafael was said to control 25 percent of groundfishing on the East Coast. Writer Ben Goldfarb described Rafael in *Mother Jones* as a "stocky mogul with drooping jowls, a smooth pate, and a backstory scripted by Horatio Alger and Machiavelli." Rafael called his smaller competitors "mosquitos on the balls of elephants."[3]

Rafael is not necessarily representative of today's fishermen, but he was the epitome and one of the last vestiges of an old-fashioned, cutthroat hunter from the "good old days" in an industry now being modernized by regulatory checks and balances to protect habitat and fish stocks.

In 2016, after an undercover sting, he was arrested and eventually indicted on charges of conspiracy, tax evasion, bulk cash smuggling, and submitting falsified records to the federal government to evade federal fishing quotas. In addition to his boats, the Codfather owned distributors on the docks. When he caught fish subject to strict catch limits, like cod or yellowtail flounder, he would report it as haddock, or some other plentiful species. He mislabeled an estimated 782,000 pounds of fish over a 4-year period, 2012–2015.[4] Rafael got away with it for years because he laundered the illegal fish through his own whole-salers in New Bedford and fish dealers in New York City.

"We call them something else, it's simple, we've been doing it for over 30 years," Rafael told two Russian-speaking undercover IRS agents, who feigned interest in buying his business. Rafael was asking $175 million, even though his books showed $21 million in assets. "This year I'll have 15 million pounds of haddock. So I can sell any son-of-a-bitch haddock if the bastards are not there. I rename them. Even when they're there, I disappear them. I could never catch 15 million pounds. It's impossible."[5]

Rafael described a deal he had going with a New York fish buyer, at South Street Sea Foods, a convicted felon, who bought mislabeled fish in exchange for bags of cash, what Rafael called "jingles." "You'll never find a better laundromat," Rafael told the *New York Times*.[6] Rafael told the IRS agents he had received $668,000 in cash from New York for his mislabeled fish; it later turned out he had worked with a local (Bristol County) deputy sheriff to smuggle bags of cash to his native Portugal, without clearing customs.[7] "You could be the IRS in here. This could be a clusterfuck, so I'm trusting you. The only thing is, I open myself because both of you is Russians and I don't think they would have two Russians. Fuck me—that would be some bad luck!"[8]

Caught on tape, the jig was up. The undercover agents were part of a joint investigation by the IRS and the National Oceanic and Atmospheric Administration (NOAA). In 2018, Rafael, 65, pled guilty to conspiracy, false labeling of fish, bulk cash smuggling, tax evasion, and falsifying federal records. He was fined $3 million, enjoined from fishing ever again, and sentenced to four years in jail—and the Feds impounded fourteen of his groundfish boats for more than a year to compensate for his past sins of overfishing. That left just seven ground-fishing boats active in New Bedford and cost its economy $500,000 a day in lost revenues and 300 jobs in the supply chain, as landings dropped by 25 percent. In a port that has seen ups and downs since the whaling era of the nineteenth century, this was a new low.

The story of the Codfather, a modern-day, self-professed pirate, is an allegory for the antiscience, wild-capture, fish industry. In New Bedford, where the fishing industry was built on its bountiful cod, yel-lowtail flounder, and scallop catch from Georges Bank and the Gulf of Maine, a cutthroat hunter illegally caught cod, lied about it, and did time—while inflicting serious harm on the whole fleet and local suppliers.

Many in New Bedford—fishermen, politicians, media, and the gen-eral public—conflated the demise of the Codfather with the demise of the cod itself, a signal that the groundfish fleet had hit rock bottom. And it wasn't just cod; yellowtail flounder was also in distress—and New Bedford had once been known as a "flounder port." Ground-fish ports all over New England—Portland, Maine; Portsmouth, New Hampshire; Gloucester, Massachusetts; Point Judith, Rhode Island—were taking a hit. The number of groundfishing vessels in New England dropped from roughly 350 in 2000 to double digits in 2020.

Meanwhile, the cod have more or less disappeared, maybe into can-yons in the Gulf of Maine, maybe to the Barents Sea in the Arctic Ocean, where cod stocks seem stable. Or maybe they have just dis-appeared after the intense overfishing of the late twentieth century. In the 1980s and early 1990s, fishermen annually landed over 60,000 metric tons of Georges Bank cod and 20,000 metric tons of Gulf of Maine cod. In 2018, fishermen caught a mere 887 metric tons of Georges Bank cod and only 504 metric tons of Gulf of Maine cod.[9]

In fact, cod have been disappearing since the Civil War. Histori-cal records indicate that massive populations of this predominantly bottom-feeding (hence "groundfish") species were targeted by Basque fishermen around AD 1000 and kept secret for 500 years.[10] In 1850, the total biomass of Atlantic cod was approximately 10.2 billion tons, according to in-depth research by the Sea Around Us project at the University of British Columbia, headed by eminent fisheries biologist Daniel Pauly. Information regarding the size of the Atlantic cod population circa 1850 was gathered from an analysis of mid-nineteenth-century logbooks maintained by a handline fleet that fished the Scotian Shelf (off the coast of Labrador), the center of the range of Northwestern Atlantic cod, prior to the industrialization of fishing.[11] By 2005, Pauly and post-doc researcher Ashley McCrea Strub estimated that this biomass had been reduced to roughly 3.5 percent of its initial size in 1850.[12]

Deepwater trawlers, which became prevalent after World War II, pierced one of the cod's protective mechanisms—depth. "Depth was once a vault for the cod, when fishing gear only went down 150 feet or so," says Pauly. "The cod could duck under that, but not now."

Massachusetts and the Atlantic cod go way back (Pacific cod is a different species), so the recent "disappearance" is a blow to the solar plexus for New England fishermen as well as New England at large. In 1642, Gloucester, Massachusetts, was given a charter to profit from the fishing of cod—a fish that can live 20 years, grow to more than 4 feet long, and weigh as much as 50 pounds. The sculptor and architect Maya Lin, who created an artistic timeline of cod, said, "We don't realize that a cod was bigger than a man in 1895."[13] In Boston, a painted carving of a "sacred cod" has hung in the state house since 1784, when it was said you could walk across Boston Harbor on the backs of cod. Cape Cod got its name from the fish.

Canada and the cod go back even farther, 500 years. In Canada, inshore small-boat fishermen noticed the cod beginning to disappear from their net traps in the mid-1980s, but the loss was initially masked by huge offshore catches taken by deepwater trawlers. It turns out that scientists assessing the stock had focused on those trawlers and ignored the nearshore fishermen.[14] In 1992, the Canadian government placed a moratorium on cod fishing, immediately putting 19,000 fishermen in Newfoundland out of work, and another 20,000 jobs were lost or severely diminished. Today, Canadian quotas are minimal, although the stock is now rebuilt to 25 percent of its 1980s level.[15]

Overfishing is certainly the primary cause of the decline, but there are other possible explanations. Brian Rothschild, the founding dean of UMass Dartmouth's School for Marine Science & Technology, noted that in the 1990s the growth rate of individual cod had declined, fish were skinnier than before, and the mortality rate had quadrupled. "The weight-to-length ratio went down, so that instead of looking like a fish, a cod looked more like a snake," he said in a talk at the New Bedford Fishing Heritage Center in 2012. "Natural mortality increased substantially during the population decline. The populations of species associated with cod also declined. So the crash was not obviously related to fishing, as declines in growth, length-weight and increases in natural mortality are unrelated to fishing."[16]

Clearly, something else was affecting the fish, perhaps nutrition, due to the lower levels of capelin, herring, and mackerel—food sources that have been scooped up by trawlers with small-mesh nets, which also collect juvenile cod. Perhaps the out-of-control gray seal population, which feast on cod, has had an effect. And, of course, warming ocean water likely reduced reproduction and drove cod to colder waters.

On top of overfishing, the Gulf of Maine is warming faster than 99 percent of the world's oceans, which is clearly stressing and changing the whole marine ecosystem. The warm Gulf Stream is extending farther up the Atlantic coast, and the cold, nutrient-rich Labrador Current from the Arctic is warming as glaciers melt. The admixture of these two super currents creates the upwelling of nutrients to feed the phytoplankton (minuscule algae) that wander near the surface of the ocean but sit at the bottom of the marine food web. It just happens that cod were one of the main pieces of the Gulf of Maine and Georges Bank ecosystems, which have been changing as currents shift and the water warms (see chapter 2).

"In really warm years, every female cod produces fewer babies than we would expect, and we also see that the young fish are less likely to survive and become adults," Andrew Pershing, at the time an oceanographer at the Gulf of Maine Research Institute, noted in *Science Magazine* in 2015. It was the first paper to explicitly link ocean warming to the cod decline.[17]

In 1994, the United States followed Canada's suit and closed three major areas of Georges Bank, a 6,600-square-mile area on the rich continental shelf (shallow submarine plateau) that has long been one of the world's hallowed fishing grounds. Cod migrate back and forth between the United States and Canada across the Hague Line that marks sovereign waters on the Eastern edge of Georges Bank. To a much lesser degree, cod also migrate between Georges Bank and the Gulf of Maine, and NOAA, a division of the Commerce Department that runs NOAA Fisheries (also called the National Marine Fisheries Service), considers them different stocks in its assessments. Besides Atlantic cod stocks in the United States and Canada, other stocks are found in Iceland, the North Sea, Celtic Sea, and White Sea (part of the Barents Sea). An Arcto-Norwegian stock is in another part of the Barents Sea.

The New England Fisheries Management Council, one of eight regional councils in the United States that manages fisheries, recommended the closure after scientists determined that the fishery could be saved only if fishing in certain areas was reduced to zero. The 1993 catch of cod, haddock, and flounder was down 23 percent from the previous year, which itself had been a down year. Other changes in management included days-at-sea restrictions, an increase in net mesh sizes (to let juveniles escape), and a vessel buyback program to reduce the size of the fleet after the government inadvertently expanded it with subsidized loans in the 1970s and 1980s. In addition to cod, fishing for scallops and yellowtail flounder was also scaled way back. The flounder stock was dangerously depleted, and the bulk of scallops were dangerously small, many below harvestable size.

Fishermen didn't like this, even though fishermen sit on the Council. "One scientist says one thing and another scientist says something else," Gloucester fisherman Jay Spurling told the *Christian Science Monitor*.[18] "They're not even out on the water; they don't see the things we see. So few people eat fish and the ocean is so big, I think they're making a huge mistake."

The decision set in motion a seemingly never-ending battle that engaged at various times regulators, fishermen, environmentalists, politicians, and the courts—a battle of rolling lawsuits that began in 1992 and ran through 2005. In 2000, five environmental groups brought suit against NOAA Fisheries for not doing enough to prevent over-fishing. In 2001, US District Court Judge Gladys Kessler ruled against NOAA Fisheries and ordered it to come up with a solution. In 2002, Judge Kessler imposed the most restrictive fishing limits ever on New England fishermen, closing more areas to fishing and cutting the days-at-sea limit from 88 to 70. The judge later abandoned the order, saying it would cause too much economic pain, and deferred to a new plan agreed to by environmentalists and fishermen.[19]

In 2002, during this legal wrangling, fishermen discovered that the R/V (research vessel) *ALBATROSS IV* (R 342), a scientific-survey vessel, had incorrectly set its trawl net and generally mismanaged the tow. NOAA's Northeast Fisheries Science Center admitted that over the previous two years the survey trawl net had been incorrectly set, according to the Fishing Heritage Center in New Bedford. Need-less to say, such revelations infuriated fishermen, who had for years suspected invalid stock assessments. Adding fuel to the fire, NOAA Fisheries claimed the faulty surveys had no impact on stock assess-ments. Fishermen and local media dubbed this fiasco "Trawl-Gate."

In 2004, NOAA Fisheries began a 10-year rebuilding plan for Gulf of Maine cod. The plan held until NOAA Fisheries declared in 2008 that the stock was healthy and headed toward recovery. "Stock pro-jected to rebuild rapidly," stated the report. But that didn't happen, as in 2011, another study suggested the stock was in dismal shape and would not rebuild by 2014. Apparently, the 2008 report, which cited data from heavy cod spawning in 2005, overstated the number of spawning fish by 300 percent. As always, the fishermen were see-ing something different on the water. Gloucester fisherman Vito Gia-calone saw it as another instance of fishery science conflicting with "all the other indicators of common sense."[20] He said fishermen were catching more cod in less time, in more areas, and with a wider range of age and size.

In 2010, NOAA Fisheries switched from a days-at-sea regulatory regime to a catch-quota regime, which limited the volume of fish any boat could take in a year. That was another dagger in the hearts of fishermen—hunters had seen grounds close and open and close, and were being told when, where, and how much to hunt. Later, in 2015, they were told to take government observers on board—and pay for them! In 2020, NOAA Fisheries had 891 observers, all professionally trained biological scientists.

In 2014, the United States announced that the Gulf of Maine cod rebuild would be extended to 2024, and the rebuild of Georges Bank cod would be extended until 2027. John Bullard, then the administrator of NOAA Fisheries' Greater Atlantic Region, appearing at a hearing of the New England Fisheries Management Council in 2014, was harangued by fishermen about the surveys that had led to various restrictions. One said, "You lie for a living!" Bullard responded: "You owe me an apology. I'm probably not going to get one, but I deserve one!" Later he said, "Hunters go where the fish are and scientists have sampling protocols; they look for consistent patterns in grids across a large region rather than single sightings. That's a recipe for distrust between scientists and fishermen."

In 2014, government scientists saw cod reduced to 1 percent of its 1980s biomass, while fishermen saw big aggregations, notably right outside Gloucester Harbor. Fishermen had said the same thing in 1994, when Georges Bank was shut down. Raymond Mayo, a marine biologist for NOAA Fisheries at Woods Hole at the time, called this a perception problem. "You see some cod and assume this is the tip of the iceberg," he told Mark Kurlansky, author of *Cod: A Biography of the Fish That Changed the World*. "But it could be the whole iceberg."[21]

"The cod were aggregating, which is what they do when there aren't many of them left," said Bullard after the 2014 announcement. They may have been visible in pockets, especially in the Western Gulf of Maine, one of cod's main spawning grounds, but they were otherwise scarce. This observation conforms to the "Allee effect," first described in the 1930s by its namesake, Warder Clyde Allee, who suggested that aggregation can improve the survival rate of individuals and that cooperation may be crucial in the overall evolution of social structure. At the time, the traditional theory of population dynamics was that a species will grow more slowly at a higher density and faster at a lower density. But Allee demonstrated that the reverse holds true when a population density is low and *under duress*. Individuals, he said, often require the assistance of others for more than simple reproductive reasons in order to persist, just as animals hunt or defend against predators as a group.[22] This would not have been news to Charles Darwin, who had written in *On the Origin of Species* that "a large stock of individuals of the same species, relative to the number of its enemies, is absolutely necessary for its preservation."[23]

American landings of Atlantic cod were worth $118 million in 1991; by 2014, when the Codfather was passing off cod as haddock two years before his arrest, cod landings were worth a mere $9 million—what NOAA Fisheries' Bullard called "the biggest collapse of a fish species in such a short timeframe in more than 100 years."

"Rusty Red" Scallops: Once Hunted, Now Harvested

"The groundfish industry has contracted significantly on the East Coast, as everybody knows, and what's left of it is concentrated in New Bedford, but its overall share of the landings in the port are quite small," New Bedford Mayor Jon Mitchell said in 2017. "Less than 10 percent of the value of the annual landings of the port of New Bedford come from groundfish these days."[24]

That is the hard truth: The iconic cod had really become a small part of the food value chain in the Greater Atlantic Region (ranging from Cape Hatteras to the maritime boundary with Canada). The real money is in lobster and scallops, worth an estimated $668 million and $572 million, respectively, in 2019. Nationally, the top-value fishery is wild Pacific salmon, followed by lobster, crab (of various types), and Atlantic scallops.[25] The top-volume fish in the United States is typically Alaskan pollock, which is often the top catch in the world (annually vying for that honor with Peruvian anchoveta). The future of groundfish on the East Coast may be in hitherto underutilized species, such as skate, monkfish, redfish, dogfish, and Atlantic pollock, along with haddock, a boom-and-bust species (now booming).

For the moment, scallops have replaced groundfish—yellowtail flounder even more so than cod—in the New Bedford value chain and made it the most valuable fishing port in the United States for the past 20 years. In 2019, the Port of New Bedford recorded $451 million in landings, more than 80 percent from scallops. The price of scallops has more than doubled since 2002, now ranging from $10 to $15 a pound at auction, depending on size. At one point in 2021, the price hit $30 a pound—wholesale. At the daily Buyers and Sellers Exchange (BASE) auction in New Bedford, 150,000 pounds or more of scallops are electronically bought by bid in less than an hour. It is hard to imagine that 22 years ago several scallop grounds were closed to fishing.

The story of scallop success is in many ways the inverse of the cod story. New Bedford scallopers are hunters turned harvesters. They are now essentially wealthy ranchers—wealthier than any New Bedford fishermen since the whalers in the nineteenth century—rotating and harvesting scallop beds as if they were rotating crops on farmland. The tactics changed around 2000, after the terrible downturn of the 1990s.

After a peak catch of 37 million pounds in 1991, scallop landings along the East Coast plummeted to less than 10 million pounds in 1994. In 1993, federal agents wearing bulletproof vests (they had been threatened by fishermen in the past) raided twenty-two scalloping boats and seized $126,220 worth of scallops. Six boat owners were charged with catching undersized scallops.[26] Meanwhile, other boat owners were smuggling cocaine and pot into New Bedford, which has been home to sin and sinners since the 1660s and the Puritan Age.

"Rum was unloaded here [in the 1660s] and sent by small boats and wagons to buyers from Maine to Rhode Island," writes Rory Nugent in *Down at the Docks*. "The harbor was condemned from the pulpit by the Puritans' chief guide on the path to salvation, Reverend Increase Mather; later, his son Cotton burnished the setting by denouncing the waterfront as Lucifer's kingdom." Two centuries later, whaling ships brought chests of opium home from India, Arabia, and China, making New Bedford the nation's top import center for opium and hashish, says Nugent. During Prohibition, seaplanes working for Joe Kennedy, the patriarch of the Kennedy political clan, would unload illicit alcohol from boats in the middle of Buzzards Bay in the dark of night and fly it back to distribution points in New Bedford, where an intricate system of tunnels connected the waterfront to sites in the business district (such as the old Cultivator Shoals bar, now the Rose Alley Ale House, on the waterfront). Kennedy's "office" in a small cove in New

Bedford Harbor was affectionately called "Big Joe's Mudflats." In the 1960s, the drug of choice was pot. In the 1970s, coke and heroin were in demand.[27] In the 1960s and 1970s, the Mafia treated New Bedford like a cash machine for junk, dope, gambling, and prostitution.[28] In the 1980s, bust after bust uncovered tens of millions of dollars worth of marijuana on fishing boats.[29]

Illicit trade and criminal behavior are clearly nothing new in New Bedford and have a storied past. But in the 1990s, the smuggling was largely borne of a desperation to put boats to work, rather than a desire to make a quick, illicit, tax-free, buck. The industry was on the brink. And it was going to get worse.

At a 1994 New England Fisheries Management Council meeting to determine how to protect yellowtail flounder, Bullard from NOAA Fisheries recounted a scalloper blurting out that there were plenty of flounder around: "When I go scalloping, I can catch 30,000 pounds of yellowtail." That same year, a judge presiding over a lawsuit brought by the Conservation Law Foundation said that if the Council wouldn't protect groundfish the court would manage the fishery, says Mike Sissenwine, who was the senior scientist of NOAA Fisheries at the time, and later the science and research director of the Northeast Fisheries Science Center. Council members moved to close off several portions of Georges Bank and the Nantucket Shoals to fishing for cod, flounder—and scallops.

"Scalloping was basically an open-access industry through the 1980s," said Ronald Smolowitz, a marine scientist and a founder of the Coonamesset Farm Foundation, which conducts scallop research. "There was very little science telling you which way things were going and very little enforcement to make sure the management measures were working. By 1994, we had hit a low point. There was no place to go but up."[30]

In 1995, one year after the closures, researchers piloting remotely operated vehicles saw something unexpected: The muddy bottom was littered with market-sized scallops, rusty red and round as saucers.[31] By 1996 and 1997, NOAA Fisheries knew the scallops had come back, but the New England Fishery Management Council hadn't reopened the closed grounds because there was no plan to protect the yellowtail flounder. "The fishermen also knew scallops were abundant in the closed areas, because they had likely been fishing there illegally," says Sissenwine.

That may be true, but the scallopers were suffering economically. The opportunistic Codfather, who always had "jingles" to spare, had even swooped in to buy three scallop dredges for pennies on the dollar in 1995. A third of the vessel owners were facing bankruptcy and desperate to return to their hallowed hunting grounds. To further reduce landings, the New England Fisheries Management Council cut the allowable days at sea and the number of crew on a vessel.

With areas on Georges Bank and the Nantucket Shoals closed, pressure built on the remaining open areas, especially in the mid-Atlantic. "We were looking at 51 days-at-sea in 2000," said Bobby Bruno, owner of a New Bedford scalloper. "That was not enough to survive. We had to do something. We came together to show that there were adequate scallops out there."[32]

A small group of scallop boat owners formed the Fisheries Survival Fund. A founder of the fund, Marjorie J. Orman, owner of a Fairhaven, Massachusetts, settlement house, later testified in court that the proposed restrictions on fishing "were so severe that they threatened to reduce scallop fishing to levels at which the vessels could not cover their costs and economically survive."[33]

The Fisheries Survival Fund solicited help from Brian Rothschild, who was then dean of UMass Dartmouth's new graduate School for Marine Science & Technology. Rothschild remembers standing in the Fairhaven Shipyard on a snowy day when a group of scallop fishermen came up to him. "They said, 'Brian, what can you do for us? We're going broke.'"[34]

Rothschild began advocating for an "experimental" permit to allow limited fishing for research purposes in the closed areas. After some misfires with the application, Sissenwine and Rothschild co-convened a session at Woods Hole to organize a series of dredge surveys of the closed areas on Georges Bank using commercial scallopers. Steve Murawski, a NOAA Fisheries scientist working out of Woods Hole Laboratory at the time and now at the University of South Florida's College of Marine Science, led the scientific effort and worked with the scallop industry on survey logistics—which included both sampling randomly selected locations and "depletion tows" over the same area to estimate the efficiency of a scallop dredge. Paul Rago, a biologist at the NOAA Fisheries Northeast Science Center, had successfully deployed the technique the year before for a survey of surf clams. "You do one dredge after another and the number of scallops you see on dredge number six or seven gives you an idea of the stock's abundance," says Rothschild. Multiple dredges of the same territory compensate for the fact that one dredge only tells you what it caught, not what else is "down there." One tow shows the relative mass compared to other areas, but not the total abundance.

"On the randomized tows, we were also getting good data on the catch rate of yellowtail flounder by location," says Sissenwine. Those data eventually helped set quotas on yellowtail bycatch when the closed beds were opened—the first time bycatch quotas had been used in New England. Tracking catches in real time definitely helped cut down the accidental capture of yellowtail flounder. By 2016, scallopers were catching only 5 percent as many flounder as they had landed in the 1990s.[35]

The two-week dredge survey in late summer of 1998 used New Bedford scallopers, chosen by lottery, including Malvign Kvilhaug, Bobby Bruno, Herman Bruce, and Marty Manley. The captains, who were from the Fisheries Survival Fund, donated fuel, food, and vessels. In exchange for their time, the captains were allowed to keep 10,000 to 14,000 pounds of scallops to cover costs and pay for observers to assure that data were accurate and complete. The project went well until analysis of the data began and disagreements arose about the "efficiency" of the dredges, which affected the estimates of abundance. In short, the regulators and fishermen ended up with different math. "Different players perceived their roles differently and had different motivations for how they wanted to release the data. Different estimates of scallop biomass were coming out that may have created false expectations," says NOAA Fisheries' Murawski.

Forging ahead with his interpretation of the data, Rothschild implored Senator Edward Kennedy (D-MA) to get involved. He called a "summit" in New Bedford and invited William Daley, then the secretary of commerce, who oversees NOAA Fisheries, to attend. Representative Barney Frank (D-MA), a big supporter of fisheries, was also involved. Back in D.C. after the summit, Daley, who had veto power over the New England Fishery Management Council, pushed to open the closed areas to scalloping, overriding concerns of environmentalists and the New England Fisheries Management Council, according to the *Boston Globe*.[36] In June, 1998, part of Closed Area II on Georges Bank was opened to scalloping, with restrictions on both scallops and yellowtail flounder. For its role in reopening the beds "without adhering to the mandates of the 1996 Sustainable Fisheries Act," the Commerce Department was later sued by the Conservation Law Foundation (along with the Center for Marine Conservation, National Audubon Society, and Natural Resources Defense Council). This was part of the aforementioned series of lawsuits brought by a variety of environmental NGO plaintiffs.

Writing an op-ed in the *Standard-Times* in 2010, Congressman Frank reflected on Daley's pivotal role. "He based his decision on data presented by the seafood industry in New Bedford, which turned out to have been accurate and we benefitted from an increase in scallop quotas without any negative effect on the stocks."[37] By 2001, NOAA Fisheries proclaimed the fishery "rebuilt." In fact, NOAA Fisheries scientists in Woods Hole had predicted that the stock would quickly rebuild to levels never before seen as a result of protecting small scallops.

With that first 1998 survey on the books, the focus shifted to two other areas that had been closed since 1994—Closed Area 1 and Nantucket Lightship (Shoals). In regular surveys, vessels sample throughout the sea scallop's range, looking at relative abundance and stock condition, collecting data at hundreds of stations from the mid-Atlantic through Georges Bank. The August 1999 survey with commercial vessels was more intensive, occupying some 500 sites in and around just these two areas. "What resulted from this collection of intensive spatial data was a graphic description of critical habitat and an array of policy options set out in much more detail, with what fishermen perceived as more reliable information," said Murawski.[38]

The School for Marine Science & Technology and New Bedford boats were not part of the 1999 surveys; the Virginia Institute of Marine Science played the academic role. Meanwhile, the New Bedford group was already heading in a different direction. Kevin

Stokesbury, a research associate at the School for Marine Science & Technology, who had joined the NOAA Fisheries survey project in September 1998 to do data entry and analysis, began to promote the idea of a video analysis as a more efficient, immediate, and less intrusive way to survey than dredging. After the debate over the efficiency of different dredges, Stokesbury didn't think doing more "depletion tows" would contribute further knowledge, according to a 2000 report by the National Fisheries Conservation Center. "I told Brian I had surveyed scallops in shallow water by scuba diving and thought it could be done in deeper water with video," said Stokesbury. "Brian said, 'Prove it.'"[39]

Besides side-stepping the controversy over the efficiency of tows, a video survey didn't require an experimental permit for fishing. With some preliminary drawings (with help from Gil Fain, an engineering student), Stokesbury and scallopers used PVC pipe to build a pyramid that could hold lights and a camera—and roll along the sea bottom. After testing it in shallow water, they took the design to welders. "Kevin had the ideas, fishermen know how to modify gear," said scalloper Bruno. The result was a 700-pound, steel pyramid rigged with lights and cameras, with cable feeds back to computer screens and video recorders in the wheelhouse.

Dropping the steel pyramid off the stern winch of a commercial scalloper (Danny Eilertsen on the *Liberty*, Chris Wright on the *Huntress*, and Gabe Miranda on the *Friendship*), the first small-scale scallop surveys showed those same rusty-red, market-sized scallops that the autonomous robot had seen in 1995. "The drop-camera system Brian and I developed using video worked like a charm," says Stokesbury. "It's hard to argue with a picture of scallops on the sea floor."[40] In a 2002 paper on the surveys, Stokesbury wrote that the density of the scallops was the highest and their size was the largest ever seen on Georges Bank.[41] Sissenwine said that results from the dredge survey and video survey were "very consistent."[42]

Researchers completed the surveys in August and provided estimates of abundance to the scallop-plan development team in September. The New England Fishery Management Council used both video and dredge data to devise management measures that allowed limited opening of Closed Area 1 and Nantucket Lightship in 2000.

Murawski later described the story of the scallop fishery's rebound as "a great collaboration between the scientific, regulatory, and academic communities." The cooperative effort laid the foundation for the NOAA Fisheries Research Set-Aside program, which sells scallops to provide money for continued research and development. The New England Fishery Management Council amended its Sea Scallop Fishery Management Plan to formally establish rotational area management. Dvora Hart, NOAA Fisheries' lead assessment scientist for sea scallops since 1999, wrote in 2005 that rotational closures "are much more likely to improve scallop yield than permanent closed areas." Hart has developed a simulation model that is now the primary forecasting tool used by the New England Fishery Management Council to aid in management of sea scallops, whose populations are a function of good recruitment years.

"Recruitment" in fishing refers to the process by which juvenile fish survive and grow into adults. Atlantic sea scallops grow to sexual maturity in 2 years and produce up to 270 million eggs at a time, so the stock can rebuild in a short time, as evidenced by the surge in scallops between 1994 and 1997. Since 2000, the Atlantic sea scallop has had three very good recruitment years. In 2003, there was a huge scallop recruitment that essentially floated the industry for a decade. In 2012, video data showed another good recruitment in Georges Bank, and in 2013 one in the mid-Atlantic. NOAA Fisheries' Hart refers to these two classes as "Lake Wobegon" classes, a reference to Garrison Keillor's *Prairie Home Companion* radio show, "where all the children are above average."

From 2004 to 2011, the scallop resource numbered about 8 billion, says Stokesbury. Based on surveys from 2016 to 2018, Stokesbury and N. David Bethoney estimated 34 billion scallops over 70,000 square kilometers of the US continental shelf, roughly the entire range of the species.[43,44] While using a different metric—tons of scallop meats—the NOAA Fisheries Northeast Science Center in its 2018 stock assessment suggested similar growth: In 2017, there were 317,334 metric tons of scallop meats in the ocean, by far the largest number since 2008, when there were just 125,025 metric tons.[45]

In 2013, the East Coast scallop industry received a Marine Stewardship Council accreditation for sustainable practices, the top honor in the industry. At the time, NOAA Fisheries' Bullard told the *Boston Globe* that scallopers "have become tremendous stewards of this resource."[46] Ross Paasché, president of the American Scallop Association, said, "For too long, activists have blamed all of the ocean's woes on fishermen. This certification provides solid evidence that fishermen are capable of being guardians of the ocean's future."[47]

But no one knows whether the fishery's good luck will continue—whether recruitment will remain strong, and how severe the impacts will be when ecological conditions change, and how fast that change will come. "Recently, growth has slowed," NOAA Fisheries' Hart told the Scallop Committee of the New England Fishery Management Council in late 2020. "Abundance is dropping faster than mortality or fishing would indicate. A lot of places have smaller scallops, what I call the 'Peter Pan syndrome.' Some are in areas that are muddy, without strong currents that stir up the phytoplankton scallops live on. And there's not been much recruitment since the 2012 and 2013 classes." As a result, catch limits and days-at-sea for 2021 were lowered, with expected landings of 40 million pounds, compared to 60 million pounds in 2019.

"The scallop fishery is not in trouble, but what happens if the scallops start to decline?" asks the School for Marine Science and Technology's Rothschild. "Fish populations do that all the time."[48]

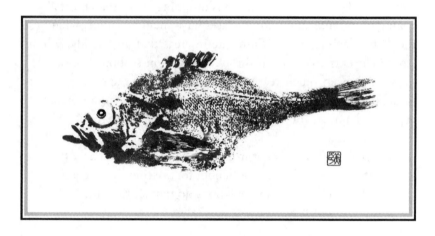

ACADIAN REDFISH

Chapter 2

Changing Rules
for a Changing Ecosystem

*We have known since the beginning of the twentieth century, when
F. I. Baranov developed the principles of quantitative fisheries
science, or at least since World War II and the giant fisheries closure
that it entailed, that excessive fishing reduces fish populations
and eventually causes them to collapse but that reducing fishing is
sufficient, in most cases, for them to recover (given time).*

—Daniel Pauly, *Vanishing Fish*

In 2012, the Department of Commerce declared the groundfish
industry in New England and New York an "economic disaster."[1] Senator Edward Markey (D-MA) said the disaster was the
"underwater equivalent of a drought." Five years later, there were more
groundfish surveyed than there had been 25 years prior. That is an indication of how difficult it is to manage fisheries—to get the science, the
data, the fishermen, and the regulators on the same page—especially
when the climate is throwing one curveball after another.

Yes, the cod and flounder had been fished down to low levels, with
ocean warming a possible factor. But scup, pollock, haddock, ocean
perch (redfish), silver hake, skate, plaice (porgy), butterfish, black sea
bass, John Dory, monkfish, whiting, and dogfish were and are healthy

if not abundant groundfish stocks (the scientific term for groundfish and other creatures living at or near the bottom of the sea is demersal). Of course, none are yet as valuable as cod, which still gets more than $2 a pound off the boat, with the rest well under that and some below 50 cents a pound. And then, of course, there are lobsters, scallops, Jonah crabs, red and blue crabs, surf clams, ocean quahogs, mackerel, bluefish, striped bass, Atlantic herring, swordfish, mahi-mahi, albacore, and bluefin tuna. Seafood is abundant in the northwest Atlantic Ocean.

That is not what was predicted in a 1998 paper in *Science*, called "Fishing Down the Marine Food Webs."It argued that the world was fishing out the high-trophic (top of the food chain) and high-value fish like tunas, billfish, and sharks, and moving down the food chain toward less valuable fish at lower trophic levels. "Before long, we'll all be eating jellyfish sandwiches," said Daniel Pauly, the lead author and director of the Sea Around Us project at the University of British Columbia. This paper has been cited more than 5,000 times, one of the most cited fisheries-science papers ever. Pauly is one of the most cited *scientists* in the world.[2]

Pauly may well be proven right over the long term, given his credibility in the field, but some 12 years later this "fishing-down" idea was largely debunked by Trevor Branch, a scientist at the University of Washington's School of Aquatic and Fishing Science. He said that lower trophic species, such as oysters and scallops, were quite valuable and perhaps even more vulnerable to fishing than the high-trophic predators.[3] Branch et al. suggested that, rather than "fishing down marine food webs," people were collectively, in fact, moving up to a higher trophic level.

That may seem like an academic food fight, but it is worth noting because the "fishing down the food web" meme is lodged in the public's psyche, due to a barrage of environmental attacks over the last three decades, some of which were certainly justified. But a 2020 paper in *Nature* ("The Future of Food from the Sea") paints a much more encouraging picture of fish as a sustainable food source for a growing world population, expected to near 10 billion by 2050. The authors state it this way:

As food from the sea represents only 17 percent of the current production of edible meat, we ask how much food we can expect the ocean to sustainably produce by 2050. Here we examine the main food-producing sectors in the ocean—wild fisheries, finfish mariculture and bivalve mariculture—to estimate "sustainable supply curves" that account for ecological, economic, regulatory, and technological constraints. We find that under our estimated demand shifts and supply scenarios (which account for policy reform and technology improvements), edible food from the sea could increase by 21–44 million tons by 2050, a 36–74 percent increase compared to current yields. This represents 12–25 percent of the estimated increase in all meat needed to feed 9.8 billion people by 2050. Increases in all three sectors are likely but are most pronounced for mariculture [discussed in part 2 of this book].[4]

That is the global perspective, which is based on a lot of unknowns about climate, policy, technology, and enforcement of regulations, not to mention the proven track record of humans as hunters and predators. Back to New England and the mid-Atlantic: the fact that there are more groundfish than 25 years ago, while encouraging and counter to public perception, is not *overly* impressive, as the actual biomass for most stocks is a fraction of what it was 50 or 100 years ago. Cod, for example, as Pauly quantified, is 3.5 percent, at best, of its 1850 biomass (see chapter 1). Pauly refers to a "shifting baseline," another one of his oft-cited theories, wherein each generation remembers what resources nature provided when they were young but forgets to account for the much richer natural world their ancestors inhabited.[5]

Given its relatively recent history of faulty surveys and cod-stock mismanagement—failing to regulate the cod fishery before it was effectively fished out of American waters—you might think that the United States is a laggard in fisheries management. It is not. It is widely regarded as a global model for modern-fisheries management. In its "Fisheries of the United States 2019" report to Congress, NOAA Fisheries said that since 2000, 47 fishing stocks that had been "overfished" (the stock is too low to rebuild if fishing continues) have been "rebuilt" (meaning that fishing within certain limits can recommence).[6]

Those stocks were rebuilt in spite of a 21 percent increase in catch. Referring to this dynamic, Jane Lubchenco, former NOAA Fisheries administrator and a coauthor of the *Nature* paper cited earlier, said at the Society of Environmental Journalists 2020 conference: "It *is* possible to end overfishing."[7]

As has been shown in numerous cases globally, a fish stock that is left alone will generally rebuild in 10 or so years, all other things (such as ocean warming and acidification) held equal—which is certainly not the case with Gulf of Maine cod, now in its second 10-year rebuild. But rebuild stories happen all over the world. In the mid-Atlantic and New England, the beloved striped bass has been down for the count several times and has always rebounded. "The story hasn't changed, stocks go up and down," says Brian Rothschild of UMass Dartmouth's School for Marine Science & Technology. "Striped bass is a great example—when I was a grad student at Cornell my professor had a grant to figure out why the bass population was so low. A few years later he got a grant to figure out why it was so high. The same thing happened in Scandinavia with herring, at one time the biggest catch in the world."

Then there's the swordfish story. In 1998, the Natural Resources Defense Council and SeaWeb, in collaboration with other environmental organizations, launched the "Give Swordfish a Break" campaign. During the campaign, hundreds of chefs signed the pledge, promising not to serve swordfish in their restaurants; numerous businesses, including hotel chains, cruise lines, grocery stores, and airlines, stopped selling North Atlantic swordfish. The campaign was declared a success and officially ended in August 2000. Two years later, swordfish populations in the North Atlantic were declared to have reached 94 percent of full recovery.[8] In 2012, NOAA Fisheries proclaimed that the North Atlantic swordfish population "has become one of the most sustainable seafood choices thanks to a 1999 international plan [with the International Commission for the Conservation of Atlantic Tunas] that rebuilt this stock several years ahead of schedule."[9]

Despite the largely negative popular perception about fisheries management, data on American fishing overall is surprisingly positive, at least relative to the rest of the world. In 1999, NOAA Fisheries listed 98 stocks as overfished; 20 years later, in 2019, the number of overfished stocks was essentially cut in half, to 46. Overall, 93 percent of American marine-fish stocks were *not* subject to overfishing (the rate of harvest is too high) and 81 percent were *not* overfished.

"The government never uses the term 'abundant' to describe a stock," says Laura Foley Ramsden, co-owner (with her husband, Peter) of Foley Fish, a processor and distributor with plants in Boston and New Bedford. "They force you to use a double negative, as in, 'not overfished' or 'not overfishing.'" Globally, by contrast, more than 30 percent of all stocks *are* overfished—either "collapsed" (less than 10 percent of their unfished biomass) or shut down to rebuild—and more than 50 percent are subject to overfishing.

"The United States has the best fisheries management regime in the world. It's not often you say the United States is the best at something, but this is the case," says the French-born Pauly. "The Magnuson-Stevens Act is proactive and enforces rebuilding within 10 years."

The Magnuson-Stevens Act: A Model for the World

The 1976 Magnuson-Stevens Fishery Conservation and Management Act (Magnuson), named after Senators Warren G. Magnuson of Washington State and Ted Stevens of Alaska, was the first piece of major legislation to regulate federal fisheries. Prior to the law, it was each man and boat for himself, from whatever country, to hunt to his heart's content, as long as foreigners respected the sovereign 12-mile territorial limit.

Overseen by NOAA Fisheries, Magnuson initially focused on protecting the domestic fishing industry from foreign competition. Magnuson established an exclusive economic zone of the United States, extending 200 miles from the coast. That was six years before the United Nations Convention on the Law of the Sea mandated a 200-mile economic zone for every country (and its territories) with a coast.

The United States acted in the mid-1970s because Russian, East German, Polish, and Spanish factory ships were raiding waters off the coasts of Washington State, Alaska, and New England. On the West

Coast, Pacific salmon and pollock were the targets. On the East Coast, namely Georges Bank and the Gulf of Maine, cod, haddock, hake, and herring were the targets. At the time, the capacity of the foreign factory-ship fleet to scoop mega tons of biomass from the sea and freeze it, with ships that could stay at sea for weeks or months at a time, far exceeded that of the Americans, who were largely fishing from day boats or trawlers on 10- to 14-day trips.

"Try to imagine a mobile and completely self-contained timber-cutting machine that could smash through the roughest trails of the forest, cut down trees, mill them, and deliver consumer-ready lumber in half the time of normal logging and milling operations," wrote William Warner in *Distant Water*, his chronicle of post–World War II fishing in the North Atlantic. "This was exactly what factory trawlers did—this was exactly their effect on fish—in the forests of the deep. It could not long go unnoticed."[10]

In 1975, for example, NOAA Fisheries reported that there were 133 foreign vessels fishing on Georges Bank, an area larger than the state of Massachusetts about 60 miles east of Cape Cod. With shallow waters full of upwelling and sun-fed nutrients, the sandy plateau sits 300 feet higher than the larger Gulf of Maine that stretches north toward the Bay of Fundy. In the 1970s, people on Cape Cod could see Russian ships from their shores (eerily reminiscent of the 1966 comedy movie, *The Russians Are Coming*), and American fishermen were known to carry guns when they fished on Georges Bank, like rag-tag Patriots fending off well-funded British troops and sailors. Magnuson decisively ended that era.

Magnuson was built on the principle of fishing a given species, such as cod or flounder, to its maximum sustainable yield. World Wildlife Fund describes maximum sustainable yield for a given fish stock as "the highest possible annual catch that can be sustained over time." Biologists differ on what that amount is, and it clearly varies by species and region, but noted fisheries biologist Ray Hilborn (University of Washington) considers it to be between 20 and 50 percent of "un-fished abundance."[11] The eight regional Fisheries Management Councils (New England, Mid-Atlantic, Pacific Northwest, et al.) generally set annual catch limits at 75 percent of that number, as a conservative hedge against the inherent uncertainty of stock assessments. If scientists set the size of a given stock at, say, 1 million metric tons and the catch rate to sustain maximum sustainable yield is 300,000 metric tons, the allowable catch would be 75 percent of that, or 225,000 metric tons.

Clearly, there is both art and science to determine the sustainable yield for any given stock. To begin with, the size of the stock (its "biomass") and the number of adults must be accurately estimated through a variety of survey mechanisms—a difficult tabulation for an underwater organism that is constantly on the move to find food or hide from predators. John Shepherd, a British Earth-systems scientist, is often quoted as saying, "Counting fish is like counting trees, except they are invisible and keep moving."[12] Eric Schwab, an oceans expert at the Environmental Defense Fund and a former head of NOAA Fisheries, later added, "And they eat each other."[13] Indeed, cod eat lobsters and clams and scallops; dogfish eat cod and mollusks; juvenile cod eat juvenile haddock and vice versa. Lobsters and starfish eat scallops and voracious gray seals eat just about everything (and are protected by the Marine Mammal Act of 1972).

A Changing Ecosystem

These biological realities, however confounding and difficult to observe and quantify, are known. Perhaps a bigger problem for wild-capture fisheries is climate change, which is quickly overtaking overfishing as the biggest challenge, evidenced by rapidly warming and acidifying waters. "We have relied on the oceans to mitigate climate change—they have absorbed 90 percent of the excess heat we have produced and 30 percent of our CO_2 emissions," says Jim Leape, codirector of the Center for Ocean Solutions at Stanford University. "The result, however, is that ocean waters are becoming warmer and more acidic, which threatens to undermine the very foundation of the ocean food web and cause upheaval in ecosystems from coral reefs to the Arctic."[14]

"As we have decreased fishing, the relative contribution of climate change and its impact on forage fish has increased," says Jon Hare, science and research director of NOAA's Northeast Fisheries Science Center. "When we were fishing at higher rates, these other factors were less noticeable."

Between 2003 and 2018, the Gulf of Maine warmed a shocking seven times faster than the rest of the world's oceans.[15] In "normal times," not so long back in human memory, the cold, nutrient-rich Labrador Current from the Arctic met the warmer Gulf Stream on the eastern edge of Georges Bank. The intersection of the two dominant currents creates the "heartbeat of the Atlantic Ocean," says Hillary Scannell, now an oceanographer at the University of Washington, who studied with Pershing, author of the 2015 *Science* paper linking ocean warming to the decline in cod, at the University of Maine.[16] Sunlight that penetrates the shallow waters (20 to 125 feet deep) of Georges Bank creates an ideal environment for phytoplankton (microscopic algae) and zooplankton, tiny free-floating creatures such as krill, which eat phytoplankton. On Georges Bank, phytoplankton grow three times faster than on any other continental shelf. The fact that phytoplankton and zooplankton are primary producers at the bottom of the food chain explains the historic legacy of Georges Bank as one of the most pre-eminent fishing grounds in the world.

Phytoplankton feed the zooplankton, which are then eaten by the larvae of fish such as cod, haddock, yellowtail flounder, and multiple other species. Georges Bank also hosts many marine birds, whales, billfish, tuna, sharks, dolphins, and porpoises. The combination of tides and the Labrador Current create a clockwise flow around the perimeter of Georges Bank and then northwest into the Gulf of Maine, circulating eggs and larvae throughout as the Gulf Stream veers northeast toward the North Sea above Europe.[17]

But these are not normal times, with the Arctic warming three times faster than the rest of the world. As Arctic ice melts around Greenland, fresh and warmer water, which is less dense than cold water and remains near the surface, dilutes the power of the Labrador Current and allows the Gulf Stream to nudge farther North in the Gulf of Maine. "If you're turning down the cold spigot, you're going to feel more of an effect from that warm water," says Scannell. Plus, the Gulf of Maine has a C-shape, like a bathtub with no escape hatch.

"The first time we used the term 'heatwave' in the oceans was 2012," says Kathy Mills, an ocean scientist researching the effects of ocean temperature at the Gulf of Maine Research Institute, who also worked with Pershing on the 2015 *Science* paper. "The heat wave extended from Cape Hatteras to Iceland and lasted an entire year. That was followed by heat waves in 2016, 2018, and 2020."

Ocean heat waves are marked by temperatures over 5 days that are warmer than the 90th percentile based on a 30-year historical baseline period. The heat has brought seahorses, squid, butterfish, and great white sharks into the Gulf of Maine, far north of their typical range, and driven northern shrimp, once a profitable winter harvest for lobstermen, out of the Gulf.

Cod have been severely affected. "Failure to recognize the impact of warming on cod contributed to overfishing," wrote Pershing et al. in *Science*. "Recovery of this fishery depends on sound management, but the size of the stock depends on future temperature conditions. The experience in the Gulf of Maine highlights the need to incorporate environmental factors into resource management."[18]

This rapid rate of warming clearly surprised fisheries' regulators, who might have restricted the cod catch 5 or 10 years earlier had they known this. Whether that would have made much difference, even at the margins, is unknown but seems unlikely. The only good news is that the Atlantic cod stock is not close to extinction; for the moment, at least, cod stocks are healthy in Icelandic waters and in the Barents Sea, a small part of the Arctic Ocean off the coasts of Norway and Russia.

Another iconic species endangered by climate is lobsters, in many years the most valuable fishery in the United States, which have a temperature threshold of around 70 degrees Fahrenheit (although they prefer 60 degrees, according to Mills). In Long Island Sound and Southern New England, where lobsters once thrived but are now scant, temperatures easily exceed that threshold. Lobsters have effectively been moving north as recruitment (survival to adulthood) and abundance decline around Long Island and Southern New England. "Some people think lobsters are actually walking up toward Canada, which they could, but that's not typically the case," says Mills. "Instead, they are failing to successfully spawn in warmer waters. We're expecting a downturn in Maine, but we can't say with surety when that might happen. The lobsters may also be moving offshore."

Squid were once ephemeral sightings in the Gulf of Maine, but since the heat wave of 2012 lobstermen and other fishermen have shown more interest in targeting squid. The squid capital, however, remains Point Judith, Rhode Island, whose big boats go past Nantucket and down south to the mid-Atlantic Bight for squid. Might they have to think about heading north in a few years? And might mahi-mahi, the colorful dolphinfish that loves Gulf Stream waters (75 degrees or higher), become a fixture in New England waters? They have been caught off Massachusetts in recent years. Great white sharks have been rarely sighted off the Maine coast, as they prefer water temperatures above 60 degrees, but there was a fatal great white attack in Maine's Casco Bay in the summer of 2020, the first ever in the state.[19]

"A number of continental-shelf species are extending or shifting northward or into deeper waters," says NOAA Fisheries' Jon Hare. "The Gulf of Maine is an inverted mountain range, not so deep that oxygen is an issue, with fish and invertebrates moving deeper into colder water. In every region, there are winners and losers. In the Northeast, some of the likely winners are black sea bass, summer flounder, and scup."

The intensity and scale of fishing efforts clearly have an impact on the size of fish stocks, but focusing on fishing alone ignores the impacts of environmental change, habitat degradation, and international fishing. And it is not just in the Gulf of Maine. The warm "blob" in the eastern Pacific Ocean that spread up the coast from Southern California to Alaska in 2014–2016 reduced the number of spawning Coho salmon returning to their natal rivers. In the summer of 2021, an estimated 1 billion sea creatures died on the coast of Vancouver, British Columbia, and that number is likely an undercount, according to researcher Christopher Harley of the University of British Columbia. Says Malin Pinsky, a marine biologist at Rutgers University, "We can see the [dead] mussels because they're on the shoreline, but to a large extent, oceans are out of sight, out of mind."[20]

Both Chinook and Coho salmon have also been affected by habitat degradation caused by drought, which affects riverine spawning habitat. In fact, during the past 5 years, the secretary of commerce has declared severe salmon "fishery disasters" on the West Coast due to factors beyond the control of fishery managers.[21] "In 2019, salmon moving from the ocean into rivers during a heat wave encountered lethal temperatures as they re-entered fresh water and suffered heart attacks," says Kelly Harrell, the chief fisheries officer at Sitka Salmon Shares, a community-supported fishery in Sitka, Alaska (see chapter 4).

The disaster of climate change may be too big a problem for Magnuson to address, but it clearly has done a good job of addressing the disaster of overfishing. Many environmentalists would say Magnuson has not been enforced rigorously enough. Many fishermen would say that the regulations responsible for this success are onerous and require a legal mind to parse. There is truth on both sides. Moreover, there are inevitable unintended consequences, as a review of the law's evolution shows.

From "Race to Fish" to "Annual Catch Limits"

The original 1976 Magnuson law certainly stopped foreign fleets from taking "American fish" from the continental shelf—the relatively shallow, nutrient-, micro-algae-, and plankton-rich waters where most fish are found worldwide—but it didn't stop American fishermen from doing so. In the 1980s, the government subsidized fishermen with low-cost loans to replace old wooden boats with more advanced steel trawlers and technological gear, such as fish-finding systems, improved electronics, and more efficient nets, which led to increased domestic overfishing.

In the late 1980s and into the 1990s, landings tumbled. "If John Cabot were alive today, he would not recognize Georges Bank," said Congressman Gerry Studds in 1991. As the representative for Cape Cod and New Bedford, and a House sponsor of the original Magnuson law, Studds was widely admired and respected by fishermen. "Instead of a sea swarming with majestic cod, he would find dogfish. Instead of flounder, he would find skates. Instead of a fishermen's dream, he would find a nightmare."[22]

Shortly thereafter, environmental groups sued the federal government, claiming that the Commerce Department didn't enforce its own rules against overfishing. Over time, environmental groups would apply increasing pressure on NOAA Fisheries to write and enforce stronger restrictions. The "days-at-sea" regime enacted in 1993 led to a so-called race to fish, in which boats would fish incessantly in good and bad weather to scoop up as much fish as possible before their competitors could, which inevitably led to accidents and death.

In 1996, in the middle of severe scallop, yellowtail flounder, and cod restrictions, Magnuson was amended as the Sustainable Fisheries Act. This put the spotlight on conservation, which the 1976 law had clearly not accomplished. The new law mandated that managers quantitatively define "overfishing" and "overfished," and create annual status listings by species. "They still haven't nailed this, as there are at least seven definitions of 'overfishing' floating around out there," says Rothschild, who worked with NOAA Fisheries to implement the original Magnuson in 1976. The law also required that managers establish plans to rebuild overfished stocks within 10 years. A typical rebuilding plan allows fishing to continue at a reduced level (thirty-eight stocks or stock complexes were in rebuilding plans in 2020).

In 2006, Magnuson was again amended, as the Fishery Conservation and Management Reauthorization Act. This rewrite really changed the way fisheries operated, starting in 2010. The new law called for a change from the days-at-sea regime by setting Annual Catch Limits and allocating catch shares to captains or boats for the multispecies groundfish industry. For some species, such as scallops, monkfish, and skate, days-at-sea limitations were set in certain areas, without catch limits. Former NOAA Fisheries' administrator Jane Lubchenko says the 2006 fisheries reform is "one of the least appreciated environmental success stories of the last few decades."[23]

The main policy making and enforcement mechanism of the original Magnuson was the establishment of eight regional Fisheries Councils, composed of fishermen, state fishing agencies, local politicians, scientists, conservationists, and other citizen stakeholders—and one NOAA Fisheries representative. This mandate for participatory fisheries management is unique to the United States and functions as a kind of representative democracy. Such distributed power was necessary because the United States has the second-largest exclusive economic zone in the world (after France). The zone covers 70 degrees of latitude, and several oceans and seas, with radically different ecosystems that would be hard to manage at the federal level. "This approach was decentralized and stakeholder-driven," says John Bullard, former Greater Atlantic Regional Fisheries administrator for NOAA Fisheries. "Think about how complex fishing management is, given the number of species and habitats and geographies, and the cultural traditions and histories. It's complex and the management system has to be a good fit for all those things. If we're going to manage scallops differently than groundfish we are going to let the people affected by the decisions make the decisions. This was revolutionary."[24]

In the 2006 reauthorization, each regional council had to specify annual catch limits for nearly all stocks under its management, based on the "best available science," a term clearly open to broad interpretation. "NOAA can do one survey and when contested in court, a judge can rule in favor and the fishermen can't argue," says Richard Stavis, formerly the chief sustainability officer at Stavis Seafood, a 94-year-old multinational company with headquarters on the Boston Fish Pier. This is known as the "Chevron defense," wherein a judge defers to an administrator's expertise when the law is not explicitly clear.

Each regional council had to establish specific mechanisms for enforcement of the catch limits through restrictions of fishing gear (type and mesh size of nets), reduced crew sizes, and partial or full closures of a fishery by region (such as Nantucket Lightship Closed Area and Western Gulf of Maine Closed Area). The closed areas are primarily designed to protect spawning grounds.

The catch-quota system allows fishing-boat captains with permits for a given stock to buy quota, or a certain amount of catch (pounds) per year. There is a bit of a gamble involved—you buy quota at a given price per pound, predicting that you will be able to sell the fish for more than what you paid in advance. Captains can sell or lease catch-quota to other captains. Annual catch limits (or "individual transferable quotas," as they are called in many parts of the world) have been effective in curbing overfishing everywhere they have been deployed—from Iceland in the 1970s to New Zealand in the 1980s to the Pacific Northwest in the 1990s—and effectively ended the destructive and dangerous "race-to-fish" syndrome.

Another enforcement mechanism is electronic monitoring. The United States, as do many countries, has a nationwide vessel-monitoring system for boats longer than 50 feet, so that regulators can see when vessels move into "closed" areas. In general, vessels holding permits in certain fisheries are required to turn on their vessel-monitoring signal and report to NOAA Fisheries regulators each time they go to sea—and then to report the amount and type of catch they are carrying back to port. This information is then checked by inspectors when the catch is offloaded in port.

In 2010, when the NOAA Fisheries Greater Atlantic Region phased out most of the old days-at-sea system, which had gradually been reduced from 225 to 50 days, in favor of annual catch limits, it also introduced sectors. This new concept in the Greater Atlantic Region was designed to enforce compliance with catch quotas. Sectors are voluntary cooperative groups of three or more independent vessels with permits to fish for a certain species or in a certain region. Catch quota for the sector is divided up between the boats and collectively managed. All seventeen sectors present their plans to NOAA Fisheries for approval and are then responsible for policing themselves—in theory. This clearly did not happen in Sector IX, whose president, Carlos "the Codfather" Rafael, was not stopped by other members of the sector from exceeding quota and mislabeling fish.

A large sector-allocation system was first trialed by trawlers fishing for pollock in the East Bering Sea in 1998. "This has been spectacularly profitable," writes Ray Hilborn in *Overfishing*.[25] "During the earlier race-to-fish [regime] the season was short, on-board factories were jammed, and then boats sat idle for many months. Now, far fewer boats work a much longer season, and because they are not racing each other, the amount of usable product for each ton of landed catch has almost doubled. Profits have soared accordingly."

Most species found on the continental shelf in federal waters are managed by regional fishery-management councils. However, highly migratory species, such as Atlantic tunas, swordfish, sharks, and billfish, are found throughout the Atlantic Ocean and must be managed both domestically and internationally. NOAA Fisheries has primary authority for developing and implementing an Atlantic-management plan in concert with international organizations, such as the International Commission for the Conservation of Atlantic Tunas. In the western Atlantic Ocean, bluefin tuna live in both subtropical and temperate waters, ranging from Labrador to northern Brazil.

Since the late 1940s, Massachusetts has been one of the top states for commercial landings of bluefin tuna, as well as harpooned swordfish. The daily retention limit for bluefin tuna in New England in 2020 was one large medium or giant bluefin tuna per vessel per day or trip, caught by rod and reel or harpoon (no long lines or nets). The number of open days varies according to the catch and is adjusted dynamically during the year.

By and large, the catch-quota and sector systems have worked well, although probably better for the fish than for the fishermen. The system's rules are agonizingly complex. To be a fishing-boat captain today, you need a legal mind and an accountant's attention to detail. "I'm not sure it's well publicized how stringent the regulations are, and how comprehensive the research is into where and how to fish," says Foley Fish's Laura Ramsden.

But fishermen know and aren't exactly happy about it. "The management system went off the rails in the early 2000s, with micro-management," says Frank Mirarchi, a fisherman from Scituate, Massachusetts, who started as a deckhand in 1967 and later served on the New England Fisheries Management Council in the early 1990s. "I went from 88 days at sea to 52, then they added in closed areas, gear limitations, and limited-access areas. What is this, I asked? It's un-American. When I started, it was basically the Wild West, you could do anything you wanted, and people did," says Mirarchi.[26]

For the many who started fishing as independent hunters, free to roam the seas, the increasingly stringent regulations since the mid-1990s have been a bitter pill to swallow. "We'll have an observer on board, the NOAA officer on the pier, you get boarded by the Coast Guard, you get boarded by the Environmental Police—sometimes in a single day you'll have three people going through your catch," says Kevin Norton, another Scituate fisherman. "They treat us like criminals, when the reality is anyone left in a small boat is doing the right thing. They can't afford not to."[27]

The open-access fishing of the old days—anyone with a boat could fish anywhere that is legally open—led to the "tragedy of the commons" and a precipitous decline in the number of fish. Something had to change after the precipitous decline of fish stocks in the 1990s. But, as with any complex system, when you solve one problem you are quite likely to create new ones.

One problem is the creation of so-called choke species. For example, if you target haddock, you are also likely to catch cod; catch limits on cod are more restrictive than on haddock so cod serves to limit—or "choke"—the catch of haddock. If you target scallops, you are also likely to catch a lot of yellowtail flounder; as with cod, the limits on yellowtail flounder can end up limiting scallop catch. Before annual catch limits, targeting one species led to inevitable "bycatch" of other species; in some cases, this bycatch is the limiting factor. "To have every species at maximum yield at one time is not attainable," says NOAA Fisheries' Hare. "We're trying to do something that can't be done, which is why we're developing multispecies models that take into account fishery interactions (the catch of cod with haddock) and food-web interactions (striped bass preying on menhaden)."

With strict quotas in place since 2010 and the number of choke species, it is difficult to fish any stock to its maximum sustainable yield. "The entire groundfish industry, even with new investments, even with Carlos [the Codfather] out of the picture, even with new technology, is harvesting a fraction of available groundfish," says Ed Anthes-Washburn, New Bedford's former port director. By avoiding cod, for example, fishermen are landing a mere 10–15 percent of their haddock quota, which is essentially leaving good seafood protein—not to mention millions of dollars—in the ocean.

The industry has significantly consolidated in the last two decades. Experts predicted catch shares would lead to this consolidation, as the biggest players were assigned quota based on their historical catch records (from 1996 to 2006) and smaller, independent boats that had poor records or had fished for multiple species were assigned precious little quota, which forced many fishermen out of business.

The quota and catch-share system amounts to a privatization of the oceans—the diametric opposite of the "tragedy of the commons."

"We were saying, 'catch shares are going to lead to consolidation, catch shares are going to lead to integration, catch shares are going to lead to corruption,'" said Scott Lang, who was mayor of New Bedford when catch shares took effect.[28]

In 2017, to limit such consolidation, the New England Fishery Management Council developed Amendment 18, which limits the number of permits and annual groundfish allocation an entity can hold.[29] While it is possible for anyone to buy quota from a willing seller, the cost may be prohibitive and restrict both new and young entrants from joining the industry. It also puts older fishermen nearing retirement in the driver's seat.

"Say a fisherman in Washington or Oregon wants to retire and sell, say, a Dungeness Crab permit for $200,000," says Luke Sawitsky, VP-Investments at Catch Invest, a Cape Cod–based nonprofit with national reach that offers concessionary loans to small-boat owners to buy permits and quota, an effort to anchor assets in small coastal communities. "The seller wants cash, so the buyer needs $200,000 or a loan. But the mortgage industry doesn't do fishery loans—fishing is hunting and highly cyclical—without a very high interest rate. Does an independent fisherman take out a risky loan and maybe put up his permits as collateral? If it doesn't work, he loses everything."

The result is that when a fisherman wants to retire and cash out, the most likely buyer is a well-capitalized company, not an independent fisherman. And there is no shortage of opinions on the matter. "When you see consolidation, you see less volume of fresh fish, which is what's happened in the Pacific Northwest," says Foley Fish's Ramsden. Kanae Tokunaga, director of the Coastal and Marine Economics Lab at the Gulf of Maine Research Institute, says, "There are some interesting management mechanisms to set aside a portion of quota to guarantee new fishermen can enter industry." Stavis Seafood's Richard Stavis says, "I'm pessimistic about New England, thinking old fishermen will sell out for pennies on the dollar and big players will take over and reap the rewards. They're in a box and the question is, 'How can they get out of the box?' Ground fishermen somehow have got be more like scallopers and figure out when and where to fish." Kate Masury, executive director of Eating with the Ecosystem, a nonprofit promoting independent fishermen, coastal communities, and underutilized species, says, "With transferable catch shares, we're setting ourselves up for another Carlos Rafael. We're giving ownership of permits and quotas to businesses that have nothing to do with the community. Meanwhile, the Conservation Law Foundation and The Nature Conservancy are buying up quotas to prevent fishing altogether. These are two extremes, and I don't like either."

Rothschild of UMass Dartmouth suggests a lack of fairness in that many owners of quota have found that they can "lease it out for windfall profits" without even going fishing. That has happened in New England as well as Alaska, where retired "armchair" fishermen lease their quota to working fishermen while they play golf in, say, Florida or Arizona. In essence, by acting in accordance with the mandates of the 2006 Magnuson revision, NOAA Fisheries is managing a group of fishermen who "won the lottery" when they were grandfathered into the quota system based on their historical catch levels. The system may be good for the fish, which is best in the long run for fisheries and the ocean, but it isn't necessarily good for the average (or young) fisherman in the short run.

Fishery advocates, economists, and working-waterfront proponents agree that consolidation could severely reduce the number of independently owned small boats. That, in turn, could turn working waterfronts into an upscale tapestry of condos and taffy shops. Consolidation could also affect pricing, the same way Walmart does, given the ability of highly capitalized firms to squeeze the market. It is clear that the 2010 reforms have created winners and losers, which is inevitable in any complex system. But it has also significantly reduced overfishing and accelerated stock rebuilding, putting the industry on a more sustainable trajectory.

"Whatever the negative perceptions of fishing, and that's mostly what we get, the real story is that the United States has spent a lot of money and time to become a global leader in sustainable fisheries. This is true even for swordfish and tuna, which are not sustainably fished everywhere, but are within our 200-mile zone," says Jared Auerbach, founder and CEO of Red's Best, a Boston-based market-maker that buys and sells fish from hundreds of small boats. "It's not too sexy, so it doesn't get much coverage. But it should be a point of pride for Americans. If they knew about the Magnuson law and the exclusive economic zone—just those two things—it would change outdated perceptions."

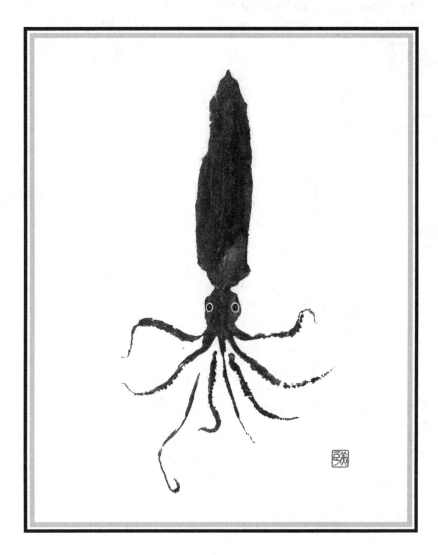

Squid

Chapter 3

As the Cowboys of the Sea Fade Away, a Postindustrial Fishery Emerges

I got the data. I got the fish. I know people want it.
—Jared Auerbach, founder and owner, Red's Best

Humans have always been effective predators, having wiped out most of the bison and whales in the world, even with relatively crude nineteenth-century tools. As fishing industrialized, evolving from sail to steam to diesel to hydraulics, from cotton and hemp to steel and synthetics, every improvement made it easier to raid the ocean more efficiently. That also resulted in habitat degradation, depletion of iconic species, and mortality of unwanted species or accidental bycatch.

Until recently, large-scale commercial fishing has effectively been *industrial* fishing, carried out with high-tech tools by the last commercial hunters of wild food in the world. Industrial hunting maximizes production with minimal regard for resource depletion or side effects, what economists call "externalities." In the United States, along with much of the European Union, United Kingdom, Australia, and New Zealand, industrial fishing peaked in the early 1990s (in Iceland it peaked in the 1980s) and has since been phasing into a more postindustrial mode. Fishermen still use highly effective new technologies, but they apply a different mindset, with an emphasis on sustainability, on extracting more value from less production, and on minimizing biomass depletion and other negative externalities, like habitat degradation. The cowboys of the sea have a new postindustrial mindset.

The Codfather was a true cowboy of the sea, an aggressive hunter and a ruthless businessman, who focused on maximizing revenues and profits without regard for any impact on the resource or the larger fleet. For all his extralegal activity and ruthless bravado, Rafael was not unique on the docks. Some say he was just colorful. Some even say he epitomized the American Dream, an immigrant who hit the jackpot. However he is judged, he certainly did keep the port of New Bedford and the local supply chain humming, with his forty-plus boats and huge catch volumes.

The high market value of scallops, with 100,000–150,000 pounds sold at auction on most days for $10–$15 a pound, has made New Bedford the top-value port in the United States for 20 years. Meanwhile, at the same auction, the coveted cod might go for $2 a pound and the less loved hake or redfish for 50–70 cents a pound. In many ways, the scallop industry is a poster child for postindustrial fishing. The fishery pioneered a collaboration between scientists, policy makers, and fishermen more than 20 years ago. It pioneered a rotational "inventory-management system," opening and closing beds based on the "best available science." The Atlantic scallop industry was certified by the Marine Stewardship Council in 2013, the same year New Bedford's Eastern Fisheries, the largest scallop processor and trader in the world, earned the British Retail Consortium certification, a global standard for food safety. Fleet Fisheries, another big New Bedford scallop producer, has multiple certifications for sustainability.

But scallops alone do not make a bustling industry or port; scallop boats are managed by a days-at-sea regulatory regimen (24 days per boat in 2020, with some other small catch allowances in certain areas), which doesn't generate enough business to keep the port infrastructure intact.

The decline in revenues in New Bedford when the Codfather's boats were banned from fishing for 18 months—$500,000 a day and 300 jobs lost—indicates that ice and fuel providers, along with shipyards, riggers, engineers, and gear technicians, just don't have enough steady business without a larger fleet spending more time at sea. Only groundfish boats, which spend more time on the water despite lower catch values, provide a consistent level of demand for services.

"Even if one species has a down year or down decade, a multispecies port can survive," says Ed Anthes-Washburn, former director of the Port of New Bedford. "A port can't survive on one species."

If the demise of the cod was the apparent nadir of New Bedford's groundfishing fleet, a phoenix arose from the ashes in the form of Blue Harvest Fisheries. In 2015, Blue Harvest, a new company with private-equity backing (Bregal Partners) bought a fleet of eight scallop boats from Peabody Corporation, based out of Newport News, Virginia. In 2016, the year Rafael was arrested, Blue Harvest acquired Harbor Blue, a New Bedford–based fishing company with seven more boats that targeted scallop, swordfish, tuna, crab, lobster, and surf clam. In 2018, Blue Harvest bought Atlantic Trawlers in Portland, Maine, which included five vessels and quotas for haddock, ocean perch (redfish), and Atlantic pollock. This is clearly emblematic of consolidation in the fishing industry, which is a separate issue (see chapter 2).

In short order, Blue Harvest replaced the Codfather in the port's ecosystem, just as dogfish has replaced cod and other overexploited groundfish in the marine ecosystem. Blue Harvest is a different kind of player, a postindustrial model for the future of wild-capture fisheries. It is by no stretch the only such example, but it is symbolic of the industry's transformation and an indication that new players are playing a different game.

Initially, Blue Harvest was buying permits (along with the boats) for the high-value scallop industry, as well as bluefin tuna and swordfish. But it quickly bought a large processing facility that handled a lot of "refreshed" Pacific cod and flatfish. Refreshed cod is headed and gutted in Alaska and frozen at sea, then shipped to New Bedford for filleting and distribution into food-service and retail sectors.[1] Soon after that, Blue Harvest bought an even larger processing plant on Herman Melville Boulevard once owned by High Liner, a big Canadian fish processor. Blue Harvest consolidated scallop and third-party groundfish processing under that roof, with Safe Quality Food certification, a globally recognized standard. In 2020, as a coup de grâce, under new CEO Keith Decker and with the approval of NOAA Fisheries, Blue

Harvest bought twelve vessels and twenty-seven fishing permits from the imprisoned Codfather (who became quite rich in jail and has gone on a real-estate buying spree since his 2021 release).

A year earlier, Quinn Fisheries, a successful scallop and boat-services company owned by Charlie and Michael Quinn, father and son, had bought six of Rafael's scallop vessels for $40 million, doubling their fleet to twelve.[2] Equally important, they had previously bought the vacant, 14-acre industrial plant of 147-year-old Revere Copper and Brass, a company started outside Boston in 1801 by Paul Revere. The Quinns are converting the newly dredged waterfront site into a new "inner-harbor" destination with a commercial shipyard for building and repairs—another phoenix from the ashes and a sign that the industry is coming back from a 20-year nightmare.[3]

Blue Harvest began retrofitting aging boats with new gear and electronics, as well as "super-chilling" water tanks that keep fish fresher, longer. At the time, only a handful of harvesters in New England had super-chilling capacity, which keeps fish at 31.8 degrees Fahrenheit in an ice slurry to lock in freshness without freezing (fish typically freeze at 28 degrees). Larger, international fish companies, like the 92-year-old Boston-based Stavis Seafoods and fishing vessels in Iceland, have used super-chilling and flash freezing for more than a decade, but it is a big investment that is only justified by consistently high volumes of fish. In addition to its premium products of scallops, tuna, and swordfish, Blue Harvest continued to diversify by targeting abundant but underutilized fish certified by the Marine Stewardship Council (MSC), such as haddock, Acadian redfish (ocean perch), and Atlantic pollock—all from the Gulf of Maine and Georges Bank.

In another break with the past, Blue Harvest is also taking proactive steps to ensure transparency, always an issue in fishing. An investigation of seafood fraud by Oceana, an international ocean-conservation advocacy organization, used DNA tests to determine that 33 percent of the fish it inspected was mislabeled. Fish labeled snapper and tuna were the least likely to be what their purveyors claimed they were.[4] Working with the Gulf of Maine Research Institute—collaboration between scientists, fishing companies, and fishermen is becoming more common in the postindustrial age—Blue Harvest joined a pilot program to test electronic at-sea monitoring of catch, bycatch, and discards, which were previously overseen by human on-board observers. Not only does electronic monitoring with video cameras, GPS, and sensors reduce labor costs, it provides more accurate and actionable data for reporting—about the areas fished, and the size and species of the fish—that helps inform policy makers and regulators. Blue Harvest also launched a voluntary dockside monitoring program, using a third-party company to routinely verify and share with NOAA Fisheries the species, volume, and weight of each vessel's catch. In 2020, Blue Harvest was the only harvester in New England using dockside monitors.[5]

"Blue Harvest is taking advantage of the new technologies entering commercial fisheries for processing, finding stock, monitoring catch," says Kanae Tokunaga, director of the Gulf of Maine Research Institute's Coastal and Marine Economics Lab. "New players like Blue Harvest, with more capital and training, can better utilize new technologies. Older men with older boats are not as receptive to technology. We have a bifurcated industry, with old and new."

Michael Rubino, senior advisor for Seafood Strategy at NOAA Fisheries, suggests that industry and regulators might want to examine ways to consolidate or streamline the use of new technologies and data streams to modernize the seafood value chain. "For example, NOAA requires fishermen to report catch of fish from federal waters. Much of that reporting is transitioning from paper to electronic formats. With growing market interest in tracking catch from boat to consumer, large supermarkets want full traceability with barcodes linked to production, processing, and distribution data. Instead of fishermen reporting the same data to several organizations, couldn't we combine all this electronic data into one stream using blockchain-type technologies to maintain confidentiality of data from individual fishermen?"

One of the weaknesses of the regulatory system that allowed Rafael to get away with his illegal practices for so long is that his company was vertically integrated, owning both the harvesting vessels and the dealers that purchased the catch. Rafael, for example, rarely sold his fish at the New Bedford Buyers and Sellers Exchange (BASE) auction, because that would have made his illegal catches public information. With his own distribution company, Rafael could ignore or falsify reporting. In 2021, two former BASE auction employees, Peter

Medeiros and Nelson Couto, alleged that BASE owners Richard and Raymond Canastra did sometimes offload and weigh Rafael's fish, which Rafael then had delivered to his own business. The Canastras allegedly asked their employees to initially prepare accurate bills of lading for species for which Rafael had limited quota (like cod)—and then falsify them by listing haddock as the catch if the environmental police were not on the scene.[6]

Like Rafael's former business, Blue Harvest is vertically integrated. Blue Harvest intended from the start to build a modern, transparent company, but its corporate structure is one of the reasons the company thought it so important to start using dockside monitors and electronic at-sea monitoring. "There's been a lot of negative press generated over the last five years about the East Coast fishery. And we felt that dockside monitoring was a way that we could add credibility to the fishery and what we're doing," says CEO Decker.[7]

Blue Harvest has been a shot in the arm for New Bedford. "You need a big company to develop the supply chain—so that if you land 50,000 pounds of fresh fish you can find buyers and processors," says Anthes-Washburn. "Blue Harvest can process 100 million pounds a year, and that will guarantee consistency of supply and price. Most of the groundfish guys don't have the same level of investment in gear and technology, like flash freezing or cold-water storage, which you need to compete against high-quality frozen whitefish from Iceland or around the world. If a buyer can get high-quality frozen product to sell in 3 months or fresh fish to sell in 7 days—for most buyers, frozen fish is a no brainer." And once that happens, it is hard to switch back. When the availability of fresh drops below a certain threshold, it is replaced by frozen and rarely switches back.

Iceland, for example, can deliver hook-and-line haddock into Boston cheaper than New Bedford can deliver it to Boston—even though it's 2,400 miles away compared to 60. "Iceland's fishermen collaborated to secure public money to help rationalize its fleet—they cut it in half to modernize it and added processing plants to drive down cost and improve quality," says NOAA Fisheries' Rubino.

"We've lost our share of the market," Scituate fisherman Kevin Norton says. "We can't compete with a piece of haddock from Iceland that is perfectly filleted, perfectly proportioned, that sells for $3 a pound. That's what's putting us out of business, even more than the regulations, even more than NOAA."[8]

Blue Harvest sells both fresh and frozen product. Stavis Seafoods and Bristol Seafood in Portland, Maine, both big traders, source globally for certified products and generally sell frozen. Bristol, for example, imports cod and haddock flash-frozen within 4 hours of catch from Norway to Portland, where it is thawed, filleted, and hand-trimmed. With a new Individual Quick Frozen tunnel, it then flash freezes the fillets again for retail. It once offered 1,400 fish products but has reduced its line to four—scallops (from around the world), Atlantic salmon (farmed), Norwegian cod, and sockeye salmon (from the Pacific). It sells both fillets and prepackaged frozen "heat and serve" bags under the My Fish Dish brand. "A lot of people are uncomfortable cooking seafood at home, so we're trying to make it easier to do," says Irene Moon, VP-Marketing at Bristol. Stavis Seafoods, by contrast, which owns fifty fishing vessels in different parts of the world, has a drop-down menu on its website that shows it can find and deliver virtually any seafood from anywhere, if verified as "sustainable."

One of the things that distinguishes Blue Harvest, which also sells frozen scallops, haddock, pollock, and ocean perch for retail, is that it is selling *domestically* caught and processed fish. Stavis Seafoods also buys squid from an American partner, Seafreeze Ltd., in North Kingston, Rhode Island. Seafreeze itself has two high-capacity freezer trawlers that can hold up to 350 metric tons—mackerel, squid, butterfish (the so-called MSB fishery), and herring. And its land-based cold-storage facilities have capacity for 23 million pounds of fish. This is industrial in scale—but postindustrial in approach.

The Rhode Island squid fishery, like Atlantic scallops, is certified by the Marine Stewardship Council. To achieve certification, fisheries undergo a long and expensive (up to $100,000) initial approval process, then an annual $75,000 audit to ensure compliance with catch quota and other regulations. Companies like Walmart and MacDonald's (Alaskan pollock) only buy and sell certified fish, so the certification has some clout, but lack of certification doesn't mean a given fish or fishery isn't sustainable. It just means the fishery hasn't paid for the certification. "And even a certification says nothing about what happens to the fish once it's landed," says Foley Fish's Laura Ramsden.

SeaFresh USA, another Kingston, Rhode Island, processor, is similar in many ways to Blue Harvest—with state-of-the art processing facilities, and, in addition to squid, an emphasis on local and often underutilized fish, such as monkfish, skate, and scup. Sea Fresh USA's signature product is both fresh and frozen Rhode Island calamari, as well as whole squid; it also offers sushi-quality tuna and fluke. Most squid landed at the Port of Galilee in Point Judith, Rhode Island, is frozen and sent to China for processing because it generally arrives in massive catches in the spring—the so-called Mother's Day Massacre—overwhelming local processing facilities. Squid is also painstakingly difficult and expensive to process.

Most seafood companies either harvest or source their fish and then take orders from buyers. Foley Fish takes orders from buyers before it sources the fish. Foley Fish, which owns no boats, has operated with a postindustrial mindset since 1906, when Michael Frances Foley opened a fish shop near Faneuil Hall in Boston to sell fish "fresh off the boat." Even today, Foley Fish buys fish that is at most 2 days out of the water, processes it in Boston or New Bedford, then ships it around North America by refrigerated truck the next day. Redfish, pollock, monkfish, and skate are shipped fresh in tins with ice. Only shrimp and squid are frozen before shipping. Foley also sells lobster, shrimp, Atlantic salmon, calamari, and swordfish.

In the 1950s, Michael's son Frank opened a "model fish plant" in South Boston, setting a new industry standard for quality control. Before government regulations for fish processing, the Foley plant was featured by the National Marine Fisheries Service in its educational pamphlets. In the 1980s, Frank's son Mike took over and opened a second plant in New Bedford. Mike's daughter, Laura Foley Ramsden, the current co-owner of Foley's, with her husband Peter, is the fourth-generation Foley in the family business.

Foley Fish is mostly wild and local, sourced from the Gulf of Maine and Georges Bank, except for farmed salmon from the Bay of Fundy in New Brunswick and wild shrimp from the Gulf of Mexico. "The Bay of Fundy Atlantic salmon is our most popular item," says Ramsden. "The value add for us is feed and freshness. It's a 10-hour drive back to our plants, much fresher than salmon from Norway, the Faroe Islands, or Chile, not to mention a smaller carbon footprint. Chilean salmon gets deep chilled before flying and it thaws en route. Plus, all the feed is dry pellets. The flavor profile is not there." Foley Fish is maniacal about flavor profile and has a tasting kitchen to sample flavor before it ships. The kitchen doubles as a venue for its 3-day "School of Fish" training programs for chefs, fish purchasers, and restaurant owners.

The Foley process starts with trained buyers, who will only take a day-old fish off a 7-day boat, and who use probes to check the color and firmness of the meat. Foley also buys at the BASE auction in New Bedford—and is often the first buyer to show up in the early morning to inspect the fish. It sends trucks every day to New England's top ports and providers, many of whom have been part of the Foley network for decades. "Last in, first out, that's what distinguishes us. We take orders, get the fish, and pack it to order," says Ramsden. "We grade the fish when unloading and take only the best fish from each boat."

Foley doesn't add chemicals (to stave off bacteria) or water (to add weight), as many processors do. Instead, Foley packs its fish in super-chilled "flake" ice (at 15 degrees Fahrenheit) while it awaits processing. On the conveyor belt for cutting, the fish is sprayed with chlorinated water to kill bacteria and increase shelf life. "Foley's is the only one in the city that does that and it's their claim to fame," says Phil Mello, plant manager at Bergie's, the largest independent processor in New Bedford. "Mike Foley, back in the day, would call customers a week later to see if the fish were holding up. If you're going to spend the money to buy from Foley's, you've got to know how to take care of the fish."

Once cut, Foley packs the fish in tins that conduct cold to maintain proper temperature during shipping. Freshness is all predicated on temperature control, ideally between 28 degrees (where fish freezes) and 32 degrees. "I tell people to count on the day they receive the fish plus three to eat it, although the maximum shelf life is 14 days from harvest."

The name of the boat that caught the fish goes on the invoice with a QR code. "People were initially jazzed about the name of the boat, but that's not what worries customers," says Ramsden. "Traceability is important, but we are MSC-certified and get audited. Every species we offer is harvested in accordance with strict fishery-management measures and tightly managed by federal, state, or international authorities. What people are nervous about, above all, is the freshness of the fish and the taste. In places like Chicago, Detroit, and Atlanta, the idea that we are on the docks adds more value." Buyers are a mix of specialty retailers, hotels, resorts, country clubs, restaurants chains, and institutions, like Tufts University.

Foley Fish is preindustrial, at least as far as fishing goes, which makes it postindustrial. Foley Fish, like Stavis, predates the intense industrial fishing that began after World War II with repurposed Navy ships. If the economic model still works, why change it?

Or, if you want to get into a tight business, why not start with a new model? In 1982, two New Bedford guys, Mark Bergeron and Sonny Stanley, got into the fishing business—with a pickup truck. They rode around at night to docks around New Bedford and bought fish direct off boats, mostly the underutilized fish that weren't sold at the auction. Bergeron and Stanley were known as the "Night Riders."

Two years later, Bergeron and Stanley formed Bergie's Seafood, dedicated to offloading boats from New York to Maine, 364 days a year, 24 hours a day, and processing and distributing the fish. They first rented the plant, then bought it. Bergie's is now the top independent offloader in New Bedford—but now the boats come to them. Roll up the large back door of Bergie's and you could jump right into the harbor, which is where the boats tie up to offload.

"We have boats that just fish for us, a lot of out-of-state boats, and they don't go to auction. Why? You can go offshore and never see a boat," says Bergie's Mello. "Minute you come in and put fish on display at the auction everyone sees what you got and they try to figure out where you were fishing." Fishing is probably not as competitive as it was back in the old free-market, open-access days, because of the intense regulations, but it is by its nature a very secretive business.

Like Foley, Bergie's looks for the best fish it can find, soaks it in brine, hand cuts it, then ships it fresh by truck to Canada, Florida, Texas, and points in between. Today, Bergie's offloads all North Atlantic species, including haddock, cod, yellowtail flounder, greysole, Georges Bank and Nantucket Channel flounder, fluke, sea dabs, hake, pollock, ocean perch (redfish), dogfish, and monk. The plant can process 20,000 pounds of fish daily.

In 2008, roughly 25 years after the Night Riders made a name for themselves, Red's Best started in Boston with a similar model. Boston native Jared Auerbach had fished in Alaska after college in Colorado then returned home and started gillnetting for codfish out of Scituate, yellowtail on Stellwagen Bank, and monkfish out of Rhode Island, with some lobstering on the side. He was looking for a way to enter a tight, insular industry that was contracting under new regulations, rather than opening its doors to young entrants. "I could have made a living some other way, who knows how, but I really loved the fishing industry," says Auerbach. At the time, he had not heard of Bergie's or the Night Riders. But he had a very similar idea: Buy fish off the docks in multiple ports from small, independent fishermen, and process and distribute those fish. Unlike more particular buyers, such as Foley, Auerbach would take any kind of fish in any quantity—from 30,000 pounds of haddock to one striped bass or bluefin tuna, la crème de la crème. The trick was grading it and finding an appropriate market based on the quality. Auerbach had the entrepreneurial zeal and independent mindset of the old individualistic, free-market fishermen. He was a cowboy of the dock.

Headquartered on the Boston Fish Pier, the oldest continuously operated fish pier in the United States (since 1914), with another plant in New Bedford on Herman Melville Boulevard—"I've got the greatest addresses for a fish business: Boston Fish Pier and Herman Melville Boulevard," he likes to say—Auerbach started buying fish off small boats in Gloucester, Chatham, Martha's Vineyard (via Woods Hole), New Bedford (all in Massachusetts), and Point Judith, Rhode Island. Like the Night Riders, he started out with a small, refrigerated van. It was a way for him to break into the tight-knit, insular business and support independent fishermen. Today, his pickup has morphed into an army of small trucks and three eighteen-wheelers that drive fish to Boston or New Bedford for processing and distribution.

Auerbach's idea quickly took hold, proving his business concept of an aggregate, direct unloader of independent fishing boats, but it quickly created a major headache: accounting and payments. Offloading up to 1,000 boats a week, with a huge range of product, and figuring out what and how to pay the fishermen was a big problem. "We had a lot of scraps of paper, napkins covered with blood and dirt or worse, and four-part carbon copies," says Auerbach. "Fishermen and truckdrivers don't much like paperwork, so the numbers weren't always reliable. I was up all night making the numbers work."

"The boat would get a copy at the point of unloading," Auerbach told the *New York Times* in 2016. "The government would get a copy. I'd file a copy. And then I'd write in the prices." As for paying the fishermen, "I'd have to get checks and then match the checks to the paperwork and mail them. It was an absolute nightmare that wasn't scalable."[9]

Auerbach developed an app to track the unloading, by boat. And because he knew that data-reporting was super annoying for boat owners, he gave them the data in electronic form. "It saved them time, helped them track landings against their quota, and the clear data developed transparency and trust with Red's Best," said Auerbach.

It also helped Red's with inventory management. When a truck offloads a boat, the driver records the catch onto a wireless tablet with a mobile printer. "The driver puts the catch data directly onto the internet, and our whole staff can see in real time what fish is being loaded onto our truck," Auerbach says. That means they can begin to find a market for it.

Trust is key because Red's Best doesn't pay fishermen when it unloads their boats. Fish prices fluctuate daily based on raw supply-and-demand economics, one of the few things about fishing that hasn't changed. A verifiable technology platform helped to clear settlements at the end of each week. The data also allowed Red's Best to better match supply and demand on the trading side.

With the system in place and improving over time, Red's Best was able to scale its business by handling more and more little transactions. In 2019, Red's Best offloaded and bought 10.7 million pounds of fish and 3.5 million pieces of shellfish from 823 different fishermen, which accounted for 29,000 individual transactions. On its busiest day, July 25, Red's Best offloaded 378 separate boats—not the kind of business you want to run with four-part carbon copies.

Those numbers show that Red's Best is a powerful aggregator of supply. In 2012, Auerbach began to address the other side of the coin—demand. Once the data app was up and running, Red's added a QR code that links to a URL with data on the species, boat, and captain. It puts that code on every "Red's Best" box it ships. "Providing the data is really a way to tell a story and less about traceability, because people already trust us to provide high quality local fish. Fishermen are compelling American figures that consumers want to connect with. Telling a story gives us the ability to influence consumer demand, to de-commoditize the fish. Americans are so good at taking a swimming fish and putting it in a white Styrofoam box in 24 hours."

"The supply chain used to be supply driven," says Auerbach. "The chef or food service tells me what they want. If they want cod, I work backwards to get cod. That used to work 30 or 40 years ago, but with today's regulations and quota there's a lot more variation in the catch. The best fishermen in the world don't know what they're going to catch when they leave port. That's the romance, that's the draw. For me, if it's legal to land, give it to me."

New Bedford's Anthes-Washburn uses almost the exact same line: "If it's legal, we land it in New Bedford." Both of which, of course, harken back to the iconic slogan of Legal Sea Foods: "If it isn't fresh, it isn't legal." The legal element is what really makes today's fishing industry postindustrial, for without legal regulations that are followed and enforced, all you've got is a bunch of hunters doing what they do best without regard for the consequences, or "negative externalities."

But that still leaves the demand side of the equation that Auerbach has been working on. The problem is, a lot of people still want their cod and flounder, or their imported salmon and shrimp. The United States imports $6 billion worth of shrimp, much from very questionable Southeast Asian farms, which is more than the value of *all* the fish it exports. Auerbach, along with a lot of others, is working on reducing demand for imports and building demand for domestic fish of all sorts. To that end, he's got a couple of big fish on the line, including Harvard University (see chapter 4).

"I got the data. I got the fish. I know people want it."

WHITING

Chapter 4

Eating with the Ecosystem

*What unites fishermen, fishmongers, entrepreneurs, food-systems
leaders, and seafood consumers in this movement is a passion
to infuse a new set of values into how we catch, process, sell,
eat, appreciate seafood.*

—Sitka Salmon Shares, Sitka, Alaska

The "foodies" are way ahead of the "fishies" in glorifying fresh, local food, and experimenting with new vegetables and cuts of meat. But the fishies are now following a similar playbook and beginning to influence the way fish is sold and prepared.

The locavore movement started in earnest in June 2005, during the San Francisco celebration of World Environment Day. A group of women—Jen Maiser, Jessica Prentice, Sage Van Wing, and Dede Sampson—unveiled the Local Food Challenge: spend a month eating only food produced within a 100-mile radius of your home. The women called themselves the "locavores" and encouraged others to join their quest for a more sustainable food system. For many in the sustainable-food movement, which had been growing for a couple of decades at that point, the globalized food system presented serious environmental problems. Moreover, the locavores argued, food produced in industrial systems was less healthy and less tasty. Local farms must go beyond organic to use a variety of agroecological farming practices, local being key. By 2005, the organic label was already being misapplied—a form of "greenwashing"—often to food produced on the other side of the world on an industrial farm.[1]

The fishies, needless to say, or the New England Seafoodies, as one Facebook group is called, were definitely a bit behind the locavore foodies. In 2011, author Paul Greenberg told Oceana, the international ocean-advocacy group, that it was not enough to have a closed echo chamber of marine conservationists talking to one another. "There has been a food reform movement going on in this country for nearly 40 years now," said Greenberg. "We need to tie fish and seafood reform to that groundswell. And, well, I wrote *Four Fish* [a 2010 book that was a *New York Times* bestseller] to be that bridge between the foodies and the fishies. So, if you are a fishie and you know a lot of foodies, try to bring them onboard to the fishie cause."[2]

In 2012, a Massachusetts Maritime Economy report said that "the seafood industry has been slow to jump on the locavore/direct marketing movement," with only a "few niche companies." It also noted that 90 percent of landed groundfish is sold into commodity markets and may pass through as many as twenty hands between boat and plate.[3] In 2016, the *New York Times* wrote that "beyond Maine lobster, Maryland crabs, and Gulf shrimp, fish has been largely ignored by foodies obsessing over the provenance of their meals, even though seafood travels a complex path. Until recently, diners weren't asking many questions about where it came from, which meant restaurants and retailers didn't feel a need to provide the information."[4]

These statements are generally true but obscure the fact that the locavore fishie movement was sparked in 2007, two years after the Local Food Challenge. The Port Clyde (Maine) Community-Supported Fishery, modeled after community-supported agriculture groups, was the nation's first. It was started by the Midcoast Fisherman's Cooperative, representing the only groundfish fleet between Portland and Canada.

Josh Stoll, who grew up near Port Clyde in Downeast Maine, the easternmost part of the state between the mouth of the Penobscot River and Canada, took the idea down to North Carolina, where he was a graduate student in environmental management at Duke's Nicholas School of the Environment.

"Much to my surprise, I found a lot of similarities between Downeast Maine and Downeast North Carolina, the rural waterfront towns east of the Durham Triangle," says Stoll, now a professor at the University of Maine, specializing in ecosystem-based fisheries management, seafood distribution and trade, community resilience, and aquaculture. "They were both small communities trying to hold onto economically important fisheries but feeling lost and losing ground. Eastern Maine is a one-trick pony with lobster; Carolina is quite diverse, with shrimp, blue crab, and flounder nearshore; oysters, clams, and scallops in deeper waters; and snapper and grouper offshore. Fishermen knew whom they sold to, but no one really knew where the fish went after that."

Stoll, along with other Duke graduate students, began to organize a community-supported fishery in North Carolina, starting with a connection to Carteret Catch, a fishing trade group that rallied its members behind the idea. It was actually an idea that Stoll had been thinking about years before he heard about the Port Clyde Community Supported Fishery. "Interestingly, Port Clyde had learned from a failed attempt to start a similar support group in North Carolina, and when I learned about this connection, I saw a different way to structure it in North Carolina that ended up working," says Stoll.

Under the auspices of Duke University, the Walking Fish Community Supported Fishery started in 2009, linking fishermen on the coast to consumers in Durham. Stoll was excited to get the first three or four checks from new members in his mailbox, then ten checks the following week, and then a note from the post office: "Come talk to us." Walking Fish had received a stack of 400 checks from people signing up for Walking Fish, far too many for the pilot project to support.

"People have forgotten where their food comes from," said Pam Morris, a former fisher who was president of Carteret Catch, about Walking Fish when it started. "And they are fed so much propaganda about the commercial fishing industry. We can help dispel that directly."[5]

As with community-supported agriculture groups and the locavore food movement, Stoll and other graduate students saw buying directly from local fishermen as crucial to support local incomes, enhance sustainability, and build a values-based seafood movement that might reconnect harvesters to consumers.

About the time author Paul Greenberg mentioned the idea of converting foodies into fishies, and about the time when Jared Auerbach, founder of Red's Best, was trying to solve the demand side of the fish-distribution system, community-based models started popping up all over North America—Abundant Seafood in South Carolina, Off the Hook in Nova Scotia, Skipper Otto's in British Columbia, Cape Ann Fresh Catch in Massachusetts. What had started in Maine and North Carolina was part of a bigger movement, the first hint of a sea change in fish distribution. An estimated 80–90 percent of the seafood we eat in the United States is imported (some of which has been exported for processing and returned). The average boat-to-plate journey is over 5,000 miles, according to Slow Food USA. These are hallmarks of globalized, industrial food and seafood systems that are slowly being refashioned.

Ten years ago, a lot of community-supported fishery startups were reinventing the wheel without support. To accelerate the movement, Stoll started a networking platform in 2011 called Local Catch, with a "clunky, handmade" knowledge-sharing website. It had no funding, no formal structure, and no institutional base. But its member base grew and grew, starting with the first of three national summits in 2012.

By 2018, when Stoll was a tenure-track faculty member at the University of Maine, he brought Local Catch under the university's umbrella. In 2020, Local Catch received a $500,000 grant from the U.S. Department of Agriculture and hired its first salaried employee. At the end of 2020, more than 200 members with more than 500 distribution drops belonged to the Local Catch network—with a big cluster in New England but the fastest growth on the West Coast.

The Local Catch story is positive, but a positive story is not news. Illegal, unreported, and unregulated fishing, and pirates like the Codfather, typically get the headlines. In 2018, the sustainable-seafood movement got the headlines, thanks to Sea to Table, a revered and early mover in the sustainable fish movement that had started in 1996. A family-run, fish-distribution business in Brooklyn, New York, Sea to Table sold nationwide to celebrity chefs and restaurants, as well as consumers and institutions.

Sea to Table had allegedly mislabeled fish, not unlike the Codfather, a form of co-optation by a "sustainable" purveyor that the locavores had identified with the organic label some 15 or more years earlier. The resultant Sea to Table scandal rocked the Slow Fish movement, an offshoot of the international Slow Food movement.

In 2018, after intense winter storms left East Coast harbors thick with ice, some of the country's top chefs and trendy restaurants were offering sushi-grade tuna supposedly pulled in fresh off boats landing in Montauk, New York. "But it was just an illusion," reported the Associated Press, after a lengthy investigation. "No tuna was landing there. The fish had long since migrated to warmer waters." Reporters had set up cameras and shot more than 36,000 time-lapse photos of Montauk Harbor, at the tip of Long Island, showing that no tuna boats had docked in the ice. DNA samples suggested the yellowfin tuna had actually come from the other side of the world. Reporters also traced the company's supply chain to migrant fishermen in foreign waters who described labor abuses (pay of $1.50 a day for 22-hour shifts), poaching, and the slaughter of sharks, whales, and dolphins.[6] (See chapter 12 for more on illegal fishing.)

While some industry insiders say Sea to Table's fraudulent labeling *could* have been the result of an honest mistake, most lamented the stain it cast on the otherwise transparent, local-catch movement. "There's tension between lack of verifiable sourcing and consumer demand; people want traceable tuna but they want it in December," says Luke Sawitsky, VP-Investments at Catch Invest, who was a fish buyer in Alaska during the scandal. "People were saying, 'Yes, this really hurts the sustainable-fish movement. You can't even trust the traceable companies.'"

But the movement has been growing close to 15 years, and there is a lot more good than bad about it. In 2008, when Stoll was organizing Walking Fish in North Carolina, a similar support group was forming in Massachusetts. Cape Ann Fresh Catch was started by the Gloucester Fishermen's Wives Association and now claims to be the largest support group in the United States. It is fitting that the nation's oldest fishing port was at the tip of the spear in remaking the fish-distribution model.

Members sign up in advance for a certain portion of fish—1 pound, 2 pounds, or a whole (3–5 pound) fish; they select anywhere from 4 to 8 weeks in any of six 8-week seasons; and they choose to pick up at one of twenty locations or get home delivery within 50 miles of Gloucester. You don't know what type of fish you will get until you receive an email on the day of delivery noting the name of the vessel—and a recipe.

In traditional markets, fishermen target species that fetch the highest price. Targeting more abundant species and offering their catch at a fixed price per pound for the season helps relieve stocks stressed by global commodity-market forces, giving species and ecosystems time to recover and replenish. And the upfront money members pay gives fishermen better financial security.

Sitka Salmon Shares, formed in 2011 in Sitka, Alaska, has similar values to other community-supported fisheries but has stretched the model and the definition of "community." With 20,000 members, many of whom are in the Midwest—cofounder Nic Mink was a professor of environmental studies at Galesburg College in Illinois when he started Sitka Salmon Shares after a trip to Alaska with college students—the group is one of the fastest-growing community-supported fisheries in the country. Sitka Salmon Shares clearly expands the definition of fresh and local into frozen, domestic, and direct.

Sitka Salmon Shares is modeled much like a cooperative, with more than twenty fishermen owners (holders of equity) who harvest sixteen species of fish. The focus is on four types of wild salmon, but also sablefish, Pacific cod, halibut, and various crustaceans, depending on the season. "Diversity across fisheries is always important in wild fisheries but more so now, with the climate issues," says Kelly Harrell, chief officer of Fisheries and Sustainability, who is a national leader in the values-based fish world.

In 2015, its fourth year, Sitka Salmon Shares built its own processing plant and distribution center, infrastructure that allowed it to capitalize when COVID hit in spring of 2020. Sitka Salmon Shares has also invested more than $1 million in freezing technology to lock in a "fresh-from-ocean" taste (salmon is frozen at –30 degrees Fahrenheit or lower) and is now a vertically integrated "boat-to-doorstep" business.

Direct marketing often demands freezing fresh, either on-boat or shortly after landing. Many consumers still demonstrate a marked preference for fresh fish, often associating "fresh" with a product that is healthy, high quality, and local. But if you live in the Midwest, where a lot of Sitka Salmon Shares' members do, you definitely want your salmon flash frozen.[7]

With the fishermen-owner model, fishermen earn an average of 10–30 percent more for their harvest, which can equate to $20,000 or more extra income in a given season. "Many small-scale fishermen are often living on thin margins," says Nic Mink, chief fishmonger. Says Harrell: "The driving value is a 'community capital' approach, with the goal of increasing fishermen's equity over time."

Sitka Salmon Shares is growing and expanding nationally, which used to be unusual in the Local Catch/Slow Fish world, but times are changing with new consumer demands and flash-freezing techniques. "Within the Slow Food world, there is some antipathy to scale and more support for the 'small is beautiful' approach," says Mink. "The onus is on us to show that we can grow without compromising our values and show there is benefit to that scale."

Mink himself is a bit ambivalent about the growth trajectory but is driven by a desire to build his own supply chain—with processing plant, warehousing operations, and distribution equipment. "This is something that no other community fishery has done and it's something that we believe is at the center of our ability to deliver more sustainable, responsible, traceable, and, of course, higher-quality fish," Mink wrote in a tenth anniversary letter to members.

The local-catch movement that sparked many community-supported fisheries is part of a larger network that includes sustainability advocates, chefs, and fishmongers. A key advocate in New England is Eating with the Ecosystem, a Rhode Island–based nonprofit that engages marine scientists, commercial fishermen, chefs, and seafood businesses to promote a "place-based approach to sustaining New England's wild seafood."

Eating with the Ecosystem is very much in sync with the Local Catch and values-based seafood movements. A key element of that is the idea of persuading people to "eat like a fish"—eating what the ocean provides, adopting a supply-based, rather than a demand-based, approach. But it's not easy to do because it is often hard to find the abundant and sustainable species, which are crowded out of retail and restaurant markets by the fish that people demand—farmed shrimp and salmon from the other side of the world, or the old favorites like tuna and cod that are in short supply.

At least 100 edible wild species thrive in New England. But how often are species like butterfish, scup, John Dory, dogfish, periwinkles, sea robin, skate, and razor clams offered for sale in the local market-place? Not so often, as a 2018 "citizen-research" survey showed. "Citizen scientists found a stark mismatch between what's swimming in local waters and what's available at local seafood counters," says Kate Masury, executive director of Eating with the Ecosystem. "This imbalance can strain the resilience of New England's underwater ecosystems and undermine the well-being of the people who depend on them."

Eating with the Ecosystem sent eighty-six people out to scour local markets for fifty-two species in all New England states and report on the availability at retail outlets. Five species led the pack in availability in the marketplace, at anywhere from 50 to 80 percent of all retail outlets: lobster, sea scallops, soft-shelled clams, cod, and haddock. In contrast, the majority of species (forty-seven) were found in less than half the outlets, and thirty-two of those species were found in less than 10 percent of outlets.[8]

"Our work focuses on five anchors: proximity, symmetry, adaptability, connectivity, and community," says Masury. "That means finding wild seafood from a marine ecosystem close by, balancing our diet with a variety of seafood, and trying new species that enter an ecosystem as that ecosystem changes. Proximity matters because you care about the local ecosystem and the local people who harvest the fish or food."

Masury is a fan of Sitka Salmon Shares and sees value in stretching the definition of local. "Even if you live in Chicago and eat fluke or squid from Point Judith or lobster from Maine, there may be five people in the supply chain you are supporting. I'd rather eat seafood in

Chicago that I know comes from a small domestic fisherman rather than from Peru or Japan. The money produced by catching that seafood supports local fishing families, and the benefit of that seafood stays within the community."[9]

One of the more powerful national advocates for a new approach to seafood is Barton Seaver. Just as Alice Waters put organic on the map in California in the 1980s, celebrity chefs are key to spreading the gospel of underutilized and sustainable fish. Seaver, who lives in Maine, has been doing that for domestic seafood since 2007. As the chef-owner of the sustainable-seafood restaurant Hook in Washington, DC, Seaver served more than 100 species of seafood in 1 year. In 2009, *Esquire* magazine named Seaver Chef of the Year for his work at Blue Ridge restaurant in D.C.[10] In 2010, as a National Geographic fellow, Seaver shifted his focus away from the restaurant business and started speaking and writing about the health and coastal-community benefits of sustainable seafood.

As the keynote speaker at a Future of Seafood conference in 2017, Seaver came up with one of his more memorable lines—"seafood is the only protein that is guilty until proven innocent." This was a reference to the stigma against seafood from the average American consumer, a stigma that seems to intensify when the concept of farm-raised seafood comes into play, which Seaver saw as "a troubling phenomenon that isn't seen nearly as often with land-based farming."[11]

"Sustainability represents the 'what, where, why, and how' fish is caught. The Who and the Why are what's important to me," Seaver began a TED talk in 2010.[12] "I want to know the people behind my dinner choices, I want to know how I impact them and how they impact me. I want to know why they fish, how they rely on the ocean's bounty for their living. Understanding this enables us to shift our perception of seafood away from a commodity to an opportunity to restore our ecosystem. What do we call this? I think we call this 'restorative seafood.' If sustainability is the capacity to endure and maintain, restorative is the ability to replenish and progress in an evolving and dynamic system. It is a more hopeful, human, and useful way of understanding our environment."

In an interview with Terry Gross on PBS's *Fresh Air* in 2017, Seaver said that just three species—tuna, salmon, and shrimp—account for

65 percent of total US fish consumption. "There's nothing unsustainable about fishing. What's unsustainable is market pressure. And that's why I think that we as consumers and as chefs need to become more educated about the wealth of diversity of seafood that's available to us so that we place our demand across a broad footprint of the ecosystem," he said.[13] In his book, *The Joy of Seafood*, Seaver writes, "For too long, we have thought about seafood as a product without provenance, a commodity that is ever the same, from places other than where we are, but we are beginning to rediscover seafood, once so dearly prized in our culinary culture, from sea to shining sea, and then forgotten by later generations."[14]

"Barton Seaver has been great for the industry," said Red's Best's Auerbach. "Barton does a really good job of connecting the influential purchasers to ground-level people like me. Without a guy like Barton, it's hard to make that connection."

Local fish shops are another big piece of the puzzle—if you know you should be eating an abundant, certified fish but can't find it you are likely to swing back to an old favorite, like frozen shrimp from Thailand, where mangrove swamps have been destroyed to create farms. Similarly, fishermen don't target species for which there is no robust wholesale or retail market demand, which means they will remain underutilized. No consumer demand and no fishing demand means minimal retail presence and low value—a vicious cycle.

Fearless Fish Market, a fish shop that opened in 2019 in Providence, Rhode Island, is out to change that. Its mission is to support local fishermen and fisheries and encourage "fearless" consumers by selling high-quality and often unusual fish that people don't see in supermarkets.

"Supermarkets don't often carry the interesting local species that are available to us in Rhode Island," says Stu Meltzer, co-owner (with his wife, Rose), who had 6 years of experience in fish distribution (Chicago) and fish shops (Boston and New Bedford) before opening Fearless Fish Market. "I thought there was an opportunity to do better."[15]

Meltzer primarily buys from dealers who buy directly from boats, except for salmon from the West Coast and Maine, so inventory depends on the daily, local catch. Supermarkets know months in advance what fish they will be selling because they have contracts with wholesalers. Fearless Fish Market doesn't know what it's going to get day to day, given the uncertainty of fishing. Thus, it posts on its website and social-media feeds a daily list of its offerings, which range from farmed Atlantic salmon to wild squid to unagi (eel) fillets to Jonah crab claws to smoked herring in wine to skate wings. "It's all in our name: We want our customers to be fearless, confident, and happy when it comes to eating and cooking fish," says Meltzer. "The sheet changes every day, that's how fishing works."

In 2020, Fearless Fish Market started its own community-supported fishery. It sends out recipes with the fish, helpful when trying to cook an unusual catch like a sea robin. "People want high-quality fish. There's a disconnect between that and the supply chain and how fish is treated," says Melzer. "People can recognize quality and are willing to pay for it. People ask, 'When did the fish come in?' That's not the question. The question is, 'How was it handled?'"

About 90 percent of Fearless Fish Market's inventory is fresh fish, with some frozen salmon from Alaska. Its top seller is salmon, mostly farmed in the Gulf of Maine. "Local bluefin tuna is also a big seller. Hake is popular as a replacement for cod or haddock, and it's less expensive. Black sea bass and weakfish are popular fillets," says Meltzer.

Fearless Fish Market is a new kind of player in the emerging fish-distribution system. It is going local and domestic in a global import world that often sources from large industrial fleets. "In the global supply chain, there are big import volumes from Thailand, Indonesia, South Korea, with possible slave labor and illegal fishing involved. That's one conversation. The other is a local high-end, artisanal fishery. We're in that small-scale artisanal world. I want to know the boat, not just to know the boat, but I want to know how the fish is treated."

To really grow the market and spread the word, however, you need institutional buyers serving a young demographic. The Red's Best–Harvard University partnership is a model for building a market through story telling.

"The Harvard story is huge, it's cool," says Red's Best's Auerbach. "Harvard was serving farmed Asian whitefish in its dining halls and getting pressure from students for more local and sustainable fish." Students wanted X, Harvard was supplying Y. In 2012, Harvard approached Red's Best for a solution to a new variation of the ancient supply-and-demand mismatch problem.

In 2013 and 2014, when fishermen were trying to figure out the mind-numbingly complex quota system (annual catch limits), Auerbach was pushing to develop a futures contract. "Say Harvard wanted Northern shrimp from Maine. Everyone did. There used to be shit-loads of it at 70 cents a pound. I said, 'I'll sell it to you for the next year at $1 a pound.' Well, that didn't work, because the next year the wholesale price went to $1.50, as the supply diminished."

Auerbach went back to the drawing board. He needed a consistent supply at a consistent price—but a supply of what? Harvard had a huge demand, with at least twenty different delivery drops, and needed to know in advance what fish it could expect. "I said, 'I don't know what I'm going to have 3 months from now, but I'll fix the price in advance—if you give me the flexibility to choose the fish.'"

This back and forth went on for 2 or 3 years, before Red's Best and Harvard University Dining Services reached an agreement. In the spring of 2015, Red's Best started with haddock and hake, then added skate wings, dogfish, albacore, swordfish, scup, cod, pollock, monkfish, redfish, black sea bass, and all kinds of flounder. "The students love it. The chefs love it. The dishwashers love it. They all love the connections to wild-harvest fisheries. It's an awesome thing. When you tell the stories of men and women producing the fish it really makes an impact. Students want to try all kinds of fish and the stories help them buy in." Red's Best uses a QR code to link to a URL with the story for the Catch of the Week, which is posted on dining-hall bulletin boards and social-media sites.

For its part, Harvard University Dining Services is proud to support both local fishermen and sustainable landings, as they tout on their website:

> Dining Services wanted to extend its local purchasing power in a way that supports the continuation of a vital New England liveli-hood—fishing! Efforts to manage fisheries and restore fish stocks in the Atlantic Ocean have instituted catch limits that sometimes challenge a New England fisherman's ability to make a viable living,

especially when consumers have a very narrow view of what species they can or like to eat. As a result, the local fishing community has dwindled over recent decades. To create a continuous guaranteed revenue stream for Boston-area fishermen, Red's Best and Harvard worked together to establish the 'Catch of the Week' program. Harvard has a standing commitment to buy a significant volume of fish (approximately 900 pounds per week), and Red's established a set price per pound for that fish without market fluctuations."[16]

On Monday, Harvard tells Red's Best if there is any change in volume. On Wednesday, Red's Best tells Harvard what kind of fish or fishes to expect, mostly fresh caught within two days. On Thursday, Harvard informs the chefs about the fish and posts "storytelling" signage. On Friday, the fish is served at lunch. The program was so successful that a second "Catch of the Week" was added for Wednesday dinner, following the same protocol.

Having refined the Harvard model, Red's now provides dining services at Tufts, Cornell, and MIT with fresh-caught, sustainable fish. The students are getting a good education in how to eat healthy, sustainable, lean protein. And Red's Best, Harvard, and other large institutional dining services have an inspiring story to tell.

The Local Catch Network has been developing since 2007 but is still what might be called an "alternative seafood network." It is an alternative network because it still represents a minuscule portion of the global, industrialized seafood supply chain, which mostly consists of tens of millions of metric tons of frozen fish flying thousands and thousands of miles. Farmed Norwegian salmon is shipped to Lithuania for processing, then flown to the United States and elsewhere; squid is frozen in Rhode Island and California, flown to China for processing, then frozen and flown to other global markets. But another variant of that alternative network is emerging, kind of a synthesis of both the local-catch and global supply chains.

During the COVID lockdown that forced many restaurants to close, there were signs of a return to a more *preindustrial* fish business, where producers and consumers interacted in a kind of Norman Rockwell-esque dock scene. When Dug Durr and his nephew, Troy

Durr, were told by dealers that local lobster markets had dried up and couldn't take on more lobster, the Durrs started brainstorming about how to sell the fish themselves. "It was scary, really. With 350 pots we were going to lose a lot of lobsters and a lot of money. We could either leave them in the water and lose them, or pull them up and have no market," says Dug Durr, who captains a boat out of Fairhaven, Massachusetts, a sister city to New Bedford on the other side of the harbor.

The Durrs decided to set up a Facebook group called SouthCoast Direct Source Seafood. "We thought the name pretty well summed it up," says Troy. His uncle Dug says, "We got a couple of hundred followers right away and then people started sharing the page. Within a week we had 3,000 followers; a week later, 7,000; a week later, 12,000."[17] Then a local radio station picked it up, calling SouthCoast Direct Source Seafood "all the rage," and the dock-to-car business took off. Dunn Vision, a documentary film company from New York, integrated SouthCoast Direct Source Seafood into its "Fast Forward" documentary about food-supply chains during the pandemic in a segment called "The Sea."

Before the Easter 2020 weekend, hundreds of cars lined up on the docks. For Father's Day weekend, the Durrs sold 2,000 lobsters; for the July 4th holiday, 3,000. "The demand got so great we called in other boats to increase the supply, which was great," says Dug. SouthCoast Direct Source started selling on a 'first come, first served' basis, but quickly switched to preordering and prepaying via Facebook. By the end of 2020, SouthCoast Direct Seafood's Facebook group had more than 17,000 followers.

That is not necessarily a sustainable model and it won't work for everyone, because selling direct requires more work by fishermen, as opposed to unloading on the dock to a dealer. But the direct transactions foretell a stronger connection between fishermen and consumers, the kind of bond between harvesters and consumers that Eating with the Ecosystem is working to foster. "Whereas the 'know your fisherman' ethic was a lifestyle choice in the pre-COVID world, it is now gaining momentum and becoming mainstream," write Local Catch founder Josh Stoll, Sitka Salmon Shares, Kelly Harrell, and Northwest

Marine Alliance's Brett Tolley and others in an academic paper on "alternative seafood networks."[18]

Whole fish were particularly plentiful during the COVID lockdown, as fishermen sometimes found it difficult to find processors for fillets.[19] "While the local-catch movement was conceived in the pre-COVID world, the pandemic only served to reinforce its underlying thesis—that the seafood supply chain was ripe for disruption," says Taylor Witkin, who organized the 2019 Local Catch Summit (with Josh Stoll) and is now the BlueTech manager at SeaAhead, a Boston-based, blue economy, startup incubator.[20]

The direct connection between consumers and fishers was never more apparent than when the Commonwealth of Massachusetts moved to stop lobstering in the winter and spring of 2021 to protect the spawning grounds of the endangered North Atlantic right whale. A write-in campaign sparked in part by SouthCoast Direct Source Seafood and other lobstermen on Martha's Vineyard led to a reversal of the ban south of Cape Cod, where whales are scarce.[21] The Durrs thanked its community on Facebook: "We did it!! You did it!! Thank you to all of you that either sent a letter or joined the Zoom meeting pertaining to the right whale closure. The volume of public response was undeniable. Normally this would have been a done deal but again the SouthCoast members stepped up to the challenge. All the owners, captains, and deckhands have been blown away by all your support! We really do have the best customers/community!"

Such networks were a bright spot in both high- and low-income countries during the early months of the COVID pandemic. In the Northeastern United States, a survey of 258 fishermen found that 60 percent reported adapting to local and direct sales during the pandemic. Even some multinational corporations, such as Cooke Aquaculture, made the same direct pivot. "Having that really direct connection takes out a lot of variability and uncertainty," said one fisherman. "You know the more hands you put in the middle the more uncertainty there is. Right? The more hands, you know, you just don't know if or when any processor is going to shut down."[22]

Companies that process and distribute what they catch, farm, or harvest are considered "vertically integrated." Vertical integration is more profitable, once you build the supply-chain infrastructure (as Sitka Salmon Shares is doing), since you're not paying other people to handle your product, and you have more oversight of quality control. That's a big advantage in a business beset by fraud allegations, a big advantage when selling a product that is "guilty until proven innocent," as chef Seaver says.

Island Creek Oysters, based in Duxbury, Massachusetts, one of the country's preeminent oyster growers and distributors, sold oysters online through its website for a decade, but with annual online sales of $2 million it was always a small part of its business—until the pandemic hit and it became *the* business. "It was always a bit of a stepchild, fairly intensive to manage and, honestly, how many people are going to shuck their own oysters," says CEO Chris Sherman, whose core business is selling to 1,100 restaurants. "In March 2020, we lost 98 percent of our restaurant business and started selling $2 million worth of oysters every month online. It became the whole business."

Luke's Lobster, based in Saco, Maine, and Brooklyn, New York, buys shellfish off docks from New Bedford to Nova Scotia and ships the raw product to its processing plant in Maine. It sells the tails to Whole Foods, picks out the knuckle and claw meat to prepare in rolls for shipping to its thirty or so shacks, whose geographical range equals that of the bluefin tuna—from New York to San Francisco to Japan.[23] It also has an e-commerce platform, selling frozen lobster, scallop, and clam dishes direct to consumers. "We freeze in a liquid nitrogen tunnel, probably the fastest, most high-tech way to freeze in the industry," says Ben Conniff, a cofounder with Luke Holden. "Freezing fast—our lobster meat goes from 40 degrees to negative 15 degrees in under 15 minutes—means the ice crystals that form in the tissue are microscopic and thus don't rupture the proteins in the lobster meat."[24]

Legal Sea Foods Marketplace is doing something similar. When owner Roger Berkowitz sold the legendary Boston-based seafood restaurant chain in late 2020 to PPX Hospitality Group (owner of Smith & Wollensky steak houses), he kept the "Legal" name to continue his fledgling online business. Legal Sea Foods Marketplace has started by selling some old favorites, like lobster, shrimp, chowder, and other dishes, also using a nitrogen-based flash-freezing technique, but it's a sure bet to diversify its offerings further. In 2011, Berkowitz held a dinner featuring fish that some environmentalists said was overfished, trying to make a point that fisheries need to be protected but some regulations were excessive and that Legal Sea Foods used only legally permitted fish at its restaurants, in keeping with the "eating with the ecosystem" ethic.[25]

Long known for its slogan, "If It Isn't Fresh, It Isn't Legal," Legal Seafoods Marketplace has a new slogan for its new flash-frozen business: "Straight from our docks to your door." "I started on the fish counter cutting fish, and going down to the pier buying fish," says Berkowitz. "Legal Sea Foods was always more in the fish business than in the restaurant business. Reconnecting to the fish business is very appealing to me."[26]

Another Boston convert to flash-freezing is Red's Best. In 2020, CEO Auerbach bought a freezer that goes as low as –120 degrees, specifically to freeze cubes of bluefin tuna for sushi. "Tuna needs to be super frozen, otherwise it won't keep its color. In a regular freezer it will be brown after a week," says Auerbach, who is one of the top bluefin dealers in the United States. When his trucks pick up a bluefin in Provincetown, Boston, or New Bedford, which they do from June to December, Red's Best can begin advertising the sushi-grade delicacy on its website for direct consumer sales while the tuna is being cut, vacuum packed, and slipped into –120-degree heaven. Very postindustrial.

"I've completely shifted my perspective on freezing," Auerbach said in late 2020, as he retools with more freezers to counteract future market disruptions post-COVID. "The pandemic forced me to re-evaluate waste—and it's so wasteful to sell fresh fish. Ninety percent of fresh fish should be frozen." Auerbach used to bend over backward to provide fresh fish as a way of distinguishing his product from the global, frozen product. "I used to think freezing connoted a commodity, but it is so much more efficient. There are a million reasons why it makes sense. Is this a zero-sum game? No. I can add value without taking it away from anyone, and so can everyone else."

Iceland has known that for a long time.

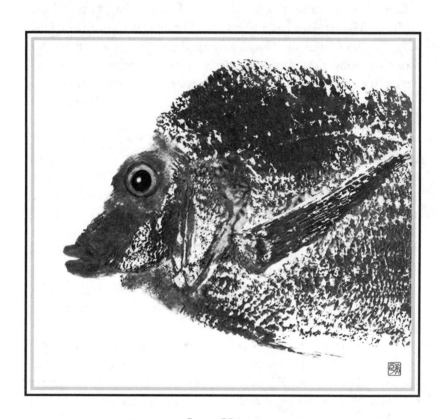

SCUP HEAD

Chapter 5

The Silicon Valley of Cod (and Other Innovation Clusters)

In Icelandic, nytin *is a positive word that describes a person who uses things to the fullest. Iceland relies so heavily on fisheries that we cannot afford to treat this resource lightly. We are getting at least 30 percent more value from cod than most developed countries. Fish is not only the fillet, but it is also fish skin becoming health products, the liver becoming omega oils and pharmaceuticals, the head and bones used in various ways—basically nothing is left for landfill.*

—Thor Sigfusson, *The New Fish Wave*

For the last 200 years or so, one of the main medicinal products derived from cod has been the strong-tasting cod liver oil that delivers vitamins A and D, and omega-3 fatty acids with their anti-inflammatory and anti-cholesterol benefits. It was first used in 1789 to treat rheumatism, and later, in 1824, rickets.[1] Today, you can buy a bottle at Walgreen's, CVS, or Amazon for around $30. It is a nice, old-fashioned home remedy and health aid. But there is an equally simple cod-derivative product that is exponentially more valuable, a twenty-first-century medical product: codskin bandages.

As fishing pressure has reduced the biomass of many fish stocks, there is an increasing effort to derive more value from fish—to increase profits for fishermen and reduce pressure on the resource. The impetus for much of the innovation in this area comes from Iceland, which is in many ways a model fishery.

If you scale and skin a codfish and process the skin in a mild manner, you can apply it to burns, wounds, and even brain and spinal dura (a tough, protective membrane). High in omega-3 polyunsaturated fatty acids, the fish skin reduces inflammation and pain, recruits the body's own cells, and is ultimately converted into living tissue. In double-blind, randomized trials, cod-skin grafts have healed wounds faster than synthetic products made from human or animal tissue, and with no risk of disease transmission. The fish skin is simply more similar in structure to human skin than other skin substitutes.[2]

Kerecis, the company that has received more than forty patents for the use of codfish skin for medical use, was founded in Ísafjörður, in the Westfjords of Iceland, right below the Arctic Circle. Kerecis now has major offices in Reykjavik, Iceland's capital, and Washington, DC. On average, Kerecis can produce eight "skin units" from one cod. Each unit sells for roughly $500, yielding a value of $4,000 per fish. The skin, often wasted, is effectively a medical wonder worth exponentially more than the fish fillet itself.

Founder and CEO, Fertram Sigurjonsson, a chemist who describes himself as a serial entrepreneur, established the company in 2009, but commercial operations didn't begin until 2013. His interest in the treatment of wounds and prevention of amputations dates to his work with prosthetic manufacturer Össur in Denmark in the early 2000s.[3]

Dr. Lee Rogers, a Los Angeles podiatrist known for preventing diabetic amputations and who has used the cod bandage on diabetic wounds, says that "the skin of the fish, once scales are removed, is strikingly similar to human skin on a microscopic level."[4] The fish skin for tissue-regeneration technology is acellular—with no fish cells to compete with human cells. This same transplantation technology is also used for hernia repair, breast reconstruction, and dura repair. "It's a 40 percent to 50 percent quicker healing process," says Rick Perez, director of business development at East Liverpool City Hospital (Ohio), which is primarily using Kerecis to help heal diabetic wounds.[5]

Innovation in Iceland

"Iceland is the Silicon Valley of codfish," says Thor Sigfusson, founder of the Iceland Ocean Cluster and its subsidiary, The Ocean Cluster House (*Hús* Sjávarklasans), a startup-business incubator on the docks of Reykjavik with around seventy companies. Silicon Valley, of course, is one of the industry clusters singled out by Michael Porter, a professor at Harvard Business School, who first espoused the "cluster theory of innovation" in 1998.[6] Many of the companies in the Iceland Ocean Cluster are developing fish-related products—such as fish-skin leather for wallets and purses, beauty creams, medicinal pills, blockchain technology for seafood supply chains, cod-liver products, and a branded fish-traceability app and QR codes. Navis is developing an electric long-line fishing vessel, alongside nanotechnology battery-maker Greenvolt, an American startup.

"The idea of Iceland manufacturing leather and health products from codfish is similar to the old expression about Russia: 'They processed everything in the pig except the squeal,'" says Brian Rothschild, from the School for Marine Science and Technology. Atlantic Leather, for example, established in 1994, is a leading manufacturer of exotic leather from fish skins: salmon, perch, wolffish, and cod. Each has its own unique character; comes in a diverse range of colors, textures, and finishes; and is good material for wallets, purses, handbags, and dresses.

Sigfusson, who has a PhD in networking, founded the Iceland Ocean Cluster in 2011. His goal was to coax people in an insular, competitive, noncollaborative industry to work with each other—and with entrepreneurs and investors who could help monetize their products. "While entrepreneurs in other industries formed diffuse networks with more contact, the seafood techs had smaller, closed networks," writes Sigfusson in his book, *The New Fish Wave*. "We wondered why we couldn't forge more of these kinds of diffuse networks in natural resource industries, such as fisheries, giving the entrepreneurs more opportunities to connect with a wider network and broader backgrounds."[7]

Over the last decade, Sigfusson has become a global leader promoting 100 percent utilization of fish to maximize the resource and its value. The basic theory is that if fishermen can derive more value from each fish, it will take the sting out of strict quotas that restrict their catch by creating new business opportunities.

Kerecis has been part of the Iceland Ocean Cluster since the beginning and is clearly in sync with Sigfusson's "100% Fish Utilization" initiative, which focuses less on the volume of fish than the value for the fish, on ways to turn waste into value. Most fisheries waste 50 percent or more of the fish; Iceland now utilizes more than 80 percent, exporting goods such as dried fish heads (for soup stock) to Africa in addition to nonfish spinoff products. In the United States, most fish gurry (offal) is used for low-value products such as fertilizer and dog food, or it is just thrown away.

Technological advances in commercial fisheries have brought considerable improvements in product yield. For instance, Icelandic fish processors have increased yield by as much as 20 percent over the past two decades. However, the fillet only makes up 35–45 percent of the cod's weight. The remainder is head, bones, skin, and intestines. Since the 1990s, the utilization of fishery by-products has increased thirty-fold, and the export value per pound of cod has risen by 400 percent. Companies within the cluster develop supplements, proteins, cosmetics, pharmaceuticals, and other high-value products from all parts of the fish.

Cod landings in Iceland dropped from 460,000 tons in 1981 to 180,000 tons in 2011, according to the Iceland Ocean Cluster, while the export value of fillets and by-products increased from $340 million to $680 million (in present dollars).[8] Arnljótur Bjarki Bergsson, a former executive at Matís, a food and biotech research and development firm in Reykjavik, ran an economic analysis of cod's value over a 30-year period. Between 1981 and 2013, the amount of money generated by cod increased by a bit more than 300 percent.[9] Less fish, much more value—a recipe for sustaining a fishery.

Iceland, like other small countries, such as Israel, Taiwan, and Singapore that have minimal natural resources, has learned to punch above its weight. To generate the value it derives from cod, of course, you need cod. And while the cod fisheries of Canada and the United States in the Northwest Atlantic have fallen on very hard times, verging toward zero catch due to moratoriums and restrictive catch quotas, Iceland has another tale to tell. Iceland started controlled harvesting rather than hunting before other cod-fishing nations and is now reaping the rewards.

Iceland's cod catch peaked in the 1960s, then started declining. Iceland introduced individual transferable quotas (see chapter 2) as the cornerstone of their fisheries-management system in 1984, 26 years before the United States. The Icelandic catch hit all-time lows in the early 1990s but has since rebounded.[10] The breeding population is now at its highest point in 40 years. Between 2008 and 2016 the catch quota for cod doubled. The annual catch now is almost exactly what it was in the 1945–1950 timeframe, before the post–World War II technology boom in fishing led to overexploitation of stocks.[11] The Icelandic cod industry is certified by the Marine Stewardship Council—the acknowledged international standard for sustainable best practices. Iceland accounts for only 1 percent of the world's global catch but 6 percent of the catch certified by the Marine Stewardship Council.

Fish skin, of course, is not the only part of the fish that is wasted. Codland, cofounded by Sigfusson in 2012, the year after he founded the Iceland Ocean Cluster, is taking care of the rest of the parts. Codland brought together seven companies with the idea of fully utilizing by-products from cod and connected them to fishing companies: Haustak, the largest fish-drying company in Iceland; Visir, a long-line fishing company; and THorbjorn, one of the largest fishing and fish-processing companies in Iceland. The fishing companies supply Codland with the raw material (waste), and the biotechnologists take over to produce fish oil, calcium, and other mineral supplements (from fish bones), and hydrologized marine collagen (also made from cod skin) for aging skin and joints.

Niceland—Oliver Luckett, founder and now chairman, was head of innovation at Disney—is a tech company that has a different relationship with cod (and other fish). Because most fish traded globally are an unbranded commodity product, Niceland is attaching a brand to fresh, wild fish from the cold, pristine waters around Iceland. Niceland traces fish from "sea to pan," packaging and shipping fish with a QR code that shoppers can scan on their mobiles and see when, where, and on what boat the fish was caught; how and when it was processed; and when it was shipped, and on what trucks and flights. The app includes photos of the capture boat and recipes. Other companies are doing this as well, but it is significant that an export is using this approach to establish credibility in the United States and other major markets.

Niceland's first export market was Denver, Colorado, through a partnership with Seattle Fish Company. The idea came about when Niceland realized that Icelandair planes flying direct to Denver had excess space in their cargo holds. Why not fill them up with fish? Those holds initially carried Niceland-branded cod and haddock, but now wolffish, redfish, and arctic char. Niceland also delivers non-Icelandic species from elsewhere, such as farmed cobia, kampachi, and ahi tuna.

Under CEO Heida Kristin Helagadottir, a prominent political adviser, Niceland has expanded far beyond the larger Denver region. Its network of distributors now includes Santa Monica Seafood, Samuels and Son (Philadelphia), Crowd Cow (for internet sales), and others. Niceland effectively serves the entire United States, including more than 160 stores in Southern California.

Iceland is probably the best exemplar in the world of a postindustrial fishery, although Norway and New Zealand are also best-practice leaders. In all three countries, fisheries are not cut off from the larger economy. The fisheries support and spark adjacent industries, such as processing, technology, and software. But the United States is playing catch-up.

Innovation in New England

As successful stories about sustainable fishing and whole-fish utilization in Iceland resonate in a world where overfishing and fish waste are concerns, Sigfusson has expanded his ocean-cluster concept to Portland, Maine; New Bedford, Massachusetts; Seattle, Washington; and New Haven, Connecticut (the Long Island Sound Ocean Cluster). The first Ocean Cluster House (Hús) outside Iceland opened in Portland, Maine, in 2020 with a mission similar to that of the Iceland Ocean Cluster: to form a peer-to-peer network in an industry that has long been secretive and insular. Like the Iceland cluster, the New England Ocean Cluster in Maine is a for-profit incubator, whereas the other clusters are nonprofits. "It would have been much easier to start a nonprofit, but it would be much harder to create the 'edge culture' that we need to drive innovation," says Patrick Arnold, founder and director of the New England Ocean Cluster. "Member companies join to get R&D, marketing insights, and partners from other companies." The Hús on the waterfront has views of boats and docks in one direction and the main drag of Commercial Street in the other, and is within walking distance of marine shops, fish shops, and restaurants—a lively collaborative environment that is the hallmark of the Reykjavik Hús.

Unlike the fish-related innovation in Iceland, startups in New England are generally focused on the larger blue-tech space. New England Ocean Cluster members include Maine Standard Biofuels, which converts used cooking oil into heating oil and biodiesel. The company is working to develop a marine-fuel market for ferries and fishing vessels, as well as a line of plant-based (nontoxic) cleaning products for boats. Already, 20 percent of Casco Bay Island Ferry Services' fuel is biodiesel. Other cluster members include Rugged Seas, which recycles used fishing bibs (foul-weather gear) into bags and other products for the retail market, and Sustainametrix, which develops models to "navigate the Anthropocene Age" and the resultant ecosystems changes. Fish-related products include Marin Skincare's marine-glycoproteins creams for people with sensitive or dry skin—a natural by-product of lobster processing (with Luke's Lobster).

The New Bedford Ocean Cluster was launched in 2017 by the New Bedford Port Authority and Spherical Analytics, a Cambridge, Massachusetts–based big-data and environmental-analytics firm, with Iceland's Sigfusson and Robert Barber, the former US ambassador to Iceland, in attendance. The New Bedford cluster is a nonprofit with a different model than the Portland cluster—more a strategic-planning network for port and coastal development than a business incubator, at least to start. John Bullard, former Greater Atlantic Regional Fisheries administrator for NOAA Fisheries, is chair; Jon Mitchell, New Bedford Mayor, sits on the Board.

The cluster is coalescing a larger network with groups such as the UMass Dartmouth's School for Marine Science & Technology, MASS Robotics, the New Bedford Research & Robotics Consortium, and other researchers, entrepreneurs, and marine businesses. Dive Technologies, for example, a firm from Quincy (a city next to Boston), is testing autonomous underwater research vehicles out of New Bedford Harbor, supported by the Defense Advanced Research Projects Agency (DARPA) and in partnership with organizations including the Center for Marine Autonomy and Robotics at Virginia Tech.[12]

In 2019, Spherical Analytics and the New Bedford Port Authority won a state-funded grant to develop a Marine Databank: outfitting multiple fishing boats with sensors to collect oceanographic data, such as temperature, salinity, oxygen levels, and abundance of phytoplankton and zooplankton. "The hypothesis is that, combined with other data sources, these oceanographic data will help captains more quickly locate target species and avoid choke species," says Chris Rezendes, chief business officer at Spherical Analytics, and a cofounder and board member of the New Bedford Ocean Cluster. "It's conceivable that better targeting would do as much to de-carbonize the fleet as switching from diesel to electric." Says Ed Anthes-Washburn, former director of the port, and cofounder and vice chairman of the cluster, "We've got a 350-boat lab in New Bedford Harbor."

In keeping with the Iceland ethic, 100 percent utilization of fish waste (gurry) is a goal. A recent presentation by Josh Riazi, a noted executive chef, to members of the New Bedford fishing community suggested a pathway to that goal. Just as chicken wings, once unwanted by-products left after carving out the more valuable Statler breasts (named after Boston's Statler Hotel) were turned into a spicy bar favorite, Riazi asked, "Why not develop a way to utilize more of the scup, a plentiful fish with a lot of waste?"

The original Marine Databank idea was that the fleet would control data to share, trade, license, or sell in a marketplace overseen by the Port Authority. It became clear that as a governmental body subject to the Freedom of Information Act the Port Authority would have to make the data publicly available, so oversight was transferred to the New Bedford Ocean Cluster. Spherical Analytics' Immutably for Maritime Trust Platform, cryptographically proofed using blockchain, assures contributors their data are safe and private. "Data are an asset," says Rezendes. "In a cyber-physical world [such as a fishing boat with sensors] they may in some cases be more valuable than the physical asset itself. Access and usage need to be tightly controlled."

Rory Nugent, author of *Down at the Docks* (see chapter 1), believes such data collection is critical to the long-term protection of ocean resources and sustainable fishing. Additionally, he thinks that the transparency of all the data is a public good that should be shared. "The data is so key to the future of both a healthy ocean and fishing industry that the government should mandate its availability to all interested parties. Ultimately, a deep data pool would be a boon to

fishermen and regulators; otherwise, we are furthering the privatization of a communal asset, the ocean, and endangering its future."

Perhaps there is a middle ground, wherein vessel captains can sell
or license certain data and maintain proprietary control over the rest.
Governments already mandate data sharing: sovereign nations require
vessel-monitoring systems to track their own fleets, and roughly
twenty governments have agreed to voluntarily supply these data to
Global Fishing Watch (see chapter 12).[13]

Another home-grown ocean cluster (not an Iceland spinoff) is
SeaAhead, specializing in "blue-tech innovation," which offers its
fifty-plus members flexible working space in Boston and Providence.
For the many members from outside New England and overseas,
SeaAhead holds regular virtual events with breakout networking ses-
sions. SeaAhead has a Blue Angels group that invests seed capital in
start-ups, and a BlueSwell program that selects certain startups for
a $35,000 grant and a 20-week training program through the New
England Aquarium's research arm. SeaAhead also has a partnership
with the UMass Boston to improve research and commercial ventures
promoting ocean sustainability, with the goal of catalyzing venture-
based innovation.

"We see blue-tech as being where clean-tech was 20 years ago or
where ag-tech was 10 years ago," says Alissa Peterson, cofounder and
executive director of SeaAhead. "We see this as a growth industry."
Blue-tech includes electric boats, solar-powered docks, autonomous
underwater robots, and marine-data collection systems, but it also
includes members in the mariculture (ocean farming) space. One of
its original members was Ocean Approved, the first commercial kelp
farm in the United States (now called Atlantic Sea Farms). Current
members include Oyster Tracker, a management platform for oyster
growers; Oyster Common, an AI-driven marketing tool for small
farmers; Akua, a kelp-food producer; BetaHatch, a Seattle-based firm
that converts mealworms into fish-feed protein; Dive Technologies,
the manufacturer of autonomous underwater vessels; and LegitFish,
a Boston-based seafood-traceability platform (used by New Bedford's
Buyers and Sellers Exchange auction, among others).

"Boston is rich in technology, people, investors, small innovative
groups, and universities. All of it together creates an environment

where you are more likely to find the right people that you need because there are so many different ways to network," says Kevin Dutt, chief operating officer of LegitFish. "SeaAhead is a big part of that."

Numerous other fishing-related start-ups in New England are connected to universities or research institutions. A science-based startup is the Marine Microverse Institute in Kittery Point, Maine, which is developing (with the University of New Hampshire and Maine Technology Institute) a fish-DNA, species-authentication test using genomic-diagnostic tools. The goal is to give large-scale, fish-industry stakeholders a way to combat mislabeling, which numerous estimates put at about 30 percent of all seafood. A related goal is to reduce illegal, unreported and unregulated fishing, and combat seafood fraud worldwide (see chapter 12).

"With the increase in mislabeling and fraud, we want to empower retailers with a field-based, accurate DNA-testing platform to accommodate a variety of commonly mislabeled species," says executive director John Bucci, a biological oceanographer with a specialization in molecular ecology. "We want to help the seafood industry distinguish between cod and pollock, or Pacific cod and Atlantic cod, or bluefin and yellowfin tuna, or wild Chinook and farmed salmon."

Marine Microverse Institute has a provisional patent on its core technology—a prepackaged assay kit designed with customized genes that differentiates between closely related fish species on a variety of test platforms. "The marker genes within the assay are designed using bioinformatics from whole-genome sequencing, which produce species-specific assays and are an improvement compared to traditional DNA tests," says Bucci. "Before this innovation, the industry relied on assays with limited capacity for species specificity."

While the Food and Drug Administration follows a paper trail to establish a chain of custody on imported fish, it does little actual DNA species-identification testing unless it has a good reason to suspect fraud. And when testing is done, samples are usually shipped to a centralized lab location that can take days to return results, which is not all that useful if you are trying to move a large volume of fish into the market.

"Seafood importers that handle thousands of pounds of fish would like to identify fish themselves rather than rely on the supplier for identification," says Bucci. "These customers can extract DNA from muscle or fin tissue from frozen blocks of fish. We have developed our assays to be compatible with field-based handheld platforms that deliver rapid results to a smart phone. For large quantities of fish, customers can use a benchtop device designed for high throughput testing."

Identifying dead fish is one thing; identifying fish swimming in the ocean is another. Given the success of Kevin Stokesbury from UMass Dartmouth's School for Marine Science & Technology in surveying and counting sea scallops on the sea floor (see chapter 1), fishermen are now asking if he can do the same for cod and other groundfish. Can he show the regulators that "the best available science" shows what they say they see?

Over the past 5 years, Stokesbury and Nicholas Calabrese, a PhD candidate, have designed a new rig to count fish flowing through a trawl net, which is more complicated than dragging a video camera on the ocean floor to snap images of sessile scallops in the sand.

A deep-sea camera with lights is affixed at the "cod-end" of the net, which is usually closed to catch cod (and other fish) but in this case is left open so the fish swim through uncaptured. GoPro cameras in the net record images of every fish passing through. That video is connected to the captain's wheelhouse, allowing observers to see fish as they swim through the net. Observers in the wheelhouse can click to take a photograph at any time. Software with sophisticated machine-learning algorithms is later used to identify the fish species and the rough number of each species.

The typical fish survey involves hauling fish on board and counting and weighing them one by one, killing most of the fish. Plus, the tow typically lasts only 20 or 30 minutes. With the open-net rig, the fish swim out the open end of the net, unharmed. And the net can stay underwater for hours, collecting far more data in less time than a typical closed-net trawl survey.

One of the problems Calabrese has been attacking is how to determine the efficiency of the net in attracting fish. This is similar to the issue that caused some tension between the New Bedford scallopers and NOAA researchers surveying scallop density in the late 1990s (see chapter 1). "If we can estimate the efficiency—the percentage of the population that enters the net—then we can get the population in a given survey area from that." Cod are known to dive and haddock tend to swim upward when they see a net, and some swim outside or above the net, and are not visible on camera. One technique to solve this problem is to use an echosounder to count cod beneath the net, but at a certain distance from the bottom it is hard to tell if the echogram is from fish or the sea floor. Thus, Calabrese is trying a different approach: a mark-recapture experiment.

"In these experiments, a large number of fish are caught, tagged, and released, then the area is fished again. The ratio of untagged to tagged fish in the second sample allows you to calculate population size. Since the video-trawl survey uses an open net we don't get the fish on deck to check for tags. Instead, we developed a Passive Integrated Transponder tag-reading system that can be placed in the net. The antennae in the net will scan any transponder tags as they pass through and record their unique ID number."[14]

While the primary purpose of these video tows is to help obtain more accurate stock assessments, the system could potentially be deployed on fishing boats to assist in decreasing bycatch. Low catch limits on "choke species" like cod have meant that millions of dollars' worth of fish, such as haddock, which are plentiful, are left uncaught every year because fishermen avoid species such as cod and witch flounder. "If we make this system smaller and more robust, we could put it on any fishing vessel. If fishermen can see in real time that they are catching a bycatch species, they could cut the tow short," said Travis Lowery, who led a survey tow in 2018. "That would be of real benefit to everyone."[15]

Counting fish is one thing, catching them is another, and killing them "with purpose" is another. A promising experiment aims to turn plain old low-value fish into high-value fish. What creates low value? In a global market that can consistently supply high-quality, frozen fish for widescale distribution—often at a price below that of domestic fish due to labor inequities or to more sophisticated processing equipment (which Iceland, Norway, and New Zealand have)—New England fishermen have trouble competing. "The way fish are traditionally handled is not good. When a fish is gaffed, tossed, bruised, or bent when it's landed, and there's not enough ice on board, the fish degrades quickly," says Jen Levin, CEO of Gulf of Maine Sashimi, a Portland, Maine, processor specializing in high-quality, wild-caught fish. "Gaffing introduces bacteria, as does gutting with rusted knives, and stepping on the fish on deck. This rough handling is rational, since fishermen are not getting good prices." Seafood is a cutthroat-pennies business. If fishermen are not getting well paid for their fish, they care less about the quality. And when buyers get poor quality, it leads to a vicious cycle of declining prices and sales.

"In 2012, when cod quota in the Gulf of Maine was cut way back, Norway had record landings and you could buy that fish in Maine grocery stores for $5.99 a pound. Meanwhile, more and more local boats stopped fishing altogether because the prices on the docks didn't make it worthwhile. 'Prices stink, so I'm not going fishing,' was the basic line. The United States is a small blip in the global seafood chain. Last year we harvested just 35 percent as much haddock as Iceland did. We're harvesting just 12.5 percent of our quota because the market prices are not good enough to incentivize fishermen. If we look at haddock harvests on both sides of the Atlantic, the eastern Atlantic harvests about 10 times as much haddock as we do here. But we do have an opportunity to compete on quality."

Ten years ago, through a grant from the Saltonstall Foundation, Levin was working at the Gulf of Maine Research Institute running its Sustainable Seafood program and looking to develop markets for "underutilized fish"—abundant species with high allowable catch limits but low demand. Levin's group was the first to refer to unloved fish as underutilized, a term now widely used by global fisheries.

Talking to major supermarket chains around the world led to a different way of looking at the problem. "If we can't compete on volume and price, we have an opportunity to compete on quality and value." This is different than the Icelandic waste-to-value initiative, but similar in that it envisions a way to get more value per pound of fish, which decreases fishing pressure.

Levin's research led to workshops on fish-handling techniques and that led to the foundational idea for Gulf of Maine Sashimi: *Ikejime*—a Japanese kill technique that translates as "kill with purpose." The kill technique can increase the value of the fish by 20 to 400 percent per pound.

"When a fish comes over the rail, the fisherman spikes the brain (behind the eye socket), instantaneously killing the nervous system. The fish relaxes, rather than flipping and squirming in a fight to live," says Levin. "That prevents lactic acid from forming, which can quickly degrade fish flesh. Blood retracts to the gut cavity where it is immediately bled. The fish go right into an ice-water slurry to prevent bacteria from taking over."

Microscopic studies comparing fish "killed with purpose" to those that just plain die after a struggle to live dramatically show the difference in deterioration. Ikejime fish ages well, the shelf life is longer, and the flavor profile can improve with age.

Because Ikejime fish are killed individually, time and labor increase. Gulf of Maine Sashimi pays fishermen a premium for their fish and sells to high-end restaurants and fish shops at a premium. "It's not a hard sell to get a fisherman to try this technique, but there are volume economics to consider. For example, if a fisherman is selling 1,000 pounds at 50 cents a pound, that's $500. If we don't have the capacity to sell that much fish, we'll, say, pay $2 a pound for 200 pounds, or $400 total." Gulf of Maine Sashimi has also developed a "whole-boat" model, buying a certain percentage of Ikejime fish as well as the rest of the catch that is well handled, but not Ikejime quality.

To train fisherman in the Japanese technique, Levin ran workshops from MidCoast Maine to Cape Cod with Chris Bean, a fisherman from Cornwall, United Kingdom. He had been a small-boat fisherman who wasn't getting the same prices at market as some bigger boats. His Japanese daughter-in-law taught him and his son the Ikejime technique, and they started selling their fish to high-end London restaurants.

"I believe proper catch handling can bring American fish industries to the next level," says Mika Higurashi, a self-professed "dead-fish specialist" who also trains fishermen and consults with processors on fish quality. "There is a huge opportunity here to build demand for more local species while also increasing their value. Proper catch handling, including the Ikejime method, onboard icing and bleeding, and careful packaging can all greatly affect fish quality."[16]

Gulf of Maine Sashimi buys fresh fish off the docks in Maine, New Hampshire, and Massachusetts, mostly from "day boats" that spend 1 to 3 days at sea. "We buy exclusively from the Gulf of Maine: a lot of monkfish, cod, hake, cusk, flounder, pollock, mackerel, and tuna. Two-day-old fish, in a salt-ice slurry, is not a problem," says Levin. "Buying direct from boats you get much fresher fish than you do at auction, because it hasn't been sitting around for a few days."

At the Portland Fish Exchange, where the majority of Maine's fish and seafood is purchased, redfish fetches an average 69 cents a pound. In contrast, Gulf of Maine Sashimi pays fishermen $2 a pound for redfish.[17] Mackerel is an even more dramatic case study in Ikejime economics. In the region, fishermen get an average of 20 to 30 cents a pound; mackerel is so cheap it is often bought for bait. Meanwhile, local, high-end chefs are importing whole, frozen Ikejime mackerel from Japan at $23 a pound. Gulf of Maine Sashimi started paying fishermen $2.50 a pound for mackerel and selling it to restaurants. "High-end distributors and chefs tell us they've never seen mackerel as beautiful as our Ikejime mackerel," says Levin.

Matt Ginn, the chef of Evo in Portland, was an early Gulf of Maine Sashimi customer. "In 15 years of cooking, including at fine-dining spots in Boston, it is consistently the best fish I have ever seen or purchased," says Ginn. "Let's show people that these sustainable species are not inferior on the plate when they are handled properly; they are absolutely delicious."[18]

"The seafood supply chain and community has typically been supported by government money and grants," says Blaine Grimes, chief ventures officer at Gulf of Maine Research Institute. "Traditional venture capital is not interested in fishing. But our seed capital and equity position can serve as a bridge to private capital, the same way angel investors do. The question is, can we make money doing this? Can we change the industry and create a new economic model? Gulf of Maine Sashimi has the potential to flip the story with end-to-end supply-chain management that creates demand for fresh, local fish. The question is whether we can create a sustainable model before fishermen go out of business."

The same question could be asked about the marine food web: Can it be restored and preserved before it is too late?

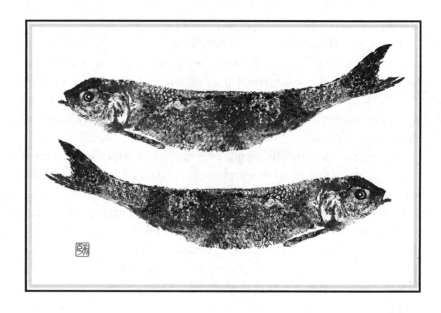

HERRING

Chapter 6

Run, Herring, Run:
Restoring the Marine Food Web

Whereas Atlantic Salmon, Shad and Blueback Herring are now
near extinction and the Alewife are threatened with extinction;
and, whereas marine species such as cod, haddock, pollock, whales,
and porpoise are dependent on such a high energy food source as the
Alewife; therefore, be it resolved that the Joint Tribal Council insist
the State of Maine immediately remove this blockage [dam] and allow
the sea-run Alewife to pass to access their ancestral spawning territory.

—St. Croix River and Alewife Resolution, Joint Tribal Council
of the Passamaquoddy Tribe, 2012

River herring—a low-trophic "forage fish" for both riverine and marine ecosystems—are a keystone species that other species depend on for food. River herring feed on phytoplankton and are eaten by larger fish. River herring (a different species than saltwater Atlantic herring) are anadromous like salmon—born in freshwater, they swim up to 100 miles out into the ocean and return upriver every 3 to 5 years to spawn, then migrate back to the ocean. Shad, alewives, and blueback herring are collectively referred to as river herring.

If overfishing is an issue, protection of rivers, and nearshore waters and estuaries, where many favored species spawn, is equally important. Elders of the Passamaquoddy Tribe in Washington County in northern Maine (along the St. Croix River, which separates Maine from New Brunswick, Canada) describe river herring as "the fish that feeds all, without which we might not have survived . . . something almost miraculous."[1] Everything eats river herring—striped bass, tuna, cod, haddock, halibut, American eel, turtles, river fish, birds and raptors, seals and whales, and fox and weasel. River herring have lipids—organic compounds with fatty acids—that are a key food for spawning cod.

Scientists are now trying to determine if the recent return of river herring after a series of dam removals over the last two decades might help to restore cod and other species that spawn in nearshore waters. "We need to have the Gulf of Maine rebuilding its food web; we need to have rivers sending billions and billions of young fish out into the ocean for species like cod," says Landis Hudson, executive director of Maine Rivers, a conservation group.[2]

In preindustrial times, the rivers of New England were silver in the spring with "billions and billions," as locals say (or, more likely, "millions and millions"), of shad, alewives, and blueback herring. Salmon swam upstream with massive schools of river herring, which hid them from the beady eyes of raptors. Other sea-run fish include the Atlantic and shortnose sturgeon, striped bass, American eel (unagi), rainbow smelt, tomcod, and sea lamprey. But, starting in the 1600s, dams restricted the upriver migration, industrial pollution over time deoxygenated the rivers, and all these stocks diminished. "In the northeastern United States, the decline of the native diadromous fish [those that swim between fresh and saltwater] is largely attributable to the construction and operation of dams," writes Tara Trinko Lake in the *Marine and Coastal Fisheries* journal.[3]

There are now roughly 22,000 dams in New England. They were first built in the 1600s to power grist mills and sawmills and, as the Industrial Revolution took hold in the late 1700s and 1800s, textile and paper mills, and then electric power plants. In 1874, Spencer Baird, the first commissioner of fish and fisheries for the United States Fish Commission, who was appointed by President Ulysses S. Grant, decried the decline of "food fish" (forage fish) in near coastal waters, although he blamed human overfishing rather than dam construction as the culprit.[4] But in 1883, nearly a decade later, Baird mentioned the "depletion of anadromous [fish that swim from rivers to the ocean] forage stock caused by dams and coastal industrialization as major factors in the demise of the coastal cod fishery."[5]

The first major dam to be removed in the United States was the Edwards Dam on the Kennebec River in Augusta, Maine, in 1999. That was followed in 2008 by removal of the Fort Halifax Dam on the Sebasticook River, a tributary of the Kennebec, further extending upriver herring habitat. In 2012 and 2013, on the Penobscot River, the Great Works and Veazie dams were removed, opening up 2,000 miles of river that had been largely inaccessible to fish migrating to spawn. The Penobscot is the second-largest watershed in New England after the Connecticut River. The Penobscot River Restoration Trust also completed a bypass channel around the Howland Dam in 2016. Hydropower production increased at six other dams, resulting in at least as much hydropower production as before the dam removals.

Removal of the Edwards Dam opened the floodgates in the United States. Since Edwards, more than 1,200 dams across the country have been removed. Edwards was one of the pivotal events of the postindustrial age because it was the first (and, to date, the only) time that the Federal Energy Regulatory Commission (FERC) overruled dam owners, who in 1991 requested permission to sign another 50-year lease, as described by Tara Lohan in the *Revelator* ("Turning Points: Big Moment in Environmental History").[6]

The Kennebec Coalition—made up of nonprofits American Rivers, the Atlantic Salmon Federation, the Natural Resources Council of Maine, and Trout Unlimited—deserves credit for this epochal event. It presented the Federal Energy Regulatory Commission with 7,000 pages about the impacts of the dam and the economic importance of a renewed fishery. In 1997, when FERC ruled against the dam owners, Maine governor Angus King said the removal of the dam would help the Kennebec "reclaim its position as both an economic asset and an ecological miracle." Much of the funding for the removal came from the Bath Iron Works, a downstream shipbuilder that was expanding its operation into prime sturgeon habitat and paid into the removal settlement as part of its environmental mitigation. Upon final approval of the dam removal in 1999, Bruce Babbitt, secretary of the interior, proudly proclaimed, "Today, with the power of our pens, we are dismantling several myths: That hydro dams provide clean, pollution-free energy; that hydropower is the main source of our electricity; that dams should last as long as the pyramids; that making them friendlier for fisheries is expensive and time consuming."[7]

Removing dams is certainly a symptom of the postindustrial age, as many dams are vestigial reminders of a bygone industrial era. The Edwards dam, for example, built in 1837 to power local mills, was generating less than 0.1 percent of Maine's electricity in 1999.[8] Moreover, dams are often a public danger—old, unmanaged dams breaking apart have caused serious damage.

The decline of fish life after the Edwards dam was built in the nineteenth century and the return of fish after its removal 161 years later provide a stark before-and-after picture of environmental damage and restorative response. Before construction of the Edwards dam, fishermen typically caught 500 salmon every year in Augusta; after the dam, they were lucky to get 5. Similarly, sturgeon landings on the Kennebec declined from 320,000 pounds before the dam was built in 1837 to 12,000 pounds a year by 1880.[9] Both Atlantic salmon and sturgeon are now endangered and no longer fished. But, since the dam removals, you can now see sturgeon jumping in the Kennebec just south of Merrymeeting Bay and the "Chops," a narrow passage with intense tidal- and current-energy where the Kennebec River intersects with the Androscoggin River (and four other rivers).

Taking down the Edwards dam opened 18 miles of Kennebec River habitat. A year later, in addition to sturgeon jumping, seals were chasing alewives 40 miles up from the mouth of the Kennebec. Taking out the Fort Halifax dam opened another 20 or so miles of the Kennebec but more importantly opened access to the whole Sebasticook River, which in 2020 had 6 million river herring—a far cry from the old days, but a huge improvement from 1999, when the Kennebec had a mere 78,000 river herring.[10]

The Penobscot story is similar. The Penobscot River and its tributaries flow east from Mount Katahdin into Penobscot Bay. It is the largest river system in Maine—draining more than one-quarter of the state—and it is the river that Henry David Thoreau paddled on while writing his 1864 classic, *Maine Woods*. On returning from a trip to the headwaters with Joe, his Penobscot guide, Thoreau asked, "Isn't it nice to be home?" Joe said, "I've been home the whole time."[11] Starting in the early 1880s, tribal leaders of the Penobscot Nation would paddle by birchbark canoe to lobby politicians against dam building. Here is Thoreau's description of the Penobscot River in the mid-nineteenth century:

> There were in 1837, as I read, 250 sawmills on the Penobscot and its tributaries above Bangor, the greater part of them in this immediate neighborhood, and they sawed 200 million feet of boards annually. To this is to be added the lumber of the Kennebec, Androscoggin, Saco, Passamaquoddy, and other streams. No wonder that we hear so often of vessels which are becalmed off our coast, being surrounded a week at a time by floating lumber from the Maine woods.[12]

Since 2010, fifteen dams in the Penobscot River watershed have been removed, thanks to the Penobscot River Restoration Trust— Penobscot Indian Nation, American Rivers, Atlantic Salmon Federation, Maine Audubon, Natural Resources Council of Maine, The Nature Conservancy, and Trout Unlimited. Fish-passage improvements have been made at another thirteen dams. Anglers now catch shad in places that were inaccessible to this excellent game fish for a century.[13] In 2020, salmon were arriving at the fifth-fastest rate since counting began at the Veazie dam in 1978.[14] River herring counts are roughly 3 million.

Since removal of the Edwards dam, dams all over New England have been coming down. In Boston, new fish ladders in the Mystic River allow herring to reach the upper and lower Mystic Lakes for the first time in 150 years. With the upper habitat reopened, the number of herring running in the spring increased from 200,000 in 2012 to an estimated 780,000 in 2019. In Buzzards Bay, the 2013 removal of the Acushnet Sawmill dam (built in the 1700s), at the head of tide 3.5 miles upriver from the State Pier in lower New Bedford Harbor, brought a dramatic increase in annual river-herring runs. In just a year, numbers increased from a few hundred before the dam removal to 10,000 in 2014, but they have since declined to 6,000–7,000, according to Mark Rasmussen, executive director of the Buzzards Bay Coalition, which has been instrumental (along with NOAA Fisheries and state agencies) in dam removals. The Acushnet River is now the only major river on Buzzards Bay that is unbroken: fish can swim all the way from the bay to the river's headwaters at the old New Bedford Reservoir.

Just as Thoreau paddled up and down the Penobscot, it was the Acushnet River that Ishmael and Queequeg sailed down in the "little" *Moss* to reach Nantucket and ship out to whale in Herman Melville's *Moby Dick*: "We borrowed a wheelbarrow, and embarking our things, including my own poor carpet-bag, and Queequeg's canvas sack and hammock, away we went down to 'the Moss,' the little Nantucket packet schooner moored at the wharf . . . hoisting sail, it glided down the Acushnet River. On one side, New Bedford rose in terraces of streets, their ice-covered trees all glittering in the clear, cold air."[15]

Up and down the coast of New England, it is clear that dam removals and river cleanups on top of 50-plus years of pollution reduction that followed the Clean Waters Restoration Act of 1966 and the Clean Water Act of 1972 have made a huge improvement in riverine ecology. In the 1960s, the Penobscot River from the timber country of Millinocket to Penobscot Bay was coffee-colored and bubbly with the refuse of chicken-packing plants, toxic effluents from pulp mills, and raw commercial and residential sewage. "It was just dead," says Glen Manuel, the state`s former Commissioner of Fish and Game, who held office through the latter stages of the cleanup. "Not a thing could live in it."

Maine senator Ed Muskie—"Mr. Clean"—was one of the fighters for the first two major pieces of environmental legislation of the period, the Water Quality Act (1965) and the Clean Waters Restoration Act (1966). The law stopped paper mills from pouring chemicals, and wastewater treatment plants from pouring raw sewage, into the river. It also outlawed log drives from the North Woods. The Penobscot responded almost immediately and continued to improve with help from the Clear Water Act (1972). Less than two decades after the Muskie-led crusade, water quality had improved from a "D" to a "B"—from unusable to swimmable.[16]

The dam removals and recovery of river health, both of which resulted in a rebound of riverine wildlife, certainly made for a success story. But it is not a straightforward one, for two reasons: (1) the initial impressive uptick in herring runs appears to have peaked and stabilized well short of historical numbers; (2) starting around 2000, the size of the herring stock crashed in multiple locations, even in rivers without dams, which generated many theories but few facts.

On the Mattapoisett River in Massachusetts, the first river in the state where counts were recorded, for example, the river herring counts dropped from more than a million in the early 1990s to 100,000 at the end of the decade to 8,000 in 2002. In 1921, when monitoring on the Mattapoisett River began, 1.85 million river herring were counted. In 2019, just 18,540 herring were counted—only 1 percent of that historic high from 100 years ago.[17]

The Connecticut River is the biggest watershed in New England, draining parts of Vermont, New Hampshire, Massachusetts, and Connecticut. In 2020, the Connecticut River Conservancy was aiming to complete nine river-restoration projects—from dam removals to culvert repairs—across all four Connecticut River states. Connecticut itself is one of the most heavily dammed states in the nation. "Many of the 4,000 dams across the state are relatively small—just a foot or two high—but they are still too tall for fish like the river herring to jump," says Steve Gephard, a fisheries biologist with the Connecticut Department of Energy and Environmental Protection. Says Sally Harold, director of River Restoration and Fish Passage at The Nature Conservancy, "A six-inch barrier is just like the Hoover dam to herring."[18]

In Connecticut, Gephard says "everything crashed" in 2020 in the streams he monitors and that he hadn't seen anything like it in his 35-year career. "Fishways that usually count 90,000 counted 8,000. Our premier run at Bride Brook was off by at least 100,000." At the time, Gephard said the quality of freshwater habitat was good and that weather, which can sometimes affect river quality and fish behavior, was not significantly different that spring from the weather in other years. "I continue to suspect that what is affecting us is something in the marine environment," Gephard said.[19] Some think the resurgence of predatory striped bass has been a factor; others blame trawlers that scoop herring into their nets as bycatch.

In Maine, the numbers of sea-run fish are much higher, because the watersheds are massive and dam removals started earlier. The Penobscot has approximately 3 million adult river herring returns a year at the lowermost trapping facility in the system—up from a few hundred before dam removals—but the estimated capacity of the watershed is upward of 20 million, says Tim Sheehan, a Research Fishery Biologist at NOAA Fisheries' Northeast Fisheries Science Center. "Over a few years, river-herring returns on the Penobscot went from 100 to 1,000 to 700,000 to 2.5 million to 3 million, but the increase has since stalled out at around 3 million," says Sheehan. "The number of returning shad is 10,000 when the capacity of the system is estimated to be upward of 3 million. Similarly, the Kennebec counts roughly 6 million river herring, when it should also be in the 20 million range, as should the St. Croix River. It means two things: that we still have a lot of habitat restoration and connectivity work to do within these systems and that there are other factors that can drive productivity. Should Maine be seeing a number like 100 million rather than 20 million? Perhaps."

Similarly, in Buzzards Bay, Mark Rasmussen and Brendan Annett, who oversee habitat-restoration projects at the Buzzards Bay Coalition, are asking the same questions. "When we were on the upswing toward 10,000 river herring in the Acushnet, I thought it would continue upward. Now, I don't know. Is it the fishing or something else?" asks Rasmussen. "I can see midwater trawlers from my office, so maybe that's a cause. It certainly is frustrating to remove dams and not see bigger gains."

The number of river herring counted is more than an academic question, given the importance of the fish to the vitality of multiple, predatory fish that feed on the herring. In 2004, Ted Ames, a lobsterman from Stonington, Maine, published a paper called "The Stock Structure of Atlantic Cod in the Gulf of Maine." He set out to determine where different cod subpopulations had spawned in the early part of the twentieth century and if that information might lead to clues about the recent disappearance of cod. Ames used an anthropological approach, interviewing older fishermen, aged 61 to 94, to determine where cod had historically spawned, based on knowledge passed on by their fathers and grandfathers. "I developed a method for validating information from fishermen to make it acceptable to the scientific community," Ames told *Maine Mag* in 2009. To develop the study, Ames combined his fishing experience with his master's in biochemistry from the University of Maine. For a while, he was also a science teacher in Mount Desert, Maine. "We documented a little less than 1,000 square miles of spawning grounds on the coastal shelf between Gloucester, Massachusetts, and Canada."[20] Ames laid out his theory in the journal *Fisheries*:

> Cod are one of three major predators of Atlantic herring. Coastal Atlantic cod also used to co-migrate in spring with alewives and blueback herring as they returned to spawn in natal rivers and streams. Baird [the first fisheries commissioner] reported that the loss of these forage stocks had triggered the collapse of the coastal-cod fishery and the abandoning of spawning grounds lying close to rivers. Such a pattern . . . opens the possibility that cod are 'programmed' to arrive at their spawning areas via their pursuit of a particular forage stock sharing a common migration corridor. The disappearance of local anadromous forage stocks [river herring] and the disappearance of nearby Atlantic cod spawning components was a coincidence that occurred in several areas, suggesting that the traditional movement patterns and arrival times of Atlantic cod may have been disrupted at their inner spawning grounds when the forage stock disappeared. If so, the restoration of coastal populations of Atlantic herring, alewives, and river herring may also be important to restoration of Atlantic cod fisheries.[21]

A year after the paper was published, Ames received a $500,000 fellowship from the MacArthur Foundation—a "genius grant"—for his breakthrough study. A year after that, Ames was profiled in a *New Yorker* story called "The Lobsterman": "Typically, a historical ecologist is an academic, a forester, or a government scientist. The only one of any prominence who is a fisherman is Ted Ames. Ames is a lobsterman in Stonington, Maine, and his scientific study is of ghost and remnant schools of fish, mainly cod."[22]

Ames read another paper that suggested cod stick to their natal spawning grounds. Like river herring, they keep coming back to the same spot. "Ah, I thought, I have all the points of origin for cod in coastal New England during the 1930s. All I had to do was figure out where they went for the rest of the year and then we would finally know something about how the fish existed 100 years ago. The question was, were they really a pandemic population—with fish evenly distributed everywhere? Or were there smaller components with unique spawning grounds and with different migration corridors? By golly, it came out that there were bodies of fish that had different migration corridors and they behaved almost like separate subpopulations."

Ames determined that when cod come close to shore to spawn the river herring are also coming in for their spring migration upriver to spawn. The cod feast on the herring and their fatty-acid lipids, which gives them the energy to spawn. But when the stocks of river herring diminished, so did the cod stocks.

"His hypothesis was that without returning river herring to their freshwater habitats we may not be able to restore cod," says NOAA Fisheries' Sheehan. "If cod over generations were reliant on river herring in the spring, when herring are removed from the ecosystem, there's got to be negative impacts."

This strikingly simple hypothesis made a lot of sense but there was no proof that it was correct. Sheehan and many other scientists have been working for a decade to prove it. Besides the science, Sheehan felt that proving a connection between dam removal and marine fisheries would really connect the two parts of NOAA Fisheries, the habitat-restoration arm and the marine-fish arm, which is a goal of Jon Hare, research director of NOAA's Northeast Fisheries Science Center.

For the last 10-plus years, Sheehan and colleagues have been looking for evidence of alewife predation by groundfish, taking stomach samples (with the Maine Department of Marine Resources) from two areas: the nearshore region downstream from Merrymeeting Bay where the Kennebec and Androscoggin Rivers enter the ocean, and the nearshore region of Penobscot Bay where the Penobscot River enters the ocean. "The idea is to see what the fish are eating and if it is changing over time with the continued restoration of river-herring populations within these areas." To date, with 1,500 samples, there is not a lot of evidence of such alewife predation, although it is higher on the Kennebec, which over time has had a larger river-herring population. Within the Penobscot Bay region, incidence of river herring consumption by groundfish predators has increased in recent years, possibly in conjunction with an increased river herring abundance.

The Ames hypothesis may be true, it may be true to a minor degree, or it may be too early to tell. This is the mystery of marine ecosystems, the mystery that engages scientists. "The question is, do you need to rebuild alewives first or cod first? Is there some critical number of alewives, like 10 or 15 million, before you really see a connection?" asks Sheehan. "Is the change linear or does it at some point become exponential, which would support the Ames hypothesis?" Sheehan and company will continue to cut open fish bellies—a biologist's delight—for the foreseeable future to answer some of these ecosystem and food-web questions.

Meanwhile, Ames has proposed a new method of coastal management, one modeled on the "collaborative-area management" plan used by the lobster industry to protect certain nearshore areas with rigorous ground rules for harvesting. "If we were to use a layered-management system like we use for lobster, the current mobile fleet wouldn't be able to target nursery or spawning grounds anymore. If fish can reproduce, then we're going to have 10 times the fish we have now. It becomes kind of like watching a popcorn popper with the lid off. Here you have this little inner area that all of a sudden is blowing fish all over the place. It's producing the way it used to historically."

That vivid description of a "popcorn popper" comes from the fisherman who was awarded a "genius grant," which has not gone unnoticed by fellow fishermen. "The good thing is, fishermen don't say, 'Oh, there's that clunk fisherman from Downeast Maine shooting his mouth off again.' They say, 'This guy knows something about the system and he's sharing it.' The bad thing is, rather than being just this guy who fishes and is sharing these ideas and things he's seen, all of a sudden, I'm this guy who knows it all and so on."[23]

One thing scientists don't know is if and when and to what extent the herring will come back, and what impact that will have on finfish. "We've got the largest river-herring population on the east coast of the United States, maybe even on the entire eastern seaboard of North America, but that population could easily be three, four times what it is now," says John Burrow, director of New England Programs at the Atlantic Salmon Federation. "So, we're continuing to work on restoring more habitat and hoping to see those populations continue to increase."[24]

Restoring the complexity of native habitat is often as important as dam removal. If lower dams are removed and quality habitat for spawning is in the upper headwaters of a river, the potential gains may be limited. Similarly, while removing dams does have a clear and immediate effect, so does widening culverts and passages under bridges.

In 2021, the Federal Energy Regulatory Commission was studying another application for a 50-year lease on the Shawmut dam in the Kennebec River, removal of which some environmentalists think might open access to the Sandy River, if effective fish ladders could be installed at other dams. "You can't just look at Shawmut in this context, you have to look at the Lockwood and Hydro Kennebec dams below it and the Weston dam above it because if we don't get salmon into the Sandy (a tributary of the Kennebec River) it's a problem, because that's where all the habitat is," says Jeff Reardon of Trout Unlimited, the sport-fish advocacy group.[25]

Dam removals get high grades from the public, as they should, but they don't necessarily radically change the situation. "Our results highlight the degree of discontinuity dams can have when quality habitat is located upstream and the compounding relationship when multiple dams are present," write NOAA Fisheries' authors Justin Stevens, John Kocik, and Tim Sheehan in a paper analyzing prospects for the endangered Atlantic salmon. "These impacts increase in systems with multiple dams in a concept called 'serial discontinuity.' Dams may impact individuals multiple times throughout their life: downstream migrating smolts, upstream migrating adult, downstream migrating spawned adult and upstream migrating adult repeat spawners. One major impact is a decreased likelihood of repeat spawning, which negatively influences population growth."[26]

One of the authors, John Kocik, chief of the Atlantic Salmon Ecosystems Research Team at NOAA's Northeast Fisheries Science Center, took NOAA Fisheries' Jon Hare on a canoe trip down the Penobscot a few years ago, to showcase what a difference taking out the dams had made to the riverine ecology. "What John told me and what I had not known is that even before the dams were constructed early settlers had 'straightened' parts of the river so they could float logs down," says Hare. "A lot of complex habitat was removed even before the dams went in." That said, Kocik says that river herring are having more luck reaching their natal spawning grounds than are salmon.

River herring interest scientists, given their "keystone" role in the marine food web. Atlantic salmon, which swim upstream with the river herring, interest investors, sport fishermen, and consumers. They both fit the postindustrial narrative: dam removals for the river herring, new farming techniques for the endangered Atlantic salmon. The two species were once connected in the marine-riverine ecosystem. The salmon, along with many other species—for better or for worse— have jumped into a new humanmade ecosystem.

PART 2

Farmed Finfish, Shellfish, and Sea Greens

Aquaculture—the cultivation of aquatic organisms and plants in fresh and saltwater—is the fastest-growing form of food production in the world. Farmed fish are increasingly important to global food security because the wild catch has been flat for the last 30 years—and keeping it flat appears to be a best-case scenario. Farmed fish accounted for 52 percent of global fish consumption in 2018. The vast majority of aquaculture is in Asia; China has always been the top producer. The United States ranks seventeenth globally in aquaculture production, behind countries such as Myanmar and North Korea, even though more than half the fish Americans eat is farmed.

This book focuses on *mariculture*—the cultivation of marine species. Mariculture in the United States is still in its infancy, but evolving fast. In 2021, there was just one ocean finfish farm (salmon) in Maine, one in Washington State (salmon), and one in Hawaii (kampachi). Offshore farming is the Holy Grail for many entrepreneurs; few have yet been permitted but several are in the application process.

New England is a hotbed for mariculture—with *land-based* barramundi, branzino, and rainbow-trout farms, and a profusion of oyster, mussel, and kelp farms. Production of shellfish and seaweed is important because they require no inputs and have a restorative impact on marine ecosystems. Several large-scale, land-based salmon farms and a kingfish yellowtail farm are planned for Maine.

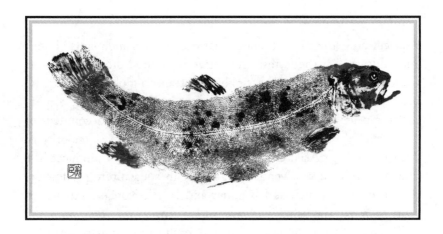

RAINBOW TROUT

Chapter 7

The Blue Revolution
and Atlantic Salmon

*The best guess of scientists is that there are 1.5 million Atlantic
salmon left in the world. To put this tragic fact in perspective, the
July sockeye [salmon] run in Bristol Bay [Alaska] in 2018 was 62.3
million fish, a record, but even a typical year is more than 40 million.
Survival is highly questionable for a species that has
only 1.5 million individuals*

—Mark Kurlansky, *Salmon: A Fish, the Earth,
and the History of Their Common Fate*

"What got me into aquaculture in the 1970s was an analysis by the United Nations Food and Agriculture Organization (FAO) on the heels of the Green Revolution in South Asia," says Sebastian Belle, director of the Maine Aquaculture Association. "The FAO looked at food supplies and said it was only a matter of time before we reached a crisis."

The Green Revolution dramatically increased yields of wheat, initially in Mexico and then in India, and of rice all over Asia. From the 1960s through the 1990s, yields of rice and wheat in Asia doubled.[1] But, in addition to selective breeding and mechanized irrigation, the Green Revolution also relied on chemical fertilizers, pesticides, and defoliants. Planting the same crops in the same fields year after year also resulted in soil degradation.

The Blue Revolution in fish production that followed initially made some of the same "industrial" mistakes as the Green Revolution. But the Blue Revolution, with help from Fourth Industrial Revolution tools, is now morphing into the larger and more sophisticated Blue Tech Innovation movement.

The first phase of the Blue Revolution in the late 1970s and 1980s was more about freshwater aquaculture than ocean mariculture, decidedly more Asian than Western, and clearly not eco-friendly. Mangrove forests in the Philippines, Thailand, and Ecuador were ripped out to make way for shrimp ponds. Carp and tilapia farms were staked out on the flood plains of the Ganges, the Irrawaddy, and the Mekong Rivers. By 1985, the World Bank, the Asian Development Bank, and a variety of other international aid agencies were pumping $200 million a year into aquaculture projects. From 1975 to 1985 world aquaculture output doubled.[2] In the 1990s, Atlantic salmon mariculture took off in Norway, with crowded nearshore net-pens that polluted the sea floor with excess nutrients and fish feces.

A 2019 report from The Nature Conservancy and Encourage Capital (a New York investment firm), suggests that the Blue Revolution needs to produce seafood in a much smarter way than it did in its early phase. "Given the significant challenges aquaculture has encountered as it's developed, the modern era should have the experience and know-how to do a much more efficient job of seafood production while minimizing environmental costs," says Robert Jones, global lead for aquaculture at The Nature Conservancy and the lead author of the report, entitled "Towards a Blue Revolution."

The authors suggest three approaches to creating an environmentally sustainable Blue Revolution: (1) nearshore, restorative bivalve and seaweed farms (see chapters 9 and 10); (2) offshore farms removed from more environmentally sensitive and active coastal zones (see chapter 11); and (3) land-based recirculating aquaculture systems (RAS). The first option is well under way; the latter two options are in the early phases of development but offer the best shot at sustainable and large-scale seafood production over the long term.

The first big test is land-based production of Atlantic salmon, which first started in Norway a decade ago and is now taking hold in the United States. If it works and is economically viable at scale, it could well be key to the future of global fish production. But first, some context.

Atlantic Salmon: Endangered but Ubiquitous

The endangered Atlantic salmon has not been fished commercially in the United States since 1948 or in Canada since 2000. The last two remaining commercial fisheries, Greenland and the Faroe Islands, agreed in 2018 with the Atlantic Salmon Federation and the North Atlantic Salmon Fund to halt commercial fishing and allow only indigenous fishing for personal consumption (through 2030).

This negotiated settlement was the best news for Atlantic salmon in decades, but the species' long-term prospects are still dim. Warming waters are a big factor; another is declining energy from salmon's primary forage food, capelin. "Energy" in this context is energy from the sun, which phytoplankton create through photosynthesis just as land plants do. The decline in capelin energy is a function of the declining energy in phytoplankton. "There's been a decrease in the number and size of phytoplankton and an increase in the number of steps to get energy from primary producers into fish, who themselves need to exert more energy," says Jon Hare, research director of NOAA Fisheries' Northeast Fisheries Science Center.

Sometime after the fact, scientists identified an abrupt decline in North American salmon marine productivity starting in 1990.[3] Katherine Mills, a research scientist at the Gulf of Maine Research Institute, initiated a follow-up study to evaluate conditions before and after that decline. In a 2013 paper, she found that around 1990, changes in salinity and temperature of the Northwest Atlantic resulted in a decrease in abundance of larger, higher-energy zooplankton and an increase in smaller, lower-energy zooplankton. Capelin are consumers of zooplankton, which are consumers of phytoplankton, and Mills reported that they had also, like their prey, declined in size and energy around 1990.[4]

A 2015 paper showed that Atlantic salmon feeding off Greenland had roughly the same diets then compared to pre-1990, but that the average energy available in capelin was approximately 30 percent lower compared to capelin pre-1990.[5] "Capelin are like high-energy bars for salmon," says NOAA Fisheries' Tim Sheehan, one of the authors of this diet study. "But since they have 30 percent less energy, salmon have to eat more capelin to get the same energy they consumed pre-1990, which means they have to expend more energy to do that, which means they need to eat more and expend even more energy. On top of that, a warmer ocean places higher metabolic demands on fish, which also requires more energy, so it's kind of a downward spiral." Numerous other marine species that relied on capelin also had reduced productivity right around 1990: various sea birds, other fish species, seals, and polar bears.

Despite the scarcity and tribulation of Atlantic salmon in the wild, there is no problem finding fillets at the fishmonger or supermarket. Atlantic-salmon aquaculture is the fastest-growing food-production system in the world—accounting for 70 percent (2.5 million metric tons a year) of all aquaculture production.

Atlantic salmon is farmed in many parts of the world—Norway, Scotland, Faroe Islands, Canada, Chile, and the United States. In the US, it is farmed in Maine, Wisconsin, Florida, and Washington State, with a California farm on the drawing board. Farmed salmon is so common that the Boston Seafood Expo, one of commercial fishing's biggest annual events, is jokingly referred to as the Boston *Salmon* Expo, with rows upon rows of pinkish-red fillets from around the world lying in state on crushed ice for buyers to ogle and inspect. It is as if the world has focused its scientific smarts on producing an edible "hologram" of Atlantic salmon to satisfy the cravings of the Western diet.

Salmon farming started in Norway in the 1970s and was shortly thereafter taken up in Maine, Scotland, and, in the 1980s, in the Faroe Islands. Salmon farming escalated in Norway in the 1990s after its herring fishery collapsed, which it does from time to time, as does the anchoveta fishery in Chile (often the top fishery in the world). "The Norwegian government made a conscious decision to promote salmon farming, linking up with an agricultural university," says Maine Aquaculture Association's Belle, a former lobsterman who was first exposed to aquaculture when he lived in Norway in the 1970s. "The founding father of salmon breeding was a professor of dairy-cow farming. Norway approached salmon farming as a rural agricultural and food-development program, not as a fishery."

Salmon are anadromous (from the Greek *ana* meaning "up" and *dromos* meaning "running") fish that spawn in freshwater and mature in saltwater before "running up" to spawn in freshwater after a year or two at sea. When farmed, they are initially raised to smolts in fresh water and then transferred to saltwater. It's a bit of a trick to replicate this natural two-step process. It starts with a large, fecund female fish that annually produces an average of 10,000 eggs, which are fertilized and incubated at a freshwater hatchery. After eggs hatch, the larvae grow into free-swimming fry and then parr, with dark vertical bands on their sides, which are vaccinated. After 18 months in the fresh-water hatchery/nursery, salmon undergo major changes that enable them to live in saltwater. Their kidneys adapt to excrete salt, and their skin becomes silvery so the fish will be less visible to predators in the ocean. Changes also occur in the eyes, blood plasma, musculature, and fat. Smolts, roughly 5 inches long, are transferred to floating net-pens in the ocean or tanks on land, where they grow out for roughly 2 years until reaching a market size of 10 to 12 pounds.[6]

Salmon consumption worldwide is now three times higher than it was in 1980. Once a luxury, salmon is among the most popular fish species in the European Union and the United States, which imported $3.9 billion worth in 2018, according to the US Department of Agriculture.[7] Salmon is popular because people like the taste, it grills well, and it is high in protein and vitamins. Like trout, albacore tuna, and sardines, salmon also contains large amounts of heart-healthy omega-3 fatty acids, which lower inflammation and blood triglycerides.

Atlantic salmon's transition from a luxury to a commodity fish is the result of widespread industrial operations. Indeed, many of the bad raps against farmed fish have their roots in the intense, industrial salmon farming of the 1990s. One rap is that salmon farming relies on fish oil and fish meal extracted from forage fish. In the 1990s, it took roughly 5 pounds of fish meal and oil to grow 1 pound of salmon, a food-conversion ratio of 5:1. Fish farmers actually prefer the fish-in/fish-out ratio, except when comparing their product to other genera, and it is now much closer to 1:1 for salmon. Another rap is that nearshore, shallow-water pollution from fish waste and the spread of sea lice—which attack the skin, head, and necks of salmon—affects the health of marine ecosystems and wild fish. (As few as eight sea lice can kill a wild Atlantic salmon smolt going to sea.) A third rap is the risk of escapement from net pens, which might have a negative impact on wild stocks; the concern is that "genetic introgression" of escaped farmed salmon to wild might reduce the survival skills of wild Atlantic salmon. Finally, the use of antibiotics, which was common in the 1990s but is less so now, upsets people not so much because it affects the taste of the fish (it doesn't) but because it potentially reduces the long-term effectiveness of the antibiotics for all treatments as bacteria develop resistance. Overuse of antibiotics for beef, milk, and farm production, of course, potentially has the same effect.

Salmon farming is rapidly changing, moving from nearshore net pens to offshore ocean pens and land-based water tanks. Fish farmers are experimenting with alternative feeds based on soy, insects, microalgae, or biotech single-cell proteins. And multinational companies (mostly Norwegian-run) are locating in the United States to move closer to their biggest market, reducing shipping costs and carbon footprint. Another reason for global expansion is that Norwegian farmers face a market at full capacity with expensive license renewal fees; in 2018, the Norwegian government took in roughly $350 million in license fees from salmon farmers.[8]

All new salmon farms built in the United States today or in planning stages are land-based, in recirculating aquaculture systems (RAS). (In Norway and China, massive offshore farms are more the norm.) A RAS uses huge tanks filled with hundreds of thousands of gallons of water, with typically 95–99 percent of the water purified and recirculated. Mechanical and biological filters remove excess waste, ammonia, and carbon dioxide. Sensors monitor temperature, acidity (pH levels), and oxygen content of the water, which must be reoxygenated before it recirculates. Any water that is not sufficiently purified for reuse is blasted with ozone to kill bacteria before it is returned to a river or the ocean.[9] Excess waste is sent to wastewater treatment plants.

RAS is basically a scientific and engineering solution to a biological problem—keeping fish alive and healthy for 2 to 3 years in a contained system until they reach market size. "Think of a RAS as a dairy barn underwater, a life-support system for an animal that doesn't live on the land," says Belle, who has helped design fourteen aquaculture projects in nine different countries and was the recipient of the 2017 World Aquaculture Society Lifetime Achievement Award. "The jury is still out on the economics of RAS; the argument has always been that no one has built one big enough to achieve economies of scale. The projects that are in the permitting process or are currently under construction will test that hypothesis."

The appeal of RAS is that it solves the problems of sea lice, excess-nutrient pollution, escapement, and cross-breeding by taking fish out of the ocean and by separating farmed from wild fish. Plus, a RAS can be built anywhere there is a good water supply and a water-discharge site, which means it can be close to major markets. Finally, it is easier to control and manage fish in a tank than fish in an ocean pen, at least in theory.

The counterpoint, however, is that a RAS is essentially a wastewater-treatment plant—capital-intensive to build and energy-intensive to run. Consider this description of a RAS project planned by Whole Oceans on the site of an old paper mill in Bucksport, Maine, from the Maine Department of Environmental Protection:

> As a whole, the project will include changes in land elevation and the construction of buildings, underground utilities, paved accessways and maneuvering areas, and stormwater management facilities. The project will also include water-supply and wastewater-treatment systems that will include new connections to domestic water and sewer lines, upgrades to a raw freshwater supply line from Silver Lake, upgrades to the saltwater intake/pump system, re-connection to existing discharge pipe(s) in the Penobscot River, new water-treatment system, new wastewater-treatment system, etc. All of this will be broken out into a series of construction phases, as it is anticipated that full build-out may take 10 years or more.[10]

Despite the capital expense, RAS potentially solves so many of the problems that have plagued large-scale, near-shore ocean farms that investors are bullish on a technology that is rapidly evolving. RAS salmon farms are certainly industrial-*scale* operations, with the intent to farm, collectively, hundreds of thousands of tons of salmon each year. Atlantic Sapphire's new Bluehouse (a "greenhouse for fish") farm in South Miami, which produced its first harvest in 2020, plans to produce as many as 220,000 tons a year by 2031, about half the current US demand.

"As one industry expert quipped to me: 'That's a lotta lox,'" wrote Michael Grunwald about Atlantic Sapphire's plans in *Politico*.[11] But hold the bagels for the moment because the operation has suffered early growing pains. In 2020, it was forced into an emergency harvest of 200,000 due to vibrations from ongoing construction. In 2021, it had a "mass mortality" event, losing 500,000 metric tons of fish, which the company blamed on "design weakness" from one of its RAS suppliers.[12] In early 2020, the parent Atlantic Sapphire in Denmark—the world's first salmon RAS, started in 2011—lost 227,000 fish.

Given that salmon need up to 3 years to reach market size, farmers need massive scale to achieve a return on huge investments or to pay back loans. Thue Holm, a Danish aquaculture expert who cofounded Atlantic Sapphire in Denmark with Norwegian entrepreneurs and is now its chief technology officer, says that if you have ever had an aquarium, you know how hard it is to keep a few fish alive indoors. The Atlantic Sapphire Bluehouse in Florida will eventually have 4 million square feet of "aquariums," most of them holding nearly as much water as an Olympic-sized pool.[13]

Despite its industrial scale, RAS is a postindustrial technology—it reuses old industrial space and land, there is little to no waste, and it relies on state-of-the-art digital tools and machine-learning algorithms to run the water, feed, and filtering systems. Energy is a major cost, but farms are piloting conversion of fish waste into biogas for energy, creating a more holistic, closed system. And there is more you do can with waste. Superior Fresh in Hixton, Wisconsin, combines a RAS salmon farm (the first in the United States) with hydroponics—the combination of aquaculture and hydroponics is called *aquaponics*—to grow greens on rafts floating in water. Nitrate-rich water is circulated to the greenhouse, where plants absorb the nutrients.

The purified water is then circulated back to the fish house. Superior Fresh produces 3 million pounds of organic greens and 160,000 pounds of salmon each year, wasting almost no water.

The latest hotspot for salmon farms is Maine—with three big RAS projects in progress. The permitting process has been slow, complex, and, in some cases, contentious, mostly concerning environmental concerns about waste and discharge into rivers and the sea.

Salmon farming in Maine is not new. It started on a very small scale in the Gulf of Maine in the 1970s and picked up in the late 1980s and into the 1990s. "But as regulations were put in place the small farmers couldn't comply with monitoring and sold out," says Belle. Aggregation in the sector culminated with Cooke Aquaculture of New Brunswick emerging as the dominant producer in 2004. Today, Cooke has marine farms stretching from Bar Harbor to Eastport, with three freshwater hatcheries in different locations, and a processing plant in Machiasport. It also has operations in New Brunswick. The Cooke farms are in the Gulf of Maine just below the Bay of Fundy, which has the highest tides in the world, assuring a strong flow of clean, cold, nutrient-rich water that accounts for the high quality of its True North salmon.

Cooke rotates the twenty-four sea sites it leases, with about half inactive at any one time for a year or two, just as traditional farmers leave fields fallow to regenerate. No salmon with a trace of antibiotics in its system can be sent to market.[14] In 2021, Cooke had an application pending to lease a twenty-fifth sea site from the state, but it was being delayed due to strong opposition from local residents and lobstermen who fear losing access to acreage at the bottom of the Gulf of Maine.[15] "As a fish farmer in Maine, you need a social license from lobstermen, which is embedded in law," says Belle. "Social policing goes back 200 years to the Lobster Wars, when gangs had territories and would start a war, burning boats and shooting at anyone who set gear in their territory."

Cooke is the third-largest salmon farmer in the world, operating farms in Washington State, Chile, Scotland, and Spain (sea bass and sea bream). It has also partnered with the We'koqma'q First Nation of Nova Scotia on sales and marketing of its farmed steelhead trout.

In 2018, after several salmon escapements that were blamed on aging net pens, the Washington State legislature voted to terminate Cooke's leases in 2025 when the current ones expire.

But farming fish in the ocean is old hat; farming on land is the new thing. Nordic Aquafarms and Whole Oceans from Norway, and Aquabang from the United Kingdom, are proposing RAS salmon farms in Belfast (54-acre industrial site), Bucksport (100-plus acre site of old paper mill), and Millinocket (old paper mill), respectively. These and other aquaculture companies have committed to an investment north of $1 billion in Maine, a state better known for lobsters and moose than foreign investment.

Whole Oceans in Bucksport, an old paper-mill town of 4,900 close to the mouth of the Penobscot River, has bought more than 100 acres and plans to invest up to $250 million for its farm and processing plant. It has received a permit to discharge 18 million gallons of water a day into the Penobscot River. The Bucksport planning board approved its permit application in 90 minutes, eager for new industry to replace the Verso Paper Mill, which closed in 2014. But in late 2020 Whole Oceans expanded its project, requiring new permits. Whole Oceans hopes to produce 20,000 metric tons of salmon a year once fully operational. It has a 15-year partnership agreement with Kuterra, a First Nation Atlantic salmon farm on Vancouver Island in British Columbia (the first RAS salmon farm in North America and the second in the world), to share technology and help train Whole Oceans employees.[16]

Whole Oceans has certainly done a better job of earning a "social license" than Nordic Aquafarms in Belfast, a town of 6,700 just 20 miles away. Belfast was once home to chicken-processing plants with flying feathers and fat (it was known then as "Schmaltzville") but has since become more of an eco-friendly, retirement haven for people seeking recreation than a destination for young people seeking jobs. "There's been a fundamental demographic shift in our coastal communities and tension between those who value recreation and those who value working waterfronts," says Belle.

The debate over Nordic's salmon farm has been fierce from the time it was proposed, with worries about environmental degradation, as well as a litigious battle over intertidal easement rights for the discharge pipes.[17] The project will rely on a steady supply of freshwater from the City of Belfast and local wells; the project will also intake nearly 4,000 gallons of seawater per minute from Belfast Bay, and treated wastewater that is not recirculated will be pumped back into Belfast Bay.[18]

Nordic Aquafarms, after 3 years of antagonistic public hearings and a couple of lawsuits, finally received four key state permits in late 2020 and the final necessary permit from the US Corps of Engineers in the summer of 2021. But Nordic, which is also planning a salmon RAS in Humboldt County, California, still needs approvals on water discharge. Nordic plans to invest up to $500 million to produce 33,000 metric tons of salmon a year.

In Millinocket, 100 miles up from the mouth of the Penobscot River, Aquabang is eyeing an old paper-mill site, unused since 2008. In its heyday of the 1970s, the Great Northern Paper Company produced 16 percent of the newsprint in the United States, according to the *Bangor Daily News*. Aquabang's site offers access to renewable hydroelectric power, clean cold water, and the industrial infrastructure of the former mill town. Aquabang looks to build six RAS facilities to produce 10,000 tons of fish a year. Because it will discharge effluents into freshwater, for which permits already exist, the approval process is expected to be more streamlined.[19]

Finally, another Norwegian-backed salmon farm is proposed for Maine—an ocean farm in Frenchman Bay, just a few miles from Mt. Desert Island and Acadia National Park. The American Aquafarms company proposes two 60-acre ocean sites and to convert a former sardine cannery in Gouldsboro into a hatchery and processing plant. The goal is to grow as much as 30,000 metric tons of salmon annually in so-called "closed pens," which look somewhat like a large salad spinner, in the middle of the bay. This "emergent technology" from Norway, said to prevent escape of salmon and fish waste—a major upgrade on the original net-pens—is now being used to farm cod in Norway.

Would-be developer Mikael Roenes, a former Norwegian stockbroker, was convicted of participating in an investment fraud worth millions of euros in 2008 and sentenced to 4 years in jail (he ultimately served two and a half years in a low-security facility). The locals are not exactly welcoming him with open arms. "This is simply a matter of the wrong place, the wrong technology, and the wrong people," local resident James Paterson said in a press release, noting American Aquafarms' proximity to Acadia National Park, not to mention ocean acreage used by lobstermen.[20]

Yet another RAS project would appear to have a better shot at success. Netherlands-based Kingfish Company (formerly Kingfish Zeeland) received its final permit in 2021 to build a RAS in Jonesport, Maine, to farm yellowtail (*Seriola lalandi*), also known as hamachi or hiramasa. The company plans to produce 6,000–8,000 tons a year in two sizes: a 1- to 2-pound whole fish, and a 5- to 6-pound fish for the sushi/sashimi market.[21] The Kingfish Company, which currently operates a RAS in the Netherlands, was the first land-based farm to receive Best Aquaculture Practices certification and the first source of yellowtail kingfish certified by the Aquaculture Stewardship Council. That pedigree, the fact that it is not in the ocean, and the local support for investment and jobs in Jonesport would seem to increase the odds of its success.

Non-fish Fish Feed

The biggest production cost for all fish farmers is feed. For finfish like salmon, the feed has historically been fish oil and fish meal made from wild stocks of forage fish—small pelagic fish that live in the upper layers of the sea, such as anchovies, sardines, menhaden, capelin, and herring. This has generated many complaints about robbing Peter (forage fish from the ocean) to pay Paul (the ravenous, predatory salmon growing to adulthood). Indeed, some reports estimate that 20 percent of wild-fish catch is reduced into fish feed.[22]

Michael Rubino, former aquaculture science advisor at NOAA Fisheries and now its chief strategy advisor, considers the argument against fish oil and fish meal a "red herring." Rubino contends that the supply of fish meal and fish oil on the global market has been relatively constant for the last 30 years, even as aquaculture production has increased by 5–6 percent per year. "It wasn't ever really an issue," says Rubino. "If salmon farmers didn't buy it, producers of pigs and chickens and pet food would. Now, aquaculture feed has been decoupled from the need for forage fish, thanks to work NOAA Fisheries, and industry scientists have done in the last 15 years."

Since 2000, the percentage of fish meal and fish oil in aquaculture overall has declined from 70 to 30 percent.[23] Many farmers have turned to corn or soy-based protein for growing fish, but these alternatives can lead to higher fish mortality and generally suboptimal growth. And farming soy and corn means often means clear-cutting pristine land, such as in the Amazon.

But a number of alternative feeds are being developed. These include insect larvae, microalgae, fermented CO_2, and biotech single-cell proteins. Fish need protein to grow, but nutritionists who design non-fish fish feed also account for about forty essential nutrients—vitamins, minerals, amino acids, and fats.[24]

New biotech alternatives are promising. Knip Bio, based in Lowell, Massachusetts, has developed microbe strains that convert ethanol, methanol, and other feedstocks into single-cell protein. KnipBioMeal combines the attributes of fishmeal and carotenoids, which give salmon its pink color. "It's really pink flour," says Larry Feinberg, co-founder and CEO. "'Knip' is 'pink' spelled backwards."

NovoNutrients, an early-stage biotech company in Mountain View, California, down the road from Google and Facebook, is looking to turn CO_2 emissions into protein for seafood farming. Its Novomeal, a nutritionally complete substitute for fishmeal, is made from the proteins of bacteria and other single-celled organisms, incubated in giant steel vessels akin to beer vats, called bioreactors.[25] The lab-created bacteria feed on carbon dioxide.

In Menlo Park, Calfornia, Calysta ferments natural gas with naturally occurring bacteria to create a protein feed called FeedKind. It has been shown to be an ideal feed supplement for Japanese yellowtail or hamachi, a sushi staple. FeedKind has also been used successfully to feed salmonoids and shrimp.

Insects are part of the diet of wild fish and crustaceans and are now being used in aquaculture. Black-soldier-fly larvae, for example, provide an inexpensive, high-protein alternative to fish-based feed. Distributed by several companies in Africa, black-soldier-fly larvae will eat just about anything, including waste, and in 14 days build up fat stores that sustain them for the remainder of their adult lives.[26] One scientific study showed that "a total replacement of fish meal with black-soldier-fly larvae meal in the diets of Atlantic salmon was possible without negative effects on growth performance, feed utilization, nutrient digestibility, liver traits, or the sensory qualities of the fillet."[27]

French company Ÿnsect produces premium oil (Ÿnoil) and meal (Ÿnmeal) from the larvae (mealworms) of *Tenebrio molitor*, a species of beetle. Both are designed for fish feed. BetaHatch in Seattle, Washington, converts mealworms and their waste into high-value proteins, oils, and nutrients for both agriculture and aquaculture.

The aquaculture industry at large is excited by these developing products—given the negative blowback about forage-fish feed—but individual farmers cite two reasons to proceed with caution. One is that they are waiting for evidence of the long-term success of the feeds. Another is that they worry about whether these new providers will scale production to provide a consistent supply of feed, because missed shipments could have a serious impact on the health of their fish. The actual ability to scale is not the issue, as the technologies appear solid—but a company needs a steady stream of large customers to justify scaling production. Thus, there is a chicken-and-egg problem hindering future development.

One more calculus to consider on the fish-in/fish-out question: If a farm can develop a large-scale aquaponics business, as Superior Fresh in Wisconsin has done, it can generate a lot of food on a small footprint of land. Superior says that for every 5 pounds of fish food it grows 5 pounds of salmon and 25 pounds of organic vegetables. This effectively converts the acronym FIFO from fish-in/*fish*-out to fish-in/*food*-out.

Whatever the feed, fish in general are a much more effective converter of food to protein than land animals. Beef has an average food-conversion ratio of 6:1, pigs, 4:1, and poultry, 2:1—while fish overall were less than 1:1 (0.82) in 2015.

Sebastian Belle attributes the food-conversion advantage of fish to their physiology. "Finfish and shellfish have two major advantages over land plants and animals: They don't have to thermoregulate, or burn calories to maintain heat, and they use air or lipids to fight gravity, which means they preserve calories and energy," says Belle. "Take the two together and it's clear why it's inherently more efficient to grow food in water than on land."

In addition, aquaculture has a much smaller environmental footprint. While land farms are essentially one-dimensional, water farms are three-dimensional, so that in terms of spatial planning the required surface area is minimal relative to the volume of the farm.

Maine, which NOAA Fisheries' Rubino calls the "the poster child for aquaculture in the United States," is a good example. The state has 3,478 miles of "tidal coastline" (51 more than California) with clean, cold water.[28] To date, just about 1,500 ocean acres are used for aquaculture in Maine, about the size of Rockland Harbor, according to Belle. And the planned RAS farms collectively account for less than 200 acres of land. In Florida, the goal of Atlantic Sapphire is to produce about 15 percent as many tons of food as Florida's citrus industry produced last year on about 0.03 percent as much land.[29] Conventionally farmed salmon already produces fewer greenhouse-gas emissions than pork and far fewer than beef, and the gap should widen as more RAS farms start generating their own power from solar panels and gasifying waste for energy.

That said, salmon are not the perfect fish to farm at sea or on land, as the grow-out phase is lengthy and expensive. That is why other entrepreneurs are trying to find the perfect fish to farm—with less upfront investment, lower costs, and faster growth.

Black Sea Bass

Chapter 8

Fish for a Small Planet

Humans tried to domesticate everything and only the good stuff
got domesticated. Aquaculture is penalized because most of it
has taken place in the scientific era, so you can apply a lot of
technology to things that maybe should not be domesticated. If we
look more carefully and determine what's a good farm animal—
what are the pigs, cows, and chickens of the fish world—we
might come up with very different answers.

—Josh Goldman, CEO, Australis Barramundi

almon is the perfect fish to sell, given voracious market demand,
but it is not the perfect fish to farm. It takes a long time and a lot
of food to reach market size. It takes a big investment and a long
time to earn out. But there are several smaller recirculating-aquaculture
system (RAS) farms in New England raising other species that reach
market faster—such as barramundi, branzino (European bass), steelhead trout, and rainbow trout. The first RAS farm in the United States,
started by entrepreneur Josh Goldman in the late 1980s, is still in full
operation in western Massachusetts.

In high school, Goldman read *Diet for a Small Planet*, Frances Moore
Lappé's best-selling 1971 book. She was the first to call attention to the
negative side effects of meat husbandry and a meat diet, and suggested
ways to ingest protein without eating meat. When Goldman went to
Hampshire College in Western Massachusetts in the 1980s, he lived
in a house where fellow students were growing vegetables in a solar

greenhouse. Goldman introduced tilapia—the African freshwater fish that was at the time becoming popular in Taiwan, China, and Southeast Asia—to the greenhouse. Besides the *Diet* book, Goldman was inspired by the ideas of the New Alchemy Institute on Cape Cod, run by two marine biologists who were looking for ways to extend food production in a cold climate. One of their ideas was a "bioshelter" with food-production systems that would mimic natural ecosystems and reuse waste to help jumpstart other foodstuffs.[1] This was aquaponics—combining aquaculture and hydroponics to grow vegetables in "fish" water—an ancient technique of the Chinese and Aztecs. At age 20, Goldman's ground-breaking research garnered a $400,000 grant from The Pew Charitable Trusts. "That money allowed me to do some real science around the notion of closed-system aquaculture, reusing water and so forth," Goldman told the *Boston Globe* in 2006. "You have this wonderful synthetic ecosystem that you're creating, and you get to play God a little bit."[2]

In 1986, when Goldman graduated from Hampshire, he and a classmate started Bioshelters, Inc., to commercially farm tilapia. At that point, almost no one in the world was farming fish on land. RAS was invented in Germany in the 1970s to grow carp and further developed by the Danish Aquaculture Institute to produce European eel (*Anguilla anguilla*). It was the success of the European eel industry that inspired Goldman and others to develop water-saving and environmentally sustainable alternatives to conventional flow-through and pond-based aquaculture.[3] (A new American RAS eel farm is discussed later in this chapter.) Goldman fine-tuned those early RAS for various species and holds multiple patents on filtration and water-reuse technologies, how to automatically remove dead fish from tanks, and low-carbon shipping methods.

But farming tilapia in the United States didn't make economic sense—most people at the time didn't know about tilapia, and it was a low-value fish with low margins for a producer. In 1989, Goldman bought land to build a fish farm called AquaFuture.[4] He started farming striped bass, a popular high-value fish but one that is difficult to farm. Striped bass are rambunctious and can be fussy about spawning. After 13 years trying to make striped-bass biology and economics work, Goldman took a break. He sold his Turners Falls farm to Hong

Kong investors. For a while, Goldman raised Arctic char in West Virginia with water reclaimed from coal-processing plants. He then set out on a 3-year quest to find the perfect fish to farm. "What's the ability to use alternative protein for feed, so we're not stuck on the fish-meal treadmill? I started to develop criteria for what the perfect farm fish looked like. It had to be docile. It had to be versatile in the ways it could be cooked."[5]

Goldman toyed with red snapper, pompano, and grouper, which caught his attention until he realized that juveniles were difficult and expensive to raise. In 2000, Goldman met Stewart Graham, an Australian entrepreneur who had eaten barramundi in an Australian restaurant and loved it. When told it was farmed, Graham wanted to start a business to produce more. Friends told Goldman he needed to meet Graham (and vice versa), who wanted to bring barramundi to the United States.

Barramundi, an Australian and Indo-Pacific fish, met all of Goldman's criteria. In 1938, the *Sydney Bulletin* described barramundi as the "King of Australian Fishes."[6] Barramundi—an aboriginal name meaning "large-scaled whitefish"—spawns in the ocean, and the fry migrate into freshwater to mature before returning to the ocean to themselves spawn. It is a catadromous species, the opposite of the anadromous salmon.

"It's an interesting fish. It's one of the first farmed white-flesh fish and it tastes pretty good," Roger Berkowitz, then the CEO of Legal Sea Foods and now the owner of Legal Sea Foods Marketplace, told the *Boston Globe* in 2010. "I have a preference for wild [fish], but Australia's the only place where they eat this fish wild. A few months ago, we started playing around with it."[7]

Aboriginal "language groups" use different words for barramundi. The Gooniyandi people from the Kimberley region of Western Australia use the name "balga"; the Wik people from the western side of Cape York use the name "Minh Wechan"; the Murrinh-Patha people from the Kimberley region use the word "Tharnu."[8] Many of these indigenous groups are now farming barramundi in the Northwest territories of Australia. That is a good sign as to the suitability and sustainability of the fish for farming. As the Passamaquoddy of Eastern Maine say, "sustenance means sustainable."[9]

Barramundi has half the calories of salmon, lots of omega-3, and not too much omega-6 (which can cause inflammation). Barramundi can subsist on a largely vegetarian diet (with a small amount of sustainably sourced fish meal) and is both docile and hardy (doesn't need antibiotics), with good tolerance for low oxygen levels in water. The food conversion ratio is 1:1 or better and the fish-in/fish-out ratio is even lower.

Goldman and Graham bought back the Turners Falls farm from the Hong Kong investors, who remained as stockholders in the newly formed Australis Barramundi company. Initially, Goldman used herring for feed but then switched to a diet of minimal fish and a large helping of vegetable matter (80 percent), including herbs such as cinnamon and rosemary. He added some fish meal as a finish food before harvest to increase omega-3 levels. Here is how Goldman described his Turners Falls Farm to *Yale Environment 360* in 2011:

> The way our plant works is basically that there are a series of five different rooms, and in each room the tanks get larger to match the growth of the fish. And each tank or group of tanks is linked to a filtration system that utilizes a combination of physical filtration, as well as biological filtration, to remove the dissolved metabolites from the fish. The fish excrete ammonia into the water, and the bacteria basically take that and turn it into a nontoxic form and ultimately bacteria put it back into nitrogen gas in the environment. [The system] utilizes very little water and the waste products are recovered, so there's almost no waste in the water leaving the facility.[10]

In 2006, Goldman "disrupted the business," his understated description of moving from Massachusetts to Vietnam, from the land to the ocean. He thought better economics would allow him to scale the production. He kept the Massachusetts operation running and traveled back and forth.

In Vietnam, Goldman switched techniques—raising fry in a land-based hatchery where he could vaccinate them by immersion and then transferring juveniles to a net pen 6 to 10 miles offshore at age 8 to 10 months. The operation has been a huge success. By 2018, he had 500 employees and was producing 3,000 tons of barramundi a year.

In 2020, retail sales increased 70 percent. Goldman flash-freezes the fish, packages it in foil with "Australis, The Better Fish" branding, and ships it by boat—unlike the millions of tons of salmon that fly all over the world—to regional and global supermarkets. In the United States, Whole Foods and Stop & Shop, among others, sell his fish.

Jessie Johnson, in her *At the Table* podcast, once asked Goldman whether global shipping was in keeping with his sustainable vision and ideals. "Local is one dimension of food, but not the answer to all problems," Goldman told her. "If we eat responsibly farmed fish, we use less water and less carbon."[11] No wonder Australis Barramundi, which uses no hormones, antibiotics, or chemicals, won a Best Choice award from Monterey Bay Aquarium for its land-based product—and was the first ocean-farmed fish to win Monterey Bay's Best Choice award, along with the coveted Aquaculture Stewardship Council stamp of approval. In 2021, the company also won Fair Trade USA certification, the first Asian finfish farmer to do so.

In 2018, Keith Wilda and James Malandrinos, owners of Blue Stream Aquaculture LLC, which operates trout farms in New Hampshire (for sale to consumers) and Cape Cod (to stock sport-fishing ponds), bought Australis Barramundi in Turners Falls. They started a new LLC called Great Falls Aquaculture. Wilda, who had studied agriculture and resource economics, had worked as a general manager for Goldman at Australis Barramundi from 2004 to 2011, and in 2006 traveled to Vietnam with Goldman to look for a farm site. Starting in 1992, Wilda was an employee of, and Malandrinos a contractor for, Bioshelters, which Goldman had left in 1989. They co-farmed tilapia and basil, carrying on the early Goldman aquaponics legacy. Malandrinos, an engineer, built a two-story, 60,000-square-foot aquaponics factory for Bioshelters; he's now building an 80,000 square-foot aquaponics facility for Blue Stream Aquaculture in Charlestown, New Hampshire.

Spencer Gowan, the current general manager of Great Falls Aquaculture, is on his second stint as a barramundi farmer. He worked under Goldman at Australis Barramundi in Turners Falls from 2009 to 2013, left for graduate school to study aquaculture at Auburn University's School of Fisheries, and returned in 2015. Great Falls Aquaculture clearly has good "barramundi genes" as it continues to farm in the nation's first and longest operating commercial RAS farm—arguably the first "postindustrial" fish farm in the United States (although Blue Ridge Aquaculture's Tilapia farm in Virginia is almost as old).

Blue Stream Aquaculture's trout farm and hatchery in West Barnstable on Cape Cod has been operating since 1860 and before that was a tannery. "It's a historic hatchery," says Wilda. "Ecology-wise, it's unique, the waters are shallow artesian wells with free-flowing water. Having been here for 160 years, it's got its own ecology with freshwater diatoms in 400 feet of sandy raceways."

Blue Stream Aquaculture's trout farm in New Hampshire is only a few years old and still being built. Wilda and Malandrinos, now partners in four fish-farm companies (including a new oyster farm planned for New Bedford Harbor outside the hurricane barrier, see chapter 9), like to build and rig their own systems. They farm rainbow and brook trout in New Hampshire and are considering adding Arctic char and steelhead trout, as well an anerobic digester to provide energy and an aquaponics farm to grow vegetables with runoff fish water. Wilda and Malandrinos have been experimenting with both systems for 25 years. A new spinoff product is Fish Brew Plant Probiotic to "give your soil naturally occurring beneficial fungi, bacteria, and protozoa that are found in our filtered fish excretions."

"I have high hopes for steelhead, it's a great alternative to salmon, with eggs more readily available. And no one in the market is doing brook trout, which is native to New England," says Wilda. "It's very similar to Artic char, so we're testing brook trout before char." Wilda has a trout hatchery on Cape Cod and Malandrinos is building a multispecies hatchery in New Hampshire. Wilda's wife, Reagan, was the first person to hatch barramundi in North America, for Australis Barramundi.

At Great Falls Aquaculture, the main business is still barramundi—mostly shipped live to restaurants and Asian markets in New York (the biggest market, at 15,000 pounds a week), Boston, Toronto, and Vancouver. Great Falls ships 6,000–7000 pounds a week, packing 300 pounds of fish into a tote lined with plastic and filled with water; the truck trip to Vancouver is 72 hours. The totes collapse for the trip back across the continent. Great Falls also sells some fillets and smoked trout from the New Hampshire farm.

Besides a more vegetarian diet, the big plus to barramundi, especially compared to salmon, is the fast grow-out—the fish reaches market size, a pound and-a-half, in 9 to 12 months. Selling mostly live, whole fish, Great Falls Aquaculture faces little competition from Australis Barramundi in Vietnam, which sells flash-frozen fillets to supermarkets around the world.

Great Falls Aquaculture is "probably the largest livestock farm in Massachusetts," says general manager Gowan. "We have 300,000 fish swimming around in here." The old tanks from the 1990s hold 130,000 to 150,000 gallons of saline water; newer tanks hold 325,000 gallons and are buried eight feet in the ground for thermal protection. The water temperature is kept at 80 degrees; sea salt (3–5 parts per thousand) is added to the water. "The fish would be fine in freshwater, but they are happier with some salinity," says Gowan. "It puts them closer to an isotonic state, where the salinity of the water is the same as the salinity of their blood, so they expend less energy regulating."

Great Falls Aquaculture's 37 fish tanks circulate more than 2 million gallons of water every hour. Ammonia in the water from fish feces is toxic to the fish. After solid waste is removed from the water, biofilters turn ammonia into nitrites and then nitrates. There is a constant flow of cleaned wastewater plus fresh water, which is pushed 60 feet underground on every circulation so that high pressure reoxygenates it. About 720,000 gallons are filtered every day, with 95 percent recirculated. Solid waste is sent to the town sewer or wastewater treatment plant; the remaining gray water is blasted with ozone to kill bacteria. Before the 80-degree water is returned to the Connecticut River it is cooled, and the heat is captured to warm fresh water. Great Falls Aquaculture is certified by the state as a Class 2 municipal wastewater-treatment plant.

All barramundi are born male and remain so for years. Although they are not sexually mature when in the tanks, they will eat each other if they don't have enough food. Part of the trick is separating fish according to size, as bigger fish go after smaller ones. Sexual immaturity is good from a farming perspective as it allows the fish to put all their energy into growth. The mortality rate is 30–40 percent from recently hatched fry to maturity, which seems high, but it is fairly standard for an animal with high fecundity, says Gowan. Great Falls

Aquaculture used to hatch its own fish, but for the last 15 years it has imported fingerlings from Australia and Israel. As with all fish farms, the major cost is feed, followed by electricity, which runs $30,000–$50,000 a month. The pellet feed is primarily made from poultry by-products, with some fish meal.

Another issue that affects all RAS farms to varying degrees is the buildup of "off flavors" that must be "purged" before slaughter or live shipping. The problem was widely encountered in the United States with catfish farms in ponds, where blue-green algae (also known as Cyanobacteria) produce metabolites that get into the fat of fish, says Jeff Silverstein, deputy administrator of animal production and protection at the US Department of Agriculture, Agricultural Research Service. Given the limited water exchange in a RAS tank, the blue-green algae produce compounds that have a very strong, earthy taste and odor that can be detected by humans at very low levels, just a few parts per billion.[12] The basic purging technique is to put the fish in clean water without food for 7–20 days. Some farms also use a finish food like that from Knip Bio, which has been designed to significantly reduce the "off-flavor" problem. Great Falls is working with Knip Bio on feed studies. "I think we can reduce the off-flavor in 48 hours," says Wilda. That is a huge deal, because the longer you purge without feed the more weight the fish lose, like apples in cold storage, and the longer the time to market.

Great Falls Aquaculture has been raising barramundi for a long time. Ideal Fish, a branzino farm roughly 100 miles southwest of Turners Falls, is a relative newcomer. Ideal Fish was founded in 2014 by Eric Pedersen, a former investment banker specializing in water deals who started an aquarium in his basement to teach his young children about the natural world. That somehow led to farming fish in "small" 800-pound tanks in the basement. "Initially, my wife was disturbed that I was doing this," he says, somewhat wryly.

Ideal Fish's "ideal fish" is not barramundi, but branzino (European bass), a popular restaurant fish from the Mediterranean that is primarily farmed (like Atlantic salmon) because the stock is severely depleted in the wild. "Other than our fish, all of the branzino served in this country is cultivated in the Mediterranean," says Pedersen.[13]

Ideal Fish has a state-of-the-art RAS facility in an old, 63,000-square-foot, military brass-button factory, using town water for its tanks. The building renovation was completed in 2016, the first fish were farmed in 2017, and the first harvest was in 2018. The salinity, level of acidity (pH), and temperature of Ideal's twenty-eight tanks are all customized for branzino, which naturally spawn in rivers. In a protected environment, no hormones or additives are required. "It produces a healthier fish that is raised in the Connecticut foodie's backyard," Pedersen says. "Consumers get a fish that is a day or two out of water and hasn't traveled all of the food miles." At full production, Ideal produces more than 5,000 pounds of fish each week, or 160 tons a year.[14]

After raising $20 million from domestic and international investors, Ideal Fish developed a $3–$5 million business selling to restaurants and high-end grocery stores. Until the COVID lockdown in March 2020, restaurants in Boston and New York were the number one market—branzino grows to "plate size" in about a year, about the same rate as barramundi—but after losing 60 percent of its revenues overnight, Ideal rapidly built out its e-commerce capability to circumvent the restaurant closures. Ideal started selling branzino through its website as well as through Amazon, and by the summer of 2020 it had recouped half its lost revenues. Ideal now also sells salmon and trout, smoked or fresh, from other farms. Aiming for 100 percent utilization (the Icelandic model), Ideal Fish smokes misshapen fish and sells bones for soup.[15]

Ideal recirculates about 97 percent of its water and gives away waste for fertilizer to farmers (it does not yet have USDA approval to sell fertilizer). Down the road, it hopes to use its gray wastewater for an aquaponics farm. It is also eyeing red snapper and sushi-grade flounder as its next products. "This is an industry that Connecticut needs to develop," says Pedersen. "Local fish production is key, sitting close to major markets of Boston, New York, and Washington, DC."

Barramundi is from Australia and Asia. Branzino is from Europe. Steelhead trout is native to the Pacific Coast. Seventy-five miles northwest of Waterbury, Connecticut, in Hudson, New York, Hudson Valley Fish Farm is farming steelhead trout, a salmonoid that is a more sustainable alternative to imported salmon. With a state-of-the-art RAS "ranch," given the acreage that is devoted to aquaponics, entrepreneur John Ng supplies restaurants and grocers with up to 20,000 pounds of fresh steelhead a week, all raised without hormones, antibiotics, or parasiticides.

Ng, the son of an immigrant from Hong Kong who built a scrapyard in Brooklyn into a multinational company, acquired his 130-acre farm in 2014. It had been a fish farm before—sea bream, sea bass, fluke, flounder, and tilapia—that ultimately failed. Ng ripped out the systems and built from scratch, finishing at the end of 2015. He had fish in the tanks in 2016 and a first harvest in 2018—more or less in sync with Ideal Fish's start-up timeline. Hudson Valley Farms recirculates roughly 4 million gallons, adding 250,000–350,000 gallons of freshwater a day. Some would say that because of the lack of saltwater the fish is technically a rainbow trout—only rainbow trout that leave rivers for the sea are called steelhead—but Ng is more focused on technical farming issues.

"We didn't have confidence in Atlantic salmon when we built," says Ng. "We thought saltwater and light control would be a problem." His steelhead are hearty eaters and stable growers, reaching 6 or 7 pounds in 16–18 months. Hudson Valley Fish Farm simulates summer's light and temperature growing conditions year-round, which shaves at least 6 months off the grow-out period.

Ng gets about 45,000 eggs monthly from West Coast hatcheries (where steelhead is native) and culls out half to keep the fastest growers. Ng feeds non–genetically modified grain-based feed with approximately 25–35 percent fish oil and fish-meal content, achieving a 1:1 food-conversion ratio. He is open to alternative feed products, but like Great Falls Aquaculture's Gowan, wants more data and a longer period of testing before switching (as well as consistency of supply). His fish have chrome-silver skin, with orange meat—roughly 60 percent sold to retailers and 40 percent to food services, with a slice to community-supported agriculture groups.

Hudson Valley Fish Farm's kill process is sophisticated and humane, if that can be said of a kill process. After a 10-day off-flavor purge, the steelhead are placed in a racetrack system with 175 electrodes along it. As the fish swim through, the electric current slowly increases until the fish are anesthetized. Stunned into unconsciousness, processors put them on a table to cut their gills and quickly bleed them. "The stress of traditional harvesting degrades the product," says Ng, who is aware of the Ikejime technique as practiced by Gulf of Maine Sashimi (see chapter 5), but feels his system accomplishes the same end. Of course, he's not on a boat pulling fish out of the water, as they do in Maine. "In traditional stun systems, a hammer hits the fish on the head and a machine cuts the gills," says Ng. "The problem is the fish struggle and don't die quickly, as a lot of fish are not stunned by the hammer."

As many other RAS farmers are now doing or contemplating, Hudson Valley Fish Farm is in the aquaponics business. Aquaponics utilizes nutrient-rich fish water to produce plants. The life-support systems of the fish farm use biomedia to convert fish waste (ammonia) into nutrients (nontoxic nitrates). These nitrates and other organic compounds make the effluent water from the fish farm ideal for "fertigating" (injecting fertilizer into soils and irrigation systems) plants.

Hudson Valley Fish Farm is not growing run-of-the-mill leafy greens, but hemp. "The advent of hemp in the last 4 to 5 years is an opportunity we couldn't resist," says Ng. "An acre of corn can yield $100, an acre of hemp, $18,000, thanks to high demand for CBD oil." Hudson Valley has the potential to use 25 acres for hemp, with five planted in 2021. The company also has 15,000 square feet of indoor space, where it controls the light cycle, and two large greenhouses (160,000 sq ft).

"We built a commercial-scale fish farm first, now we're getting into greenhouses," says Ng. "The solid waste and ammonia convert to nitrates for the crops. We built the system so that we can ventilate CO_2 into the greenhouses to keep them at 60 degrees for year-round growing. The fish farm is also kept at 60 degrees—optimal for steelhead. Land-based aquaculture is 'borrowing' the water—drop it in and drop it out—so we're not fighting farmers for water. I could put a fish farm next to an almond farm—and grow fish and almonds without using any more resources."

The idea that Ng is selling both his fish and greens to the same "locavore" shoppers through a community-supported agriculture group gives some hope that "fishies" and "foodies" might well coalesce in a broader movement (see chapter 4). Even if they don't, the aquaponics offshoot is positive from a resource-economics perspective. On top of that, there is the potential to use energy from the fish farm either directly or through an anerobic digester. The food output, water conservation, and energy conservation potentially reframe the economics of high-capital RAS farming—as well as the resource requirements for agriculture.

"For me, the two have always seemed to go hand in hand," says Wilda, who first started experimenting with aquaponics at BioShelters nearly 30 years ago. "I think what we've learned about aquaponics over the past 25 to 30 years is that you don't need quite as many fish as initially thought in order to grow the number of plants you want to grow, particularly if you're growing leafy greens or basil."[16] To grow vegetables, you need more nutrients than tilapia provides. "With trout, you produce zinc and phosphorous, and can easily grow tomatoes and strawberries," says Wilda.

Just as every RAS farm must be customized by species, so must every aquaponics system. For example, one issue with salmon, barramundi, branzino, and some steelhead is the salt and chlorides used in the fish tanks, which must be extracted before being fed to plants. This also complicates the effort to turn waste into fertilizer.

American Unagi: The Mysterious and Coveted Eel

The viability of RAS farming was first confirmed by successful efforts to farm European eels in the early 1980s, so it is fitting that this new wave of RAS farms in the United States includes an eel farm. It is run by Sara Rademaker, an entrepreneur who, like Ideal Fish's Pedersen, started in her basement to prove the concept. Like Great Falls Aquaculture's Gowan, she has a master's in aquaculture from Auburn University's School of Fisheries.

For years, Maine fishermen have caught baby eels a few years old called glass eels or elvers as they migrate upriver in the spring before river herring do. Mainers ship eels to China for $2,000 a pound—it takes about 2,500 glass eels to make up a pound—where they are grown to maturity and worth thousands of dollars more per pound. Eels are prized in Asia as *unagi* for sushi.

Rademaker is betting she can grow out the eels in a land-based RAS system in Waldoboro, Maine, and keep that value in the United States. Her company, American Unagi, is producing a clean, high-quality, high-value, made-in-the-USA product that is traceable, sustainable, and raised without antibiotics or hormones. "The species had had success in RAS in Europe, so I wasn't reinventing the wheel. And I started in my basement, where all good start-ups happen, to see if the eel would hold up."

Rademaker's first foray into farming was with catfish in Uganda and tilapia in West Africa, after which she returned to America and settled in Maine. "I knew what I wanted to do. I knew land-based aquaculture is where things are going, with warming and acidifying oceans, with the technology and lower labor costs," she says. "I had worked in Maine enough to know that it's a good place to grow a business and that Maine has become a significant aquaculture hub because of the regulatory environment and the seafood infrastructure. I just needed to find a species that worked with RAS. And there are very few species with a good track record."

As she watched fishermen scooping eels out of Maine rivers and selling them for $2,000 a pound she thought, "Why don't I just do this?" Eels are found in most rivers of the Atlantic Coast; they spawn in the Sargasso Sea, a "nocturnal forest up to 23,000 feet deep," and then small larvae-like creatures with a body "like a willow leaf" disperse, ranging from the top of South America to Greenland and across to Europe and the North Sea.[17] Glass eels have a high survival rate after being caught, and they thrive in a tank for another year or two before reaching market size. High-end sushi restaurants take about 30 pounds of eels a week.

Philosophers and scientists have been trying to figure out the eel since the time of Aristotle, who thought the eel was viviparous—capable of bringing forth a live eel without an egg. Freud spent 20 years dissecting eels looking for sex organs, without success. What Aristotle, Freud and many others missed is that eels have no visible sex organs until they need them, in the fourth stage of their life. Twenty years after Freud's failed efforts, a sexually mature silver eel was found off the coast of Sicily. However, as Rachel Carson wrote and it is still true, "No human has even seen eels reproduce, no one has managed to breed European eels in captivity; and no human has even seen an eel in the Sargasso Sea."[18]

NOAA Fisheries established an eel quota system in 2014—9,688 pounds—which has been successfully implemented and reduced poaching, says Rademaker. "I'll need about 5 percent of the quota to make the business work." A wild eel can take 5 to 30 years to reach maturity, but the eels in American Unagi's tanks can mature in as little as 7 months to 2 years thanks to her special attention and care to their habitat. "Our eels are happy; that way they grow the best and taste the best."

At her pilot farm, Rademaker had about 200,000 eels in 2020. At her new farm in Waldoboro, built in 2021, she expects to house 1,500,000 eels. Given the surge in interest in sushi, Rademaker sees a national market, which now typically imports eels from China. China itself sources eels from all over the world, some from Maine, some black market, some from Europe. "Many eels are smuggled around the world, and those being imported back into the United States have uncertain sourcing. My goal is to displace those imports with traceable American products," says Rademaker. The only thing she won't be able to do is start an eel hatchery, as no one has ever witnessed eels spawning.

RAS is a fairly well tested technology, at least for some species, but as with any complex system there is a lot that can go wrong. And the economics are not fully worked out. "RAS gives you a lot of control, but if there's a disease outbreak, you're in trouble," says Michael Rubino of NOAA Fisheries. "But someone's going to figure RAS out. And someone's going to put big investment in shrimp, which grows much faster than finfish. That could be a gamechanger."

Indeed, Bangkok-based CP Foods has bought a failed 40-acre shrimp farm on a former citrus grove in Indiantown, Florida, and established Homegrown Shrimp USA to pilot a RAS shrimp farm. In Thailand, CP Foods specializes in shrimp aquaculture, including grow-out, feed, and hatchery technologies. The company operates bio-secure, broodstock farms that achieve 95 percent survival rates, which it hopes to replicate in Florida. The company wants to demonstrate that shrimp can be grown away from salt marshes, mangroves, and other valuable coastal lands.[19] In Thailand and Vietnam, shrimp farms have been ecological disasters, ripping out mangrove swamps.

Proving the ability to successfully grow shrimp on land at scale would be an environmental plus and would potentially reduce the huge US seafood trade deficit. Americans imported $6 billion worth of shrimp in 2019.

SEA SCALLOP

Chapter 9

The Beauty of Filter-Feeding Bivalves

The billions and billions of sessile animals, like oysters, mussels, and barnacles, owe their very existence to the sweep of the tides, which brings them the food which they are unable to go in search of.
—Rachel Carson, *The Sea Around Us*

Putting aside the economics, you can debate about the perfect finfish to farm or the healthiest fish to eat, but there is not much argument about the best *seafood* to farm *and* eat. Hands down, it is shellfish, particularly oysters and mussels.

"Mussels are just about the perfect food," says Scott Lindell, a research scientist at the Woods Hole Oceanographic Institution. Lindell likes mussels because they require few inputs (just the phytoplankton they extract from the ocean) and produce few outputs (just feces that are consumed by ocean-bottom dwellers). They are high in protein and omega-3 fatty acids, fix nitrogen and phosphorus (removing them from the water), and taste great. Just 3 ounces of mussels provide 40 percent of the daily protein needed by the average person. Mussels are an excellent source of iron and B12.

Oysters may take a tad longer to grow out (depending on latitude and water temperature) but otherwise have all the same attributes—and they filter and purify more water, up to 50 gallons a day. Oysters offer 7 grams of protein for only 68 calories (leaner than mussels), which rivals lean, red meat for protein density. Raw oysters are also an abundant source of several vitamins and minerals—vitamin D, vitamin B12, iron, magnesium, phosphorous, zinc, copper, manganese, and selenium. From an economic perspective, they are in much higher demand from consumers than mussels and command higher prices.

For all their similar characteristics, oysters and mussels are quite different as a food and a crop. Mussels are edible raw for the adventurous, but they generally need to be cooked; oysters can be eaten raw or cooked. Mussels are produced at a much higher volume but sell at a much lower price than oysters. Mussels are sold wholesale by the pound (80 cents–$1.50, depending on quality and buyer); oysters are generally sold by the piece (roughly 50 cents, depending on the size). Starting and running a mussel farm is far more capital intensive than running an oyster farm, which is one reason why there are far more oyster farms than mussel farms. The other is that the New England oyster market is ten times bigger than the mussel market—$220 million to $20 million—and much better developed. Oysters have brands, depending on their "merroir" (the oceanic equivalent of a vineyard's terroir) in which they are grown, which gives them the cachet of microbrews. Blue mussels—the common mussel—have blue, black, blue-black, or brown shells, and are distinguished more by the plumpness of their meat than by their taste, although some are certainly sweeter than others. As adults, both shellfish are sessile (fixed in place) and need moving water to deliver their food (phytoplankton). As larvae or spat, oysters and mussel float until they set. Thus, protected tidal bays, estuaries, or rivers with high levels of water exchange are perfect ecosystems for shellfish farming.

More and more fishermen are hedging their lobster and groundfish bets by moving into shellfish and seaweed, says Sebastian Belle, executive director of the Maine Aquaculture Association. Sons and daughters of fishermen who can't get finfish or lobster permits are also taking up shellfish and seaweed farming. Federal permits are transferable but the market price, when available, can be hundreds of thousands of dollars. A third group of shellfish farmers comprises entrepreneurs with a science background, or scientists with an entrepreneurial streak. A smaller, fourth group is "foodie" entrepreneurs, who are looking to develop value-added products and often want their own farm to control production.

Even though some lobstermen are diversifying into shellfish, they are not necessarily as a group supportive of the number of new farms. There has been a rapid increase in the number of limited-purpose aquaculture licenses, which are pilot plots measuring up to 400 feet. Even some larger oyster farmers are worried that many small farms will be consolidated and sold to out-of-state bidders. "What's to keep us from cashing out and selling to a corporation?" asks Pat Burns, who started a cooperative of ten farmers in Robinhood Cove, in George-town, Maine. "Philosophically, we're not in that court. But could some-one do it? Yes."[1] It's definitely a hot-button issue. Belle says he's seeing more and more of the "'friends of' phenomenon," where wealthy land-owners form a group of friends in their community with a fancy name like Protect Maine's Fishing Heritage to block aquaculture projects that might infringe on their ocean views.[2]

Unlike some of today's fish farmers, who are breaking new ground with technique and species, shellfish farming has a long history. Shell-fish cultivation in China dates back 2,000 years. Likewise, ancient Romans farmed oysters in Italy in the first century and later in Britain for export back to Rome. The Japanese have farmed oysters since the seventeenth century (around Hiroshima), as have the French, focusing on their native, "flat" Belon oyster (*Ostrea edulis*).

In the United States, oyster harvesting (not necessarily farming), dates back more than 3,000 years to Native Americans in the Ches-apeake Bay region. Archaeologists have uncovered countless oyster middens that Native Americans left behind in New England. During the nineteenth century, commercial harvesting of wild oysters was a big business in the United States. At its production peak, from about 1880 to 1910, the country produced as much as 160 million pounds of oyster meat, more than all other countries combined.[3] "No evening of pleasure was complete without oysters and no host worthy of the name failed to serve the luscious bivalve," according to historian Clyde MacKenzie.[4]

By the 1890s, the world's largest fleet of oyster steamships operated in Connecticut in the New Haven area.[5] Long Island Sound was home to the famous Blue Point oyster.[6] Oyster production in Connecticut peaked in 1911. Throughout the twentieth century, both supply and demand declined—a function of overfishing, sewage, pollution, wars, storms, and disease. In 1924, for example, many oyster eaters became ill, with some dying of typhoid, mainly in Chicago. In 1927, the last of the New York City oyster beds were closed.[7] Not long after, in 1931, the now legendary Milford Lab in Milford, Connecticut, which has promoted oyster-cultivation techniques around the world, was opened to help increase oyster cultivation in Long Island Sound (it became part of NOAA Fisheries when NOAA was founded in 1970). In the 1950s, a period of intense storms and hurricanes and a parasitic disease later named MSX began to kill huge quantities of oysters in Delaware Bay and Chesapeake Bay. In the 1990s, with water warming, MSX spread into Long Island Sound and New England, and wild oysters were not on many diners' wish list.[8]

By then, the modern oyster-farming boom was just beginning. Today, there are 2,500 oyster farms in the United States, on both coasts and in the Gulf of Mexico, where oysters grow at least twice as fast as they do in New England. "Oyster bars are like cigars in the 1990s," said Christian Callahan of Ipswich Shellfish Company in 2014. "They are hot."[9] More than half a decade later, they're still hot.

Oysters Rediscovered

Oysters may be "hot" now, after nearly a century of disfavor, but the modern industry emerged slowly over 40 years until it took off in the early 2000s. In 1962, George Carey Matthiessen started growing oysters on Fishers Island, New York, off the coast of New London, Connecticut. He was an industry pioneer and innovator developing seed in hatcheries. In the 1970s and early 1980s, researchers on the Damariscotta River in Maine piloted oyster hatcheries and culture using the French Belon oyster, but they never scaled commercially.

Carter Newell, owner of Pemaquid Oyster Company (founded in 1986) and Pemaquid Mussel Farms (founded in 2008) says, "When I told people in the early '80s that I was thinking about growing oysters, they said, 'Don't do it, you'll lose your shirt.' Fifteen or 20 companies had failed in the 1970s. What I learned from Professor Herb Hidu in graduate school at the Darling Marine Center (University of Maine) is that aquaculture success is based on the right species, in the right habitat, with the right growing culture," says Newell. "They had the wrong species and the wrong culture (European oysters in lantern nets), but it was baseline trial-and-error pioneering." During the 1980s, East Coast growers switched from the Belon oyster to the native Eastern oyster (*Crassostrea virginica*).

Cuttyhunk Shellfish Farms, started by Seth and Dorothy Garfield in 1981, was one of the first commercial New England shellfish farms of the twentieth century. Cuttyhunk Island is part of the Elizabeth Islands in the middle of Buzzards Bay, between the mainland and Martha's Vineyard. Seth, who had spent summers on Cuttyhunk from an early age, got the idea of starting a farm after working for Carey Matthiessen at the Ocean Pond Oyster Company on Fishers Island in the 1970s. Matthiessen grew oysters from his hatchery in a salt pond, which he then transferred for grow out to the Cotuit Oyster Company on Cape Cod, founded in 1857.

Topographically, Cuttyhunk is like Fishers Island in that both have a protected pond that is suited for early oyster growth. The Cuttyhunk pond is tidal and exchanges water with Buzzards Bay twice a day; the Fishers Island pond is not open to the ocean except when moon tides and storms bring in enough saltwater to satisfy oyster seed. For more than 30 years the Garfields have bought oyster seed from Fishers Island—first from Matthiessen and later from the Fishers Island Oyster Farm, which is the old Matthiessen farm now run by Steve and Sarah Malinowski. (Their son, Pete, helped start the Billion Oyster Project in New York Harbor in 2014, with the goal of stocking a billion wild oysters in the city once called The Big Oyster.)

Seth Garfield, president of the Massachusetts Aquaculture Association, started farming the French Belon oyster in the early 1980s, buying seed from the Bristol Shellfish Company in Maine, but he switched to the Eastern oyster in 1989. Today, he typically buys 350,000 minuscule seed oysters (25 mm, about the size of a quarter) from the Malinowskis to plant each March. The genetically "fast growers" will reach 3 inches in July, ready for market, but "slow growers" can take up to 2 years to reach that size. "Seth was really the first entrepreneur to get involved in the industry. Previously, all the famers had been scientists," says Chris Sherman, CEO of Island Creek, one of the industry leaders. "That was a clear moment where the industry evolved."

The Malinowskis were just as entrepreneurial. Their Fishers Island Farm also started in 1981, with clams and bay scallops. The Fishers Island site was not conducive to clams, and the Malinowskis switched to Easter oysters in 1987, selling to local restaurants. "Blue Point oysters were the most numerous offering but by this time it did not have much distinction, because almost every northern oyster that found its way to a menu was called a Blue Point," says Steve. The Malinowskis got seed from Carey Matthiessen until they started their own hatchery in 1995. The Malinowski hatchery now produces 40 to 50 million seed oysters a year, all for the New England market. It sells all its own grow-out oysters direct to restaurants, as it has for 30 years. "We were farm-to-table before there was a farm-to-table movement," says Steve.

The biggest oyster grower in the Northeast is Copps Island Oysters, run by Norm Bloom and Son in Norwalk, Connecticut. Bloom's grandfather started farming oysters in 1940. In 2021, Copps Island Oysters had fifteen boats and eighteen employees. Bloom's focus has always been on Blue Point Oysters, farmed as they were in the 1800s—by dumping shells in the mouth of an estuary, letting wild spat settle on the shells, then moving the shells to beds in Long Island Sound where they grow out in 2 or 3 years. "Norm Bloom is like Budweiser and the rest of us are like microbreweries," says Steve Malinowski. "The scale of the operation is enormous."

In 1985, a few years after the Cuttyhunk Shellfish launch, Bill Mook started Mook Sea Farm in Walpole, Maine, on the Damariscotta River. Another Darling Marine Center grad, Mook worked at the Bristol Shellfish Company in the early 1980s and had sold Garfield his Belon-oyster seed. Mook Sea Farm, now one of the largest and most innovative oyster farms on the East Coast, was the first commercial hatchery on the Damariscotta River and one of the few on the East Coast. The farm produces 5–7 million oysters a year for the half-shell market (branded as Moondancers, Pemaquids, and Mookie Blues), as well as 120 million seed for growers from Maine to the Carolinas. In the early years, although he also grew oysters to market size, Mook was primarily a seed supplier for all the commercially important bivalves found on the East Coast, including the European oyster, soft-shell clams, and scallops, but for the last 20 years has focused solely on Eastern oysters.

"Part of our business model is to really attack biological problems head on," says Mook. "That's not necessarily cheap, but it increases your dependability as you go. That's something that's led us to really making a commitment to R&D." Mook Sea Farm has a proprietary system for growing microalgae to feed oyster larvae in the hatchery using a fermentation technology. The company grows 99.5 percent of its microalgae using sugar as fuel for cultures and uses large centrifuges to concentrate the cells so they can be frozen and stored. Mook claims this dense, rich feed—which he calls "green gold"—is less expensive to grow. The sugar provides both the building blocks for making new cells and the energy to drive the process. The culture is much denser compared to systems that rely on light energy, which is dependent on surface area. "If you think of the hatchery as the engine that drives our business, which it is, the microalgae are the fuel that runs our engines," says Mook, who also sells his "green gold" to other farms.

Carter Newell started another Damariscotta River farm, the Pemaquid Oyster Company, in 1986 with Chris Davis, who since 2004 has been the executive director of the Maine Aquaculture Innovation Center at the Darling Marine Center. (Garfield and Davis are boyhood friends from summers on Cuttyhunk.) Like Garfield, Newell bought his seed from Mook. Pemaquid Oyster Company starts its seed in surface trays in the upper Damariscotta River that are then bottom planted downriver when they are big enough (50 mm) to no longer be of interest to predators such as green crabs or starfish. Before harvest, the oysters are moved into specially designed rafts in cold, salty water to purge mud and silt. Pemaquid Oyster Company now grows more than a million oysters a year, keeping the scale of its operation in balance with the space available and other users of the water in the Damariscotta River. Newell is an ecumenical shellfish farmer and has also grown mussels for 40 years. "I wanted to try both mussels and oysters and see which did better," Newell says today. "Turns out, they both did pretty well."

One of the biggest oyster farms and distributors in New England and the country is Island Creek Oysters in Duxbury, Massachusetts. Founder Skip Bennett, son of a lobsterman, grew up in the Island Creek neighborhood of Duxbury. After college, he returned home in the early 1990s and started growing quahogs (hard-shell clams). The clams didn't work out so well and in 1995 Bennett turned to oysters. Bennett bought seed from ARC, a Cape Cod hatchery that has been supplying shellfish seed since 1984. In 2000, Bennett started Island Creek Oysters.

The company has grown into a nationally known, vertically integrated company, with its own distribution and restaurant network, and one of the most highly regarded brands in the country. "Island Creek is the mothership," says Garfield. As a distribution company, Island Creek sells 15–20 million oysters a year from over 175 farms to about 1,110 chefs around the country. (At least, it did before the 2020 COVID lockdown when it lost 98 percent of its sales overnight and switched to an e-commerce model; see chapter 4.) "We sell oysters from a lot of different farms but the branded Island Creek oyster comes from Duxbury Bay, the others are like a wine portfolio," says Chris Sherman, CEO. "Provenance is a big piece of oysters' success. Customers want more than one brand. Our trademark with vendors is our high touch with kitchens and chefs.

"A good bottom-grown Island Creek is the best oyster you can get, I think, but you have more control with trays," says Sherman. "It's a step up in capital, but you can take them out in the winter to increase yields, shape and quality are more consistent, inventory management is far more accurate, and they are easier to process postharvest. To bottom-plant, we broadcast single seeds on the bottom and then harvest by hand at low tide. In the wild, they'd grow in a cluster on a reef."

Blue Mussels: The High Volume, Low-Cost Shellfish

Mussels don't have nearly the storied history that oysters do. Oyster bars have not had to compete with mussel bars, except for Moules-Frites (mussels-and-fries) joints in Quebec or France. In fact, until the 1970s, when wild foods were becoming popular, mussels in the US were either considered bait or a "poor man's seafood."

If the modern oyster industry weaved a long 40-year trail of trial and error, the same is true of modern mussel cultivation. The godfather of mussel farming on the East Coast was Ed Myers, like Matthiessen a Princeton graduate, whose Abandoned Farm in Clark's Cove on the Damariscotta River, with support from Maine Sea Grant (a national NOAA Fisheries program affiliated with universities), was awarded the first aquaculture license in the state of Maine in 1973. (Taylor Shellfish Farms in Washington State started in 1890 specializing in oysters but added mussels about 30 years ago.)

Myers—a dapper dresser who often wore Brooks Brothers shirts, a bowtie, and a jaunty cap—ran his farm for 20 years. His office was a converted chicken coop; he used a 1924 Maytag washing machine to de-clump his mussels. Myers grew his mussels on ropes suspended in the water column from rafts. He built the rafts out of old telephone poles floated by plastic barrels once filled with Coca-Cola syrup. Each 22-foot pole on the raft supported fourteen ropes that dropped 24 feet into the water.[10] He later grew mussels using the Italian longline method, socking the seed in plastic mesh.

Because there are no mussel hatcheries (Downeast Institute in Maine is working to hatch golden mussels), mussels are exclusively grown from wild spat, which attaches naturally to ropes, rocks, or the sea floor in summer. When mussels reproduce, huge quantities of microscopic larvae (enough to outnumber predators and maximize chances of survival) drift around on the tide until enough calcium is laid down in the shell and they are ready to "set" on the seabed, rock, or rope. This means that two key elements of oyster growing are not needed with mussels—hatcheries or nurseries.

The dominant mussel harvester (and later, farmer) in the early days was Great Eastern Mussel Farms, in business from 1978 until 2008. As Copps Island does with oysters, Great Eastern Mussel Farms moved wild mussels from their beds to deeper, more open water, giving tiny seed mussels room to grow. During the summer, Great Eastern Mussel Farms also harvested wild mussels off Cape Cod. In 1983, it was shipping 6 million pounds a year around the country from its processing plant in Tenants Harbor, Maine.[11]

Mussel farming is a volume game from beginning to end, from spat to harvest. The mortality rate of spat in a crowded mussel bed is high because there's a connection between the density of shellfish and the supply of food. If a mussel filters 1 gallon of seawater per hour—the rule of thumb for a 2-inch mussel—and tidal currents only supply a half-gallon of seawater per hour, the mussels will grow half as fast. For mussels to grow, they either need more food or lower density, or both.

"Ideally, for fastest growth, there should be 15 to 20 mussels per square foot on the sea bottom," says Newell, who started with Great Eastern Mussel Farms as a biologist in 1982.[12] "An engineering friend of mine calls it the 'hydraulic zone of influence,' which applies to farms as well as individual mussels. If you have a 200- by 200-foot farm, the next farm (or set of rafts) should be 200 feet away." Great Eastern Mussel Farms would harvest its bottom-planted mussels in roughly 2 years (mussels grow faster on ropes than on the sea floor).

Yet another Darling Marine Center graduate and Myers mussel protégé is Bill Silkes, who graduated from Unity College in Maine. "I ended up working with Ed Myers, an incredibly interesting guy," says Silkes. "When I was there, oysters were the hot thing, with Dr. Hidu leading the charge. Myers got a grant to pilot mussels and I got involved with that."

In the early 1980s, Silkes moved to Rhode Island to set up a mussel farm in Narragansett Bay for Blue Gold Sea Farms. In 1986, he started American Mussel Harvesters in North Kingston, Rhode Island, to harvest wild mussels by dredge on the Nantucket Shoals. The company now sources wild mussels from Maine and Massachusetts and grows a small crop on its farm in Narragansett Bay. American Mussel Harvesters ships mussels by truck to its processing plant in Kingston, submerges them in its SeaWater purge system to allow recovery from the harvest and trucking trauma, and to purge bacteria lodged in their stomachs, then ships them in 2- or 10-pound bags around the country. American Mussel Harvesters is the largest mussel producer and processor in the United States.

"The blue-mussel resource is very different than it was 15 to 20 years ago, the abundance from Maine to Rhode Island has definitely diminished," says Silkes. "There are fewer mussels near shore, whether it's due to acidification, predators, disease, warming water, or some combination, we don't know. But the same thing is going on in Sweden, Denmark, and Norway." Silkes has three sons in the business, two of whom are farming oysters and mussels in Rhode Island, one of whom runs the processing plant. He's hoping to start an offshore farm in federal waters, more than 3 miles offshore (see chapter 11).

A pivot point in mussel farming occurred in the 1990s, when Newell was still working for Great Eastern Mussel Farms. He started Aquaculture Harvesters as a rope-grown division of the bottom-planting company, using the Spanish raft method. "When we heard about the longline technique, we looked at each other and said, 'There's no way we can do that,'" says Newell. Initially, ducks ate the small mussels and those that grew larger got so heavy they slid off the ropes.[13]

Joint research by Great Eastern Mussel Farms and the Maine Aquaculture Innovation Center, along with both private and government funding (a Small Business Innovation Research grant from the US Small Business Administration) helped to develop a raft, 40 × 40 feet, with a minimum of a 60-foot clearance above the lowest tide, allowing for 45-foot lines with pegged ropes. This was designed to yield more than 60,000 pounds per raft, per year. One-ton steel plow anchors on both the upstream and downstream side, anchored with steel chain, keeps the raft stable in wavy water, at least in theory.

A predator net hangs around the perimeter to a depth of 40–50 feet to prevent eider ducks from devouring the crop. Mussels are the food of choice for eider ducks, which dive to 50 or so feet. Each eider duck, prevalent in the Northeast from December to April, consumes its weight in mussels every day and a "raft" of eiders (that's not a duck joke) can collectively eat its way through thousands of dollars of mussels in a week. Take Ed Myers's word for it:

> The ducks dive to 35 feet and crush the mussels in their gizzards, sometimes getting so full that they can't fly. One mussel raft farmer spent $3,000 seeding a mussel raft with 12,000 feet of drop lines (to which tiny mussels attach themselves at their earliest stages), only to have 60 percent of his mussels eaten by ducks in two days. A leased mussel bottom area in Stonington had 60,000 pounds of seed mussels eaten by ducks in one month. Needless to say, for mussel suspension culture to succeed, the duck problem needs to be addressed.[14]

With the raft designed, Aquaculture Harvesters went on to start 10 mussel farms with Great Eastern Mussel Farms in Casco Bay, Penobscot Bay, and Frenchman Bay. That was really the beginning of the modern era in US mussel farming, at least on the East Coast.

While Newell's raft design has proved viable, it does depend on a location in protected waters. In high-energy zones, the rafts will rock and roll, and mussels will fall off the ropes. But Newell has a solution for that. In 2007, when Great Eastern Mussel Farms declared bankruptcy and ceased operations, he took the rafts and Aquaculture Harvester's harvesting-and-processing barge, *Mumbles*, and started a new owner-operated company called Pemaquid Mussel Farms. It now has farms in Belfast Bay, Stonington, the Damariscotta River, and Frenchman's Bay.

When Newell started, he realized he needed to improve the efficiency of his raft design. In Spain, the rafts produced 300,000 tons a year; in Maine, just 500 tons. The wind, waves, and ice during the winter growing season were too much. Newell started to think about a submersible raft that would sit below the high-energy wave zone, which had never been successfully done before. He got his fourth Small Business Innovation Research grant and designed a new raft system—a patent-pending 40-ton submersible raft that eliminates the risk of costly storm damage and mussel drop-off from the ropes. The new raft is capable of producing 100,000 pounds per 2-year crop.

On traditional rafts, when the mussels are ready for harvest, the ropes weigh 100 pounds. On the submersible rafts, the ropes weigh 300–350 pounds. "Tripling the yield really changes the economics," says Newell. "If you look at yield per rope, you can break even at 80 pounds per rope; at 200 or more pounds the business becomes profitable."

Pemaquid Mussel Farms spun off the raft-construction side of the business into Undine Inc., which uses the mussel company for research and development as it continues to improve the design. The mussel company has a farm in Clark's Cove, the site of Ed Myers's Abandoned Farm, and one in Lamoine, near Bar Harbor. In 2016, Pemaquid built a mussel-bagging plant in Bucksport, one of the cities expecting a land-based salmon farm.

But not everyone needs a submersible raft. If you find protected waters, the traditional floating Spanish-raft technique works, which is the Bangs Island Mussels approach. And you can bottom plant, as the de Könings do, using the "Dutch method" of bottom-planting, like Copps Island Oysters now uses. Both mussel farms are indirectly tied back to Great Eastern Mussels.

One of today's leading farms is Bangs Island Mussels, started around 2000, with technical support from Great Eastern Mussels. When Gary and Matt Moretti, father and son, bought the company in 2010, it had only three rafts. "We kind of got in over our heads," says Matt Moretti. "There's no way you can support yourself with three rafts. Dad was a transplanted Midwesterner, a nurse, and a part-time lobsterman. I was the stern man, with no aquaculture experience, but I had studied marine biology."

As the Morettis quickly learned, the mussel business is capital intensive and requires a high volume to compensate for the relatively low value of mussels. "Mussel infrastructure is expensive, with the rafts and required stainless-steel processing equipment," says Chris

Vonderweidt, manager of the Aquaculture Program at the Gulf of Maine Research Institute in Portland. Bangs Island, for example, has a de-bysser (de-bearder) from Italy, a polisher from the Netherlands, plus stainless slides to pull ropes out of the water, and automatic baggers after the mussels are cleaned up. "You need hundreds of thousands of dollars, over a million to go all in. The lesson learned is you need scale, which is why there are very few mussel farms in New England, only six or seven," says Vonderweidt. "There's demand for more supply, but the upfront investment is a barrier. An oyster farmer can start small and bootstrap."

By 2021, Bang's Island Mussels had scaled up, with twenty-six rafts spaced 50 feet apart. "We made a big jump because we couldn't stay in the middle ground, growing by one raft a year," says Moretti, who produced 750,000 pounds of mussels in 2021. "And we weren't satisfied with the company; we wanted to pay people more, provide more full-time jobs, reduce physical effort." In 2021, Bangs had eight full-time and eight part-time workers.

Some years ago, Bangs Island Mussels had started growing kelp between its mussel rafts for Ocean Approved (now Atlantic Sea Farms), the country's first commercial kelp farm (see chapter 10). The question is how close the kelp lines should be to the mussel lines to avoid fouling and to allow for proper nutrients for both—Newell's "hydraulic zone of influence." "At our flagship site (one of six), we've got twelve mussel rafts around thirty kelp long lines," says Moretti. "It's a pretty cool culmination of a long-term vision." At one site, Moretti has two 1,500-foot horizontal lines, dropped 7 feet below the surface so boats can drive over, with kelp lines hanging vertically in the water column.

"Site selection is key for mussel growth, with adequate delivery of phytoplankton and acceptable wave energy," says Moretti. "The happier the mussels, the better. If they're not bouncing around on the rope and protected from predators, they can put all their energy into the meat and not the shell. When threatened, the opposite is the case." With its continuing expansion, Bangs hopes to produce 1 million pounds of mussels a year.

In 2005, Theo de Köning, a fifth-generation mussel farmer whose family has been harvesting and farming mussels in the Netherlands since the 1700s, set out to search the world for a new farming locale.

The mussel industry in the Netherlands was mature and saturated, with little room for new farms or economic growth. After traveling the globe, de Köning fell in love with the Bar Harbor region in Maine and moved his wife and children to the New World—a mere 396 years after Henry Hudson claimed New York ("New Amsterdam") for the Dutch during his futile search for the Northwest Passage.

Theo and his wife, Fiona, started mussel farming, using the Dutch method of bottom planting (they are the only ones doing so in the United States today), under the auspices of Great Eastern Mussel Farms. When the company went bankrupt in 2008—the business had gotten too complex, with ten farms to manage over a wide area—the de Könings had to acquire new leases and find a distributor. They did both in short order and began selling to Pangea Shellfish, a Boston wholesaler started in 2001 by Ben Lloyd. The de Könings now have the largest shellfish lease in the state of Maine, spanning 157 acres. Seed is caught from managed seed beds then spread on private leases where the mussels reattach their byssal threads to the sea floor and to one another.

Just as Great Eastern Mussel Farms had done in its early days, the de Könings collect wild seed and place it in open sea beds for optimal growth. They claim that if the seed were not collected, 98 percent of it would die and that by thinning it out, they can increase the population by as much as 12 percent. Clearly, increasing the wild population is key to survival for *all* mussel farmers as there is still no hatchery seed available.

Fiona is de Köning's operations and sales manager. Alex de Koning, an engineering graduate from the University of Maine, is the processing manager and helped build a new plant in 2016. His younger brother, Max, is in high school and is a trainee boat captain. Besides their business in Maine, the de Könings continue to operate farms in Holland.

Despite all the gains made in mussel farming over the last 20 years, the United States still imports more than $100 million worth of mussels a year—frozen from New Zealand, Chile, and China, and fresh from Canada, primarily from Prince Edward Island. If the fresh-mussel market in the United States is worth $20 million today, as analysts suggest, there's plenty of room for American producers to scale supply and cut into the import market.

"I've spent decades trying to figure out why it takes 30 to 40 years to develop an aquaculture industry in the United States, when New Zealand and Scotland did it in half the time," says Newell. "New Zealand has all the same elements as Maine—a wild commercial industry, trained people, distribution, good growing environments. But New Zealand, Scotland, and Canada all focused on outcome-based research and development—how do we produce x tons; how do we create y jobs? Maine has never done that. In the United States, we're too laissez-faire."

Canada's Prince Edward Island, for example, produces 44 million pounds of mussels a year, many exported to the United States. The United States can't compete on volume, at least now, but there is a belief that Maine mussels can compete on quality. "Prince Edward Island mussel size and meat size are not up to snuff," says Bangs Island Mussels' Moretti. "I think we are distinct because of our consistent size and plump meat." His confidence stems from a 2016 market analysis by the Gulf of Maine Research Institute. "Canadian mussels have established a market in New England and North America, but because Prince Edward Island's farms have increased mussel density the perception is that the mussels have slipped in quality," says Vonderweidt, at the Gulf of Maine Research Institute. "There is an opportunity to displace Prince Edward Island mussels in the market."

Shellfish As Sentinels of the Sea

At the Pacific Coast Shellfish Growers Association meeting in 2017, Bill Mook gave an inspired talk about the threat of climate change to the shellfish industry. "Bill called for us to storm the streets to jumpstart action on climate change, kind of a 1960s style movement," says Lissa James Monberg, marketing director at Hama Company in Lilliwaup, Washington, a family-owned timber-and-oyster company dating to the 1890s. "Mook later came to our farm and we signed up as a founding member of the Shellfish Growers Climate Coalition." While out West, Mook also signed up Hog Island Oyster Company in Marshall, California, and Taylor Shellfish in Shelton, Washington, the country's largest shellfish producer, run by the Taylor family since 1890. Mook then gave a similar talk on the East Coast and picked up additional founding members: Island Creek Oysters, Fishers Island

Oyster Farm, and Rappahannock Oyster Company in Topping, Virginia. But the fledgling coalition needed institutional support.

The Malinowskis of Fishers Island Oyster Farm connected Mook to Sally McGee, a friend of theirs who was director of The Nature Conservancy's Northeast Marine Program. That led to a partnership with The Nature Conservancy, and the Shellfish Growers Climate Coalition officially launched in 2018. "The Nature Conservancy was determined to be the most politically neutral nonprofit partner," says Mook.[15]

The Shellfish Growers Climate Coalition now has 230 members from 24 states (mostly oyster farms, with some geoduck-clam and mussel farms). In addition to the founding members, other members mentioned in this chapter include Bangs Island Mussel, Maine Oyster Company, Pemaquid Oyster Company, Cuttyhunk Shellfish Farms, Pangea Shellfish, and American Mussel Harvesters.

"The Coalition is focused on climate policy, setting a price for carbon, trying to put a tourniquet on the situation," says The Nature Conservancy's McGee. "We're 90 percent focused on CO_2 pollution. The cause of acidification is different on the East and West coasts. With Mook, it's probably more runoff. On the West Coast, it's deep-water upwelling that is more acidic."

Hama can attest to that. "When the wind is from a certain direction, it pulls acidic water into the hatcheries," says Monberg. "You can predict it. This started in 2008. We first thought it was bacteria, then found it was acidity. It turns out the acidic waters now upwelling last touched the atmosphere 50 years ago—which means that even if we stopped pumping CO_2 in the atmosphere today, we'd still be feeling it 50 years from now."

In addition to lobbying, Mook is investing to reshape his production facilities to build business resilience against climate change. The centerpiece of his strategy is a new indoor facility with large tanks that can keep thousands of oysters alive during river closures. The $2 million, 9,000-square-foot facility, built 3 or 4 years ago, is essentially a land-based aquaculture farm. When there's a threat of heavy rains, such as in the aftermath of Hurricane Florence in 2018, Mook moves tens of thousands of market oysters from the river into four tanks with roughly 26,000-gallon capacities. A recirculation system can maintain high water quality for weeks without sucking in river water. "During the last closure we shipped about 20,000 oysters that we wouldn't normally have shipped during a closure," says Mook. "It's hard to get that business back when sales are interrupted." The roof of the facility has 282 solar panels to help offset an electricity-intensive operation.

Climate change is bringing other challenges. Vibrio, a bacteria that can be toxic for humans, has increased with warming waters. "We used to think that Long Island Sound was the northernmost border for vibrio, but it's moving even further north," says Steve Malinowski. Down the line, if vibrio shuts down the Damariscotta's oyster harvest for an extended period, Mook says he'll decontaminate the oysters in his new indoor facility (pending US Food and Drug Administration approval). Mook can set the tank water at an optimum temperature— warm enough that the oysters are still metabolically active, but cold enough so that vibrio reproduction rates are dramatically decreased.

It is ironic that shellfish, heralded as stewards of the near-coastal ocean environment given their ability to purify nitrogen-, nutrient-, and carbon-dense water, are also sentinels of the overpoweringly negative impacts that climate change may be wreaking on the ocean.

"Ten years ago, the oyster larvae in our hatchery in Dabob Bay (off the northern end of Hood Canal in Washington State) were dying and we couldn't figure out why," says Bill Dewey, director of public affairs at Taylor Shellfish in Seattle, a charter member of the Shellfish Growers Climate Coalition. "At the same time, it was happening to good friends of ours with a hatchery on the Oregon coast. It took a few years and a lot of collaborative research to understand that it was CO_2 emissions absorbed by the ocean that were killing our baby oysters. And it turns out we were likely the first businesses to be impacted by ocean acidification and know it. And now our focus has turned to addressing the source of the problem."

Some think that kelp can help.

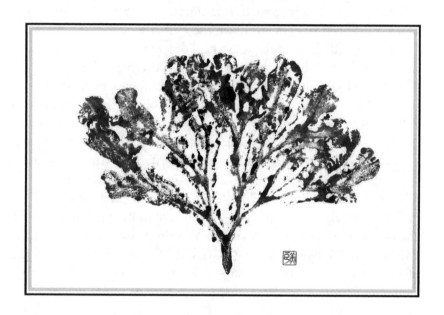

Seaweed

Chapter 10

Kelp—for Food, Fuel, Pharma

*When I started growing seaweed, people wondered what it was for.
They thought I might be growing hemp! It is a little embarrassing
for a fisherman like me to grow kelp; it's a bit like being an arugula
farmer. But kelp is what the oceans provide. What's emerging is
a new climate economy, whereby water and land shortages will
steadily drive up the cost of land-based food production. Add in the
rising costs of fertilizer and animal feeds, and we either have to farm
on Mars or grow massive amounts of sea veggies and shellfish.*
—Bren Smith, *Eat Like a Fish*

It is becoming increasingly difficult to think about shellfish without thinking about seaweed—or, more euphemistically, sea greens, sea vegetables, or sea veggies, as "restorative farmer" Bren Smith calls them. So does Charles Yarish, a professor in the departments of ecology and evolutionary biology, and marine sciences, at the University of Connecticut—who is affectionately known as Dr. Seaweed or Captain Seaweed for his deep knowledge and love of seaweed: "I call them sea vegetables rather than seaweed, because that's a more accurate description. Just like vegetables, they're high in nutrients, vitamins, and trace elements, and they're good for you, and they're delicious. They can be made into pasta noodles and are gluten free."[1]

Shellfish and kelp, which is what most sea greens are—order Laminariales, any of about thirty genera of brown algae that grow as large coastal seaweeds in colder seas—are similar in that they are basically no input/no output crops. Shellfish take phytoplankton from the ocean; kelp take nutrients. They are naturally symbiotic and increasingly grown together; seaweed absorbs CO_2, which reduces ocean acidification and makes it easier for shellfish to build their shells. Kelp is nutrient dense, rich in vitamins A and C, and minerals such as calcium, magnesium, zinc, selenium, and iron. Kelp also has a high level of vegetable proteins and omega-3 and omega-6 fatty acids. Kelp has more fiber than brown rice, more calcium than whole milk, and more iron than spinach. In 2015, *New Yorker* writer Dana Goodyear called sea vegetables "the culinary equivalent of an electric car."[2]

Kelp absorbs at least five times as much CO_2 as land-based trees or plants—along with nitrogen and phosphorous—which is why kelp forests are often called the "rain forests of the seas." Akua, a startup kelp-food company, calls its foods "carbon-negative snacks."

While mussels and oysters feed on algae (phytoplankton) as it drifts through their shells, kelp *is* an algae. (Phytoplankton is a microalgae; seaweed is a macroalgae.) And kelp is symbiotic with mussels. When Carter Newell was developing his mussel rafts in the late 1990s, he noticed kelp growing on the rafts and persuaded Maine Sea Grant to fund research about its potential as a crop. Those early trials with Maine Sea Grant extension agents spawned some of the early kelp farms in Maine.

Eating kelp is a new idea in the United States, but people in other parts of the world have been "eating like fish," as farmer Smith would say, for a long time. At a 14,000-year-old site in southern Chile, archaeologists have found cooked and partially eaten seaweed.[3] In the past 400 years, kelp has been an important part of Asian cuisine. Widely cultivated and eaten in Asia, sugar kelp (*Saccharina latissima*) is also known as sea belt and Devil's apron, due to its broad and fluted shape. Although sugar kelp takes many forms, in its classic form it looks like a giant, yellowish-brown lasagna noodle that can grow up to 12 feet long. About half the cultivated kelp in the world is sugar kelp, which grows well in the cold waters of Alaska and Northern New England.

The top-producing countries of cultured seaweed are China, Indonesia, Korea, and The Philippines. China, which began farming another species of kelp (*Saccharina japonica*) in earnest in the 1950s, is responsible for 50 percent of the world's output of roughly 30 million tons.

The first kelp farm in North America was started by Louis Druehl on Vancouver Island in British Columbia, Canada, in 1982. Referred to by some as the "seaweed guru," by others as the "kelp grandfather," Druehl never left his day job as professor of kelp, genetics, and agronomy at Simon Fraser University while he and Rae Hopkins, his wife and cofounder, kept their Canadian Kelp company going. In the United States, Yarish's Seaweed Marine Biotechnology Lab in Stamford, Connecticut, laid the foundation for the modern seaweed movement. Yarish was an adviser to Ocean Approved, the first commercial kelp farm in the United States, started in 2009 in Maine by Paul Robbins and Tollef Olsen. "In 2010, we had zero farms," says Yarish. "Today, we have 70 in New England."[4]

In the last 5 years, kelp has built a niche market in the United States as a nutritious food used in sushi, soups, salads, and even jerky and burgers. Akua started with kelp jerky in 2019, introduced kelp burgers in 2021, and is moving toward kelp sausage and kelp meatballs—another twist on the plant-based Impossible Burger and Beyond Meat burgers (more plant-based "fish alternatives" are gaining adherents and investors). Courtney Boyd-Myers, founder and CEO, says she buys all her kelp from female farmers in New England. Akua, along with Oyster Common, purveyor of an AI-based marketing platform for farmers, was in the first cohort of SeaAhead's Blue Swell Incubator Program (see chapter 5).

Curio Spice Company in Cambridge, Massachusetts, specializes in directly sourced, sustainably produced spices from around the world, including several kelp products: Wild Kelp Salt, a mixture of Maine sea salt and Icelandic kelp; Icelandic Wild Kelp, which features great umami (a Japanese "loanword" roughly translated as savoriness, one of the five basic tastes); and Salmon Sister Forest Kelp Crunch, with Alaskan kelp, boletus mushroom, spruce tips, sea salt, juniper, ginger, and sesame. Curio's Supeq Spice blend, one of *Bon Appétit*'s "15 Spice Blends We Can't Live Without," is made from 100 percent New England–sourced ingredients, starting with nutrient-rich dulse seaweed—mixed with shiitake mushroom (Maine), ginger

(Massachusetts), nettle (Vermont), and hot paprika (Massachusetts). "Supeq is good on almost everything," says Liesel Davis, *Bon Appétit's* recipe editor. "I use it on fish and rice, and other grains that get tossed into a salad."[5]

"The Supeq Spice blend was invented with the Atlantic ocean in mind, with my home in mind," says Curio founder Claire Cheney, a Massachusetts native who often travels the world in search of spices she can blend together but found these in her own "backyard." "The name comes from the word for 'ocean' in Passamaquoddy, a First Nation tribe from the northeast. Because spices are so often thought of as exotic seeds and barks from faraway lands, I wanted to create a blend that was hyperlocal, celebrating the familiar land (and sea) where I grew up. When I smell Supeq I think of walking on the beach in Maine, the tide low and the air clean and cold."

Now that kelp has been proven easy to grow, the trick is developing markets for it. Food is a driving force for kelp farmers, but there are promising companies in the bioplastics space (Loliware makes biodegradable and edible seaweed straws) and methane-free animal feed (Blue Ocean Farms). Higher-value seaweed markets for pharmaceuticals and biofuels are on the horizon.

"When you look at how we are going to feed the world population by 2050 in a way that doesn't harm the environment, there is only one pathway," says Carlos Duarte, a researcher and professor in biological oceanography and marine ecology at King Abdullah University of Science and Technology in Saudi Arabia. "To scale up seaweed farming."[6]

Ronald Osinga, a biologist at Wageningen University in the Netherlands, suggests that sea-vegetable farms totaling 180,000 square kilometers—roughly the size of Washington State—could provide enough protein for the entire world.[7] Scott Lindell, a marine scientist in the Applied Ocean Physics and Engineering Department at The Woods Hole Oceanographic Institution, frames the kelp-and-shellfish opportunity with an East Coast perspective: "We could develop all the protein and calories we need in an area as small as coastal New England and New York State."[8] To date, the United States produces 3–4 million tons of seaweed a year; it imports 98 percent of seaweed from Asia—some of it nori for sushi rolls—suggesting a huge market gap for growth.

To propagate, kelp releases spores into the water that settle on a surface—just as oysters and mussels do—and germinate into tiny plants. In a lab, where light and temperature can be controlled for ideal growing conditions, the spores grow into small plants, less than one-tenth of an inch in size, when they are wound on string around a piece of PVC pipe. The spools with seeded lines are then transferred to a nursery in seawater. At a certain point, the plants are ready to go into the ocean. The seeded line, unwound from the cylinder, is attached to a long rope, as mussel seeds are, dropped in the ocean in late fall, as mussel seeds are, and typically ready for harvest in April or May.[9]

Kelp aquaculture is certainly a darling of the blue-green economy. "Whether it's the new kale or its potential for reducing cow flatulence, seaweed is attracting a lot of attention and investment," cites a "business outlook" by the Maine Seaweed Exchange, an industry advocacy group. "Some of this attention is justified, some not so much." One negative cited is that seaweed is approved by the US Food and Drug Administration as a spice or savory, but not as a food.

Kelp is also known to act as a carbon buffer and it does appear to have a "halo effect" on water conditions in small areas. But more research is needed. The World Wildlife Fund, with support from the Bezos Earth Fund, awarded Bigelow Labs in Maine a $900,000 grant in 2021 to develop a computer model of water circulation, kelp growth, and water-quality changes that could provide a better understanding of the "kelp effect" on the ocean. Bigelow Labs is partnering with the Island Institute and the University of New Hampshire on the research side, and collaborating with Bangs Island Mussels, which grows mussels and kelp side by side (see chapter 9). Initial research has shown that primary production of sugar kelp can take up enough CO_2 to remediate local waters from ocean acidification, a process called "phytoremediation." Even more exciting is the finding that farmed mussels located within the kelp farm produce stronger shells and larger meats than those reared outside the kelp lines. "We took the mussels to the local dentist to x-ray the shells and were surprised to discover they are denser and thicker when grown with kelp," Bigelow Labs reported.[10] A Maine startup, Running Tide, is testing the idea that kelp can do more than provide a halo effect and significantly offset carbon in the atmosphere. Running Tide farms kelp and puts it into biodegradable buoys. As the kelp grows, it eventually becomes too heavy for the buoy and sinks to the bottom of the ocean where massive water pressure pushes it into the sea floor. "There are a lot of really progressive companies out there that want to minimize their carbon footprint and we can sell the carbon removal service to those companies," says founder Marty Odlin.[11]

As to kelp's positive environmental impact as a carbon sink, which is undeniable, there are limits to the efficacy of kelp, at least in the quantities grown today. "I get greenwashing fatigue when I hear about kelp—it gives people a pass, they need to do more," says Brianna Warner, CEO of Atlantic Sea Farms (formerly Ocean Approved) in Biddeford, Maine. "I like to focus on the food side. Kelp is the most efficient food to grow—one 4-acre farm produces 65,000 pounds of food, with no inputs, no freshwater, no arable land, no pesticides—just a boat, some old ropes, and some buoys. Think of it as the best food to eat—super nutrient-dense—and one that does no harm. It does mitigate some aspects of climate change, but it is not a panacea."

Ocean Approved, the country's first commercial kelp farm, was started in 2009 in Portland, Maine, by Tollef Olsen. There are now dozens of kelp farms in Maine, where the majority of the country's kelp is grown. In 2018, Olsen left Ocean Approved to join Ocean's Balance, a Maine purveyor of kelp products (butter, tea, pasta, salsa, pickles). Paul Dobbins, co-owner, left to work on seaweed advocacy at the World Wildlife Foundation.

Briana Warner took over as CEO and founded the brand Atlantic Sea Farms. Rather than directly operating its own farms, as Ocean Approved did, Atlantic Sea Farms recruits farmers, provides technical assistance and seed, and guarantees purchase of whatever farmers produce.

A former Foreign Service officer with the US State Department, Warner had been at the Island Institute developing strategies to help fishermen and lobstermen diversify by moving into shellfish and seaweed farming. "At Island Institute we made a strategic investment—let's help by building the supply chain, giving out free seed and guaranteeing purchase," says Warner. "Maine has more than 5,000 licensed lobstermen who have the equipment and the social capital, who are skilled on the water and farm responsibly. These own-er-operators are essentially an overqualified workforce who make fantastic kelp farmers." In 2021, Atlantic Sea Farms had sixteen seaweed farms extending across two-thirds of the rugged Maine Coast and twenty-four farmers (including a high school student until he left for college).

Atlantic Sea Farms' hatchery is the largest in the Western Hemisphere, and it provides free kelp seed to its farmers every fall. It grows both sugar kelp (*Saccharina latissima*), whose blades are wide with undulations near the edges, and skinny kelp (*Saccharina latissima forma angustissima*), a form of sugar kelp that is not as wide but is thicker and more durable in high-energy (waves and current) ecosystems.

Because kelp is a winter crop, it is symbiotic with summer harvests of lobster. Until relatively recently, lobstermen harvested Northern shrimp in the winter, a highly valuable species (tiny and sweet) but it is no longer a reliable harvest. If you have boats, ropes, buoys, and marine know-how, which lobstermen do, kelp farming is not complicated. The main issue is getting a lease from the state, which means keeping navigational lanes open and no gear conflict. But lobstermen have a "social license" to farm and widespread public support, which nouveau farmers often lack (see chapter 9). The typical farm is 4 acres, with 1,000-foot lines running between two mooring balls 10 to 20 feet apart with anchors on the sea floor. "Every several hundred feet there's a lobster buoy marked with 'ASF' so people know what they're looking at," says Liz Johndrow, Kelp Innovation Specialist, who previously worked on several kelp-focused projects with the Department of Energy and the University of New England. The lines are set 7 feet underwater (to allow boats to pass over), and kelp lines with spores are dropped off the horizontal lines. Kelp has predators, urchins and snails, but when they arrive in the summer the kelp has already been harvested. "Kelp must be harvested by the middle of June to make way for lobstering, but that's fine because the quality of the blades diminishes in warmer water," says Johndrow.

The new model—switching from a handful of company-operated farms to a cooperative of sixteen farms—has increased output from 30,000 pounds of kelp in 2017 to 850,000 pounds in 2021. Atlantic Sea

Farms processes the kelp, blanching and drying it, and turns it into food products for 800 retail outlets, including Whole Foods and Legal Sea Foods. Products include Ready Cut Kelp and Kelp Cubes for the freezer. "The cubes give an umami boost of flavor and have a wide range of uses—drop one in a smoothie, a sauce, soup, pesto, a stir-fry, or create a seasoned butter," wrote a *Boston Globe* reviewer. [12] In early 2020, before the COVID lockdown, national salad chain Sweetgreen worked with award-winning chef David Chang to create a sweet potato-and-kelp bowl for its menu and bought 30,000 pounds of kelp from Atlantic Sea Farms for the 6-week seasonal special. Promotion included posters and billboards throughout the country, including one in Times Square—certainly a first for seaweed. Later in 2020, the San Francisco–based Good Food Foundation, judging taste but also the crafter's achievement to produce food in a socially and environmentally responsible way, presented Atlantic Sea Farms with a Good Food award—in the *Fish* category!—for its Fermented Seaweed Salad and Sea-Beet Kraut. This shows how quickly sea vegetables are finding a spot in the culinary landscape.

"We're fermenting or freezing seaweed, and it tastes really damn good," says Warner, who is building out a new processing plant with three times the capacity of the previous plant. "The seaweed Americans typically eat is imported dry, rehydrated, then dyed with all the same chemicals found in Mountain Dew.[13] The trick for us is to grow supply and the market at the same time so we don't overproduce. We've proven the concept that we can provide a viable income source to ease the shock of lobster volatility. We're paying people well. We can see a path to profitability, but it will take time, as it does with any food company."

A few years ago, it would have been hard to imagine Americans eating fermented foods or seaweed, but now some are developing a taste for fermented seaweed as a food. Kimchi and Kombucha paved the way. "The Venn diagram between people who eat kimchi and people who are excited about beet kraut and fermented foods, and those who aren't intimidated at all by seaweed, is pretty overlapping," says Warner.

"Fifteen years ago, a nori farm failed. Ten years ago, there was nothing," says Sebastian Belle, executive director of the Maine Aquaculture

Association. "Now, Atlantic Sea Farms has shown that grow out is possible. Now that we know we can grow it, can we sell it? That will make or break the sector."

Restorative "3D" Farming

When the Canadian government shut down its cod industry in 1992, putting 35,000-plus people out of work virtually overnight, Bren Smith was one of the casualties. Born and raised in Petty Harbour, Newfoundland, Smith left school at age 14 to go cod fishing on Georges Bank (the Canadian portion across the Hague Line from the US side) and the Grand Banks. At 19, after the cod shutdown, he ventured into Northern Canada to work on an aquaculture farm. He found the industrialization—fecal pollution on the sea floor and the use of antibiotics—as bad as the worst in the agricultural industry and as bad as he had seen on a trawler that scoured the sea bottom. "We used to say that what we were growing was neither fish nor food," says Smith. "We were running the equivalent of Iowa pig farms at sea. I was working at the height of the industrialization of food."[14]

After an intense stint fishing in Alaska on the Bering Sea, Smith returned East to rethink his future. For a while, he lived in a van and worked as a lobsterman in Massachusetts. Then he was attracted by a program to lure fishermen back into the industry by opening up shell-fishing grounds in Connecticut—the epicenter of the American oyster industry in the nineteenth century—for the first time in over 100 years. Once a seagoing Canadian fisherman, Smith signed up to be an American oysterman. Once a hunter, he became a farmer, leasing 40 acres around the Thimble Islands, off the coast of New Haven. That worked fine for 7 years. But after twice losing his oyster crop in the back-to-back disasters of Hurricane Irene (2011) and Superstorm Sandy (2012), both of which buried his oysters in three feet of mud and trashed much of his gear, he again reinvented himself—as a 3D farmer of vertical, undersea gardens.

"Imagine an underwater garden where you're using the entire water column, which means we have a very small footprint," says Smith. Like the kelp farms of Atlantic Sea Farms and Bangs Island Mussels, Smith's "garden" consists of vertical lines hanging off anchored horizontal ropes. Kelp hangs off ropes next to lantern nets with scallops and mussels in sock nets. Oyster cages sit on the bottom. It is what scientists call integrated multi-trophic aquaculture, a term Smith finds a bit alienating. "I think 3D captures the imagination more than 'integrated multi-trophic aquaculture.'"[15] He calls his model of fish farming "the least deadliest catch."

To highlight his paradigm shift, Smith changed the name of his company from Thimble Islands *Oyster* Farms to Thimble Islands *Ocean* Farm. Although there have been experimental versions of multi-trophic aquaculture around New England and North America for years, Smith has effectively marketed Thimble Islands Ocean Farm as a kind of new-age fish farm in the United States, and, given his rollicking history of fishing, he certainly has the street cred to do so.

In Asia, of course, multi-trophic aquaculture is old hat. The Chinese have farmed carp in ponds for 4,000 years in conjunction with pigs and crops—composted pig manure and eel grasses feed the fish, whose composted manure feeds row crops. On the ocean, the Chinese farm abalone that feeds on kelp; abalone waste is eaten by sea cucumbers; and waste from both feeds the kelp; all three are harvested for human food. In Sanggou Bay, China, farmers produce 240,000 tons of seafood per year. More than thirty important aquaculture species, including kelp, scallops, oysters, abalone, and sea cucumbers, are grown using long lines, cages, bottom sowing, pools in the intertidal zone, and tidal-flat culture.[16] These examples of multitrophic culture maximize the utilization of space in aquaculture as they work in both the pelagic (top-layer) and benthic (bottom-layer) zones.

Thierry Chopin, professor of marine biology at the University of New Brunswick and a thought leader of the integrated multi-trophic aquaculture movement (he actually coined the term at a 2004 conference with a colleague, Jack Taylor) has worked with Cooke Aquaculture in New Brunswick, Canada, to place blue mussels and kelp downstream from salmon pens.[17] Mussels can take advantage of small organic molecules, such as the fine-powder leftovers of fishmeal, fish excrement, and naturally occurring seston (the tiny living and nonliving particles swimming or floating in the water). Seaweeds make use of the inorganic molecules and "are nutrient sponges," explains Chopin.

Integrated multitrophic aquaculture—"3D garden" *does* sound better—relies on the idea that in natural ecological communities nutrient waste from one organism is reused as food for the next. Chopin likens single-species systems in aquaculture to the dominance of monoculture systems on land. In agriculture, farmers typically specialize in one species, such as wheat, cattle, or corn. Every single-species system generates environmental and economic issues that parallel intensification. On land, the Green Revolution increased yields and increased productivity, but only in the short term. "Now soils are eroding and getting exhausted," says Chopin. "On land, we're rediscovering the value of crop rotation, fallowing, and multi-culture." It took centuries on land to refine agronomy principles. Chopin thinks that it is now time to approach farming of the sea through the development of "aquanomy."[18]

One of the marine organisms most highly prized as food—the lobster—is in fact a bottom-feeding detritivore. This technical term, Chopin says, disguises the fact that lobsters eat "the garbage of the sea . . . the excrement and dead bodies fallen on the bottom." When it comes to wild seafood, explains Chopin, "lots of what you eat is a product of recycling at sea." Multi-trophic aquaculture is an extension of this natural recycling idea, clustering fed species (such as fish) and extractive species (such as mussels and seaweeds) together so that they can exchange nutrients.[19] On Thimble Island Farms, the same holistic, zero-waste pattern holds: The mussels and oysters filter the water clean; the kelp absorbs CO_2 and nitrogen. When Smith first thought about growing seaweed, he called in Dr. Seaweed, who is also an expert on integrated multitrophic aquaculture, as an adviser.

Smith has delivered a proof of concept for 3D farming. Thimble Islands Ocean Farm, with a 40-acre plot, can produce 30 tons of sea vegetables (kelp) and 250,000 shellfish *per acre* per year—with no inputs. Smith sees his 3D garden as a way to mitigate climate change while producing food. "I'm not just a fisherman; I'm a climate farmer," he says. Smith sees kelp as a "gateway drug" that could lead to all kinds of ocean-farmed plants. "We need to push wild fish to the edges—make it an occasional treat for special occasions—and put sustainably produced bivalves and sea vegetables at the center."[20]

In 2021, Thimble Island Ocean Farms relaunched a community-supported fishery it had first launched a decade earlier, when it was the first in the nation to sell sea vegetables. Today it sells oysters, clams, kelp—even kelp bagels.

In 2013, the year after Superstorm Sandy, Smith started GreenWave, a nonprofit organization whose mission is to replicate the Thimble Island model throughout the United States and around the world, both by creating new 3D farms and by pushing the edge of what's possible on the sea, such as embedding 3D farms in offshore wind farms. "Our goal is to train thousands of new ocean farmers," says Smith. He claims that with about $30,000, a boat, and a lease to farm 20 acres of ocean (which requires approvals from state regulators and the Army Corps of Engineers), anyone can start a 3D ocean farm that produces 10 to 30 tons of kelp and 250,000 shellfish per acre in 5 months. "We want fishermen of the future to be at the front edge of jumpstarting a new ocean economy that meets the growing need for sustainable seafood, habitat restoration, and resilient communities in the era of climate change."

Smith's 3D farm concept, which started out as a business-survival strategy but quickly turned into a crusade, is designed to address three global challenges: (1) to deliver delicious and healthy new seafood in this era of overfishing, food insecurity, and fast foods; (2) to transform fishermen into restorative ocean farmers, and (3) to build the foundation for a new blue-green economy that doesn't re-create the injustices of the old industrial economy.

In this jump from "sustainable" to "restorative" farming, Smith is in sync with the mantra of Barton Seaver, noted chef and seafood advocate: "Sustainable is not sexy. Fish quotas are not sexy. *Delicious* is sexy. It was Alice Waters's secret in California. She didn't so much promote the locavore movement, she promoted delicious food—which just happened to rely on fresh, local ingredients. "'Sustainable' means keeping things the same. Why not make things better? Why not practice restorative farming? 'Sustainable' is 'do no harm' farming, working hard to keep things the same. 'Restorative' is positive. Fishermen and shell-fishermen who do this are heroes and deserve the same noblesse as does a dirt farmer. They are avatars of restoration."

Echoes Smith, "Regenerative ocean farming is growing crops that breathe life back into the ocean. No freshwater, no fertilizer, and no feed make shellfish and seaweed the most sustainable foods on the planet. But at the same time, our crops soak up carbon, nitrogen, and rebuild reef systems. So they really become engines of restoration as we're farming and trying to make a living."[21]

GreenWave's 10-year goal is to provide training, tools, and support to 10,000 ocean farmers and catalyze the planting of 1 million ocean acres. By 2021, GreenWave had trained and supported more than 120 farmers and hatchery technicians throughout New England, California, New York, the Pacific Northwest, and Alaska—and had a waitlist of 7,000 people. In 2015, GreenWave's 3D ocean farming model won the Buckminster Fuller Institute's Fuller Challenge, an ecological design prize that recognizes innovative and comprehensive approaches to solving problems created by marine degradation and climate change.

Buckminster Fuller posed a stark question to addressing social and environmental challenges: "Are we heading toward Utopia or Oblivion?" That's how the Buckminster Fuller Institute characterizes the Fuller Challenge. "Fuller challenged his contemporaries to creatively respond to the urgency of this moment by reframing the crisis as an opportunity pointing to humanity's 'option' to live successfully without compromising the ability for all of life to thrive."[22]

Beyond Food: Kelp for Pharma and Fuel

Global demand for seaweed is exploding, expected to create a $95 billion market by 2027.[23] Already, there is a long history of seaweeds providing ingredients for pharmaceuticals, which carry a much higher-value market than food ingredients, according to Dr. Seaweed. "A major extracted class is phycocolloids, such as alginates, carrageenans, and agars, products that are used, for example, in texturizing, thickening, and emulsifying, as well as a range of medical uses, including antivirals and antifungal agents," said Yarish in a 2020 talk. "Prices for derived products range from 50 cents a pound for commodity colloids up to $2,000 for specialties for pharmaceutical uses."[24]

Everything Seaweed is a new company that is eyeing the higher-value seaweed market. It plans operations in Iceland and the East Coast of the US—if it raises the $16 million it needs to begin operations. British founder Colin Hepburn, who has worked in the seaweed sector for 30 years, has an interesting business model: Harvest wild kelp in Iceland, process it there, ship it to the US for blending, sell to food companies and Big Pharma. Everything Seaweed has an Icelandic license to sustainably harvest a kelp species called *Laminaria hyperborea*, which grows naturally and abundantly on the north coast of Iceland. In the US, the processed seaweed will be finished and blended with other natural ingredients.

Alginate from this Icelandic kelp—found within the cell walls of brown seaweeds—offers a significant performance advantage over existing products, with most coming out of Norway. "This Icelandic kelp is 50 percent better than other products," says Hepburn. "It's not a new product, but potentially a more effective one. And we will process without toxic chemicals and produce no waste, which is not the norm in global seaweed processing."

Everything Seaweed is targeting opportunities in the lucrative, growing, stomach antireflux market, a high-value, $200 million segment of *Laminaria hyperborea* products. The *Laminaria hyperborea* alginates market is growing 5–10 percent annually and could be greater but for a limited global supply, particularly for antireflux products. Alginates are also an important compound in bioplastics, such as biodegradable films replacing cellophane.

Hepburn plans to harvest 1–2 percent of available kelp per year (of which 10–20 percent is typically destroyed by storms) that is 5 to 7 years old, using a "comb" to separate the older kelp from younger plants. "Bioactives don't become useful until plants are more mature and larger," says Hepburn.

Besides the alginates, Hepburn is excited about two other elements: nanocellulose ("it's strong as Kevlar and protects drug transit through the stomach") and fucoidan. The main source of fucoidan is brown seaweed, but it can also be isolated from invertebrates such as sea urchins and sea cucumbers. "Found in the cell walls of many species of brown seaweed, fucoidan has antitumor, antiviral, antiarthritic, and immunomodulatory effects," according to the Memorial Sloan Kettering Cancer Center.[25] One human study suggests fucoidan may help to enable longer courses of chemotherapy, but more studies are needed to confirm safety and effectiveness.

"Fucoidan is kind of a miracle molecule," says Jessica Chalmers, director of marketing at Everything Seaweed. "Its properties are known in Asian folk medicine, and there have been some clinical trials in Asia." Says Hepburn: "Research at the University of Rhode Island on fucoidan manufacture at a molecular level is a potential game changer. The issue is fucoidan is not that easy to make with consistently high purity." Everything Seaweed would treat antiviral and anticancer development as a secondary, spinoff business with other partners.

Applying seaweed derivatives to pharmaceutical products is not new. But growing kelp for biofuel is new and potentially exciting. The Department of Energy's Advanced Research Projects Agency–Energy (ARPA-E), modeled after the Defense Advanced Research Projects Agency program (DARPA)—has initiated a $50 million program to develop biofuels from kelp. The Macroalgae Research Inspiring Novel Energy Resources (MARINER) program estimates that the United States has suitable conditions and geography to produce at least 500 million dry metric tons of macroalgae per year. Such production volumes could yield about 10 percent of the nation's annual transportation-energy demand. That said, producing 500 million tons is a tall order because current global production is about 30 million dry metric tons.

"The MARINER program addresses a critical challenge that land production systems are unlikely to solve," says Woods Hole Oceanographic Institution's Scott Lindell. "How do we meet growing global biofuel needs and meet the 50 to 100 percent increase in demand for food expected by 2050? Seaweed farming avoids the growing competition for fertile land, energy-intensive fertilizers, and freshwater resources associated with traditional agriculture."

The MARINER project has multiple aspects and researchers, but the Lindell/Woods Hole branch is focused on selectively breeding multiple strains of sugar kelp. "Our goal is to improve productivity—size and weight of the biomass per unit area—by 10–20 percent per generation," says Lindell, acknowledging that Asian producers are far ahead of the United States in terms of developing strains and increasing biomass.

"We've learned from aquaculture to date and we're moving into selective breeding, looking for traits that will work offshore," says the University of Connecticut's Yarish, who is also part of the MARINER research team. "Terrestrial agriculture has evolved over 10,000 years; we're trying to make similar gains with macroalgae in a much shorter time."

MARINER has test sites in Alaska, Gulf of Maine, and Long Island Sound, and the best results are coming from the Gulf of Maine. "We estimate there are 1 to 6 million acres of potential 'cropland' in the Gulf of Maine, and 6 to 16 million in Alaska," says Lindell. "Let's be conservative and say 1 in Maine and 6 million in Alaska. That's a good start."

Lindell's hope is that in 20 years or less, cars may be able to use seaweed—instead of corn—as a biofuel. "If you were to take something like the space of Iowa and farm it for seaweeds, you would supply about 10 percent of the transportation needs of the United States in biofuels," he says. "Sugar kelp, in particular, is very high in carbohydrates and sugars. A fermentation process will release those sugars and they can be turned into ethanol." Of course, by the time kelp biofuels are a reality most cars *may* be electric, but even if that's the case there will still be demand for biofuel.[26] And these feedstocks and the refinements from them can be the basis for replacing fossil fuels for other uses, such as planet-friendly bioplastics and packaging.

The other way to look at the ARPA-E project is that the government is pumping $50 million into research on selective breeding for better traits and studying how technology can be deployed to harvest the seas. In the end, this will help all ocean farmers as the battlefield moves from nearshore to offshore.

"To produce enough food for a growing world, given the amount of arable land left in the world, we'd need to find and develop a new land mass equivalent to the mass of the continental United States," says Lindell. "Or we could develop all the protein and calories we need in areas as small as coastal New England and New York State. Plus, marine protein dramatically outperforms land protein in land use, water use, amount of feed, and carbon footprint. When weighing the pros and cons, the only viable solution is to join the Blue Revolution."[27]

Octopus

Chapter 11

The Holy Grail:
Farming the Open Ocean

We must plant the sea and herd its animals using the sea
as farmers instead of hunters. That is what civilization is
all about—farming replacing hunting.

—Jacques Yves Cousteau, marine explorer and conservationist

The United States has the second-largest exclusive economic zone in the world—territory extending 200 miles from the coast. Only France, with its many Pacific territories, has a bigger zone. Even more striking, the United States has 24 percent more territory underwater (4.3 million square miles) than above water (3.5 million square miles).

When it comes to aquaculture, the fastest-growing type of food production in the world, the United States' vast ocean resource clearly presents a huge opportunity for mariculture. Now, with less than 1 percent of the world's total aquaculture production (freshwater and saltwater), the United States ranks seventeenth in the world, behind even North Korea and Myanmar. Lack of aquaculture production is a key factor behind America's $16.8 billion seafood trade deficit (2018), the largest of any category except for oil and gas. "China produces 150 times what we do with fewer aquatic resources," says Scott Lindell, a research specialist in ocean physics and engineering at the Woods

Hole Oceanographic Institution. Of course, China has been practicing aquaculture for 2,500 years.

Despite punching below its weight in fish production, the United States is a heavy hitter in terms of "biomass" consumption. It ranks third in the world in its SeafoodPrint score, a metric created by Daniel Pauly, the noted fisheries biologist at the University of British Columbia. The SeafoodPrint, analogous to the "carbon-footprint" metric, measures the total impact a country has on the fish resource in the world's oceans. The metric factors in the volume and trophic level of fish consumed. A pound of tuna, for example, has a SeafoodPrint 100 times bigger than a pound of sardines, because it has consumed more forage fish.[1] The United States is a leader in wild-fisheries management but nonetheless is having a big negative impact on global fisheries.

"America needs to begin accepting responsibility for producing its own seafood," says Neil Sims, cofounder of Kampachi Farms in Kona, Hawaii, which received the first US permit to farm in federal waters in 2012. Sims, an Australian zoologist and animal biologist, is now angling to start the first offshore finfish farm in the "lower 48," 45 miles off the coast of Sarasota, Florida. "The United States is essentially eating other people's lunch [as the Seafood Print metric shows], and they won't let us do that much longer as nations like China and India get wealthier," says Sims. "It's an economic problem and a moral problem."[2]

Offshore or ocean farming does not mean the "high seas," as any farm will be on the continental shelf and probably within a reasonable distance from the coast to allow for access, even though remote management through sensors, electronic equipment, and machine-learning algorithms is increasingly viable. Ocean farming generally means waters at a remove from nearshore estuaries and bays, the locale for most mariculture to date. In the United States, "open ocean" or "offshore" is understood to be in federal waters, between 3 and 200 miles from shore.

The pioneers of American ocean farming are Neil Sims; Brian O'Hanlon, an entrepreneur from Long Island; and Michael Chambers, an ocean scientist at the University of New Hampshire. Their stories date to the 1990s, but they are still at the forefront of open-ocean farming, both in the United States and the world.

In 1997, at age 18, Brian O'Hanlon drove a U-Haul from his parents' house in Long Island to Alabama, where he rented a boat and went fishing 50 miles offshore for red snapper. He returned with a boatful, put the fish in a refrigerated tank in the U-Haul, and drove back to his parents' basement where a 2,000-gallon tank awaited. O'Hanlon's grandmother had started him on fish tanks when he was 6. He did the trip two more times and ended up with thirty surviving red snappers that grew to 10 pounds in a year. With his basement grow out as a proof of concept, O'Hanlon started a business called Snapperfarm, with the idea of farming offshore.[3]

O'Hanlon had fish in his blood. His grandfather started out working at the legendary Fulton Street Fish Market on the lower East Side of Manhattan and later moved on to other seafood distribution jobs in the industry, as did his father. O'Hanlon went to Eckerd College in St. Petersburg, Florida, and took a course with Professor Daniel Benetti, a Brazilian marine biologist studying how to spawn marine species in the lab. When O'Hanlon told Benetti about the snappers in his parents' basement, the professor insisted on visiting. "This guy is crazy," Benetti told the *Miami Times* in 2006, but he nonetheless thought O'Hanlon had a great future.[4] "I kind of grew up being force-fed fish," says O'Hanlon. "So I have this mental block. I blame my grandmother."[5]

O'Hanlon dropped out of college after a year and tried to get long-term leases to farm snapper off the coasts of South Carolina and Florida, without luck. This would be no surprise to the many scientists and entrepreneurs who have been trying to get permits in the United States for 20-plus years—the Byzantine regulatory maze is virtually impossible to successfully exit. In 2000, with Benetti's guidance, O'Hanlon found a site 2 miles off the island of Culebra, Puerto Rico—with strong currents and clean water, perfect for farming fish. It was not in federal waters, but it was an offshore habitat. O'Hanlon spent 2 years obtaining permits and building out Snapperfarm. He brought in Aquapods, floating and submersible underwater cages based on architect Buckminster Fuller's geodesic-dome concept, designed by

Steve Page of Ocean Farm Technology in Maine (now part of Inno-vaSea and headquartered in Boston). By 2003, O'Hanlon was ready to start Open Blue Sea Farms, Puerto Rico's first ocean fish farm.

O'Hanlon had been planning on farming snapper, but Benetti, then at the University of Miami, persuaded him to try cobia. He thought cobia might be "the next salmon," except with much better prospects for farming. Cobia grow from egg to 11 pounds in a year, are high in omega-3, and taste good raw and cooked. Cobia don't mind popula-tion density in a cage, which is odd because the fish don't school and are highly migratory, which is why there's no commercial fishery tar-geting cobia. A tropical fish, cobia is popular with sport fishermen in South Florida, Mexico, Belize, as well as along the East Coast of the United States in the summer. In Mexico, cobia is served at weddings.[6]

As a trial in Puerto Rico, O'Hanlon had two underwater cages—one for mutton snapper (closely related to red snapper) and one for cobia fingerlings that Benetti had flown in from his Miami hatch-ery. "You could see the cobia grow in one day, from morning to eve-ning," says O'Hanlon. "In one month, the fish weighed more than 20 grams." By contrast, the mutton snapper, at 1 month, had grown to 2 or 3 grams. Switching to cobia was a "no-brainer," O'Hanlon says.[7]

Despite some trial-and-error setbacks and shark predation, the cobia farm went well enough, certainly as *another* proof of concept. But O'Hanlon needed more volume to create a market and a business. In Puerto Rico, Snapperfarm's permits capped output at 50 tons per year; O'Hanlon fought for 6 years to increase that limit to 250 tons, again without luck. Snapperfarm needed five core permits to operate, but the company had to consult with many more agencies to obtain them. A short list of the US and state agencies involved included the Department of Natural & Environmental Resources, Environmental Quality Board, Planning Board, Army Corps of Engineers, Environ-mental Protection Agency, Fish & Wildlife Service, National Marine Fisheries Service, State Historic Preservation Office, and the Coast Guard. Investors saw the writing on the wall and O'Hanlon finally cut the cord with Puerto Rico, decrying his lack of government support and forced departure from Culebra as "a disservice to America."[8]

In 2009, O'Hanlon bought Pristine Oceans, a fish farm in Panama, with investment from Aquacopia in New York, and renamed it Open

Blue Cobia. "Aquaculture is about managing failure," Daniel Tze, founder of Aquacopia, a now closed investment firm, told *National Geographic* in 2014. "Escapes, disease outbreaks, slow growth. These are all things Brian knows how to handle."[9]

As in Puerto Rico, O'Hanlon first used AquaPods but eventually switched to Innovasea's larger SeaStations, which also provided a simplified and centralized feeding system. (Innovasea was formed by the 2015 merger of Ocean Farms Technology, which made Aquapods, and Ocean Spar, which made SeaStations.) "Both products are submersible pens designed to withstand the roughest environments found in the open ocean and hurricane-prone areas," says Tyler Sclodnick, a principal scientist and aquaculture lead at Innovasea. "When people think 'ocean' they think of big breaking waves, but it's the cyclical energy of chafing and rubbing that is destructive. In Panama, our SeaStations are set about 45–50 feet below the surface. Two anchors set in 180 feet of water keep the cage steady and provide enough negative ballast so the cage can't reach the surface."

Open Blue Cobia claims to be the largest open-ocean fish farm in the world. Seven miles off the Caribbean coast of Panama, "over the horizon," 22 submerged cages produced 2,700 tons of cobia in both 2018 and 2019—more than 10 times the 250 tons O'Hanlon had hoped for in Puerto Rico (his Panama permits allow up to 10,000 tons). Innovasea, a full-service aquaculture provider with data-analytics and remote-automation capability, distributes feed from a single point to a submerged grid of up to twelve pens. Operators monitor fish behavior with high-resolution cameras. Analysis of water temperatures provides estimates of how much food will be required. Scuba divers periodically check the nets for damage or signs of predation, but the copper-alloy mesh netting resists predators and biofouling, while allowing steady water flow.

With O'Hanlon's Puerto Rico experience as a foundation, Open Blue Cobia took off in Panama. "These fish are coming from what we like to call the next-generation open-ocean farm," says O'Hanlon. "I would venture to say that we are further offshore than any other farm in the world. We are literally over the horizon in very deep water with strong currents, far from sensitive ecosystems and areas commonly used by other stakeholders. Our water is blue, blue, blue, it is crystal clear open-ocean water, and the fish never see the same water twice. We raise our fish in waters where cobia can naturally be found. The farms are essentially located in the deserts of the sea, without environmental impact." Says Benetti, "Open-ocean aquaculture in cages is just as good as organic. No pesticides, no antibiotics, no pigments, no medicines, no nothing."[10]

The first-known scientific study of nutrient and sediment impact from an offshore fish farm essentially confirmed claims made by O'Hanlon and Benetti:

> Water column samples were collected up- and downstream of the site at various times between 2012 and 2018. Typically, no significant difference in dissolved oxygen, chlorophyll-a, particulate organic carbon, particulate organic nitrogen, nitrate + nitrite, and total dissolved nitrogen concentration was observed in the water column between the up- versus downstream samples. Similarly, sediment samples were collected at various times between 2012 and 2018. Samples were collected at up- versus downstream locations and analyzed for benthic carbon, nitrogen, and chlorophyll-a content. Some of the collected data demonstrates a trend toward sediment enrichment within the vicinity of the farm. These data are of interest to stakeholders concerned with the expansion of offshore aquaculture in the United States and other countries. To our knowledge, this is the first report of its kind from a commercially scaled aquaculture facility utilizing offshore submersible-cage technologies.[11]

At harvest, giant pipes suck mature cobia from the water and a hammer immediately knocks the fish on the head. A blade then cuts a main artery under its chin. This quick kill is similar to the method practiced by Hudson Valley Farms with its steelhead (see chapter 8)—a "percussive stunning" form of Ikejime (see chapter 5) that is designed to stop the "survival message" and restrict the amount of lactic acid that flows through the fish and tightens its muscles.[12]

Open Blue Cobia is vertically integrated and manages the entire life cycle of the fish from hatchery to harvest, processing, and shipment. In 2017, Open Blue Cobia was awarded four stars by Best Aquaculture

Practices; in 2018, it won the coveted Aquaculture Stewardship Award for top sustainable practices (feed with low fish content and no antibiotics). In 2018, Open Blue Cobia started distributing red snapper—a return to O'Hanlon's early basement days—produced by Earth Ocean Farms in the Sea of Cortez, Mexico. (Both companies, as well as Innovasea, have investment from Cuna del Mar of Los Angeles, an investment firm specializing in open-ocean technology.)

O'Hanlon is an entrepreneur and a risk taker. Neil Sims is a scientist and a risk taker. In 1990, Sims came to Kailua-Kona, Hawaii, to develop an oyster-pearl hatchery and develop pearl farming throughout the South Pacific and Southeast Asia. Over the course of the decade, he saw a bigger opportunity. Given the global decline in marine stocks during the 1990s, Sims and his partners saw a chance to apply their hatchery and grow-out expertise to produce food from the ocean.

In 2001, Sims and research scientist Dale Sarver founded Kona Blue Water Farms to develop cutting-edge hatchery methods for "difficult-to-rear" marine-fish larvae: snappers, groupers, yellowtail ("kampachi"), and amberjacks. This was roughly during the same time that Benetti was developing his cobia hatchery in Florida. Clearly, the Blue Revolution was moving to a new level—nurturing a marine organism from egg to larval to adult stage is not a simple task, but it was happening in many species all over the world.

In 2003, Kona Blue Water Farms started a fish farm in state waters, about a half-mile offshore, in 200 feet of water. In 2009, Sims sold the farm to Blue Ocean Mariculture; 2 years later, he sold them the hatchery. Blue Ocean Mariculture, at that time a research company, got a full commercial permit in 2015. In 2021, Blue Ocean Mariculture was the first American finfish farm to receive certification from the Aquaculture Stewardship Council, a comparable organization to the Marine Stewardship Council for wild fish (and the same certification that Open Blue Cobia in Panama received). Tyler Korte, who once worked at Blue Ocean Mariculture but left to help O'Hanlon set up his net-pens in Panama, returned in 2015 as VP-Marine Operations. "One of the problems with most nearshore net pens is they sit too close to the bottom and there's not a good dispersion field for nutrients," says Korte. "But the bathymetry of Hawaii is such that we can be a half-mile offshore and sit in 200 feet of water with good energy and flow."

When Sims sold the hatchery, he and Michael Bullock, a Kona Blue Water Farms executive, formed Kampachi Farms, a new company. "The overall goal of these efforts is to reduce mankind's footprint on the seas, by transitioning toward a more nurturing relationship with our seafood," said Sims, co-CEO of Kampachi Farms, a title he shares with Bullock.[13]

Kampachi Farms was the first company to get a permit to farm fish in federal waters—for a research project, not a commercial operation. Vellela Beta was seemingly a graft of ideas from Jules Verne, Buckminster Fuller, and Jacques Cousteau. (A velella is a small, free-floating marine animal that lives on the surface of the open ocean, commonly known as a sea raft, by-the-wind sailor, purple sail, little sail, or simply velella.[14]) Sims filled an AquaPod with 2,000 fingerling kampachi—raised from eggs in his hatchery—and towed the pen out to deep waters on the backside of Hawaii's Big Island, where there are constant eddies. The unmoored pod circled in eddies in waters 12,000 feet deep, far removed from coral reefs or other marine life. The "drifting fish farm," tethered to a sailing vessel that could alter course direction as needed, was named one of *Time*'s "25 Best Inventions of the Year" in 2012.[15] "The fish thrived in the research net-pen far from shore (from 3 to 75 miles out), with phenomenal growth rates and superb fish health, and without any negative impact on water quality, the ocean floor, wild fish, or marine mammals," said Sims. After 6 months, the Aquapods yielded 10,000 pounds of kampachi, which grew twice as fast as expected.

A second "over-the-horizon" aquaculture project, Velella Gamma, used the same net pen, species, and number of fish, but included a single-point mooring in water 6,000 feet deep, 6 miles offshore. An unmanned feed barge, controlled remotely from shore by an iPhone or iPad, was topped up with feed once a week.

Like cobia, kampachi have not been commercially fished. They can grow up to 3 feet and 130 pounds. Like cobia, kampachi's white meat is firm and suitable for grilling or sashimi. While kampachi enjoy squid and zooplankton, they can subsist on a full or partial plant diet. Since

2006, Kona Blue Water Farms had been testing new types of vegetarian-mixed feed, cognizant that feeding forage fish or fish meal to farmed fish was fast becoming a hot-button ecological issue. Researchers found that kampachi accepted agricultural proteins, including soy-based products, and grew as well and tasted as good as those raised on 100 percent fish-based diets. One of Kona Blue Water Farms' main collaborators on the feed project was KnipBio, the Lowell, Massachusetts, company whose single-cell protein offers a sustainable fish-meal replacement (see chapter 7) and is providing "finish feed" to Great Falls Aquaculture (see chapter 8).

In 2017, Sims's Kampachi Farms won a grant from Florida Sea Grant (a national NOAA Fisheries program affiliated with universities) to trial a new Vellela net-pen pilot in the Gulf of Mexico, about 45 miles off the coast of Sarasota. The Velella Epsilon project uses a single net pen with a single-point mooring. In 2020, however, a Florida appeals court upheld a lower-court decision saying that NOAA Fisheries did not have jurisdiction over aquaculture and could not permit the project because "aquaculture is not fishing." Sims said that "the primary goal of the demonstration project is to help the local communities in the Gulf of Mexico to understand the ancillary benefits that offshore aquaculture can bring to fisheries and to recreational tourism."[16] But the Florida judicial decision points to a much larger national issue about the future of offshore farms—the lack of a clear framework for permitting.

It is true, as the judge ruled, that NOAA Fisheries is not the sole agency in charge of aquaculture, although in 2011 a judge in Hawaii had allowed NOAA Fisheries to give Sims the first federal permit in the United States. Given the more recent ruling, it is unclear exactly which agency would have jurisdiction without a new and explicit law from Congress to replace the antiquated National Aquaculture Act of 1980. You can easily imagine senators in 1980 looking up "aquaculture" in the dictionary before voting.

Besides NOAA Fisheries, other US federal agencies responsible for regulating aquaculture (both freshwater and saltwater) include the Environmental Protection Agency, the Army Corps of Engineers, the Department of Agriculture's Animal and Plant Health Inspection Service, the Food and Drug Administration's Center for Veterinary

Medicine and its Center for Food Safety and Applied Nutrition, and the Fish and Wildlife Service—more or less the same list of suspects O'Hanlon was wrangling with in Puerto Rico in the late 1990s.

Since the National Aquaculture Act passed Congress in 1980, new bills have been introduced in 1995, 2005, 2007, 2009, and 2011, but all fizzled. In 2020, Senators Roger Wicker (R-MI), Brian Schatz (D-HI), and Marco Rubio (R-FL) introduced the AQUAA Act (Advancing the Quality and Understanding of American Aquaculture), but it had not been brought up for floor debate in 2021. It's not like aquaculture has been forgotten since 1980; it has just been unimportant, controversial, and misunderstood, at least at the federal level, with no clear sense of which agency should take the management lead.

There is clearly a strong anti-mariculture lobby in the US. Many of the same environmental groups that lobbied hard during the 1990s and early 2000s to restrict wild-capture fisheries have been just as active trying to stop offshore mariculture before it starts. For these and other opponents, two relatively recent fish-farm disasters in the United States certainly raise fresh doubts about mariculture. In 2017, 263,000 farmed Atlantic salmon escaped from failing net pens into Puget Sound (Washington State), raising fears that they might crossbreed with wild Pacific salmon. The Washington state legislature swiftly responded with a statewide ban on fish farms for nonnative species, effective in 2025 when the Cooke Aquaculture (a Canadian company) leases expire.

In 2019, at Catalina Sea Ranch, a shellfish farm that was the first commercial offshore farm permitted in the lower 48, off the coast of Los Angeles, a 400-foot mussel line broke loose and wrapped around the propellor of a small fishing boat motoring through the ranch and flipped it, drowning a 70-year-old man. An investigation showed that the operator of Catalina Sea Ranch had ignored permit requirements from the California Coastal Commission and the Army Corps of Engineers, did not perform required inspections, and failed to repair equipment. "Catalina Sea Ranch was an example of what not to do," said Diane Windham, West Coast aquaculture coordinator for NOAA Fisheries. "It's going to haunt the industry for quite a while."[17]

In late 2020, less than a year after the Catalina event, Hubbs-SeaWorld Research Institute, a prestigious research institute, and

Pacific6 Enterprise, applied for a Pacific Ocean AquaFarm, relatively close to Catalina Island. The proposed farm would be about 4 miles off the coast of San Diego, generating up to 5,000 metric tons of sushi-grade California yellowtail each year. NOAA Fisheries, the Environmental Protection Agency, and the Army Corps of Engineers are reviewing the project, with a finding expected in 2022.[18]

In New England, a handful of small-scale, ocean-farm, research projects have been permitted. Cat Cove Marine Lab, a 33-acre blue-mussel farm 7 miles off the coast of Cape Ann, Massachusetts, run out of Salem State University, got a permit in 2015 for three longlines to study the feasibility of the habitat and any protected-species interactions. ("Protected species" is primarily code for the North Atlantic right whale.) The other is a permit for multiple research projects at the Isle of Shoals, 7 miles off the coast of New Hampshire (in state waters), run by Michael Chambers, a professor at the University of New Hampshire's School of Marine Science and Ocean Engineering.

Chambers has as much experience as anyone in America in open-ocean aquaculture. In addition to projects in the Black Sea, Norway, and the Mediterranean, Chambers in the early 1990s attached submersible cages to abandoned oil platforms in the Gulf of Mexico to farm red drum and pompano, with funding from the Occidental Petroleum Company. At the Oceanic Institute in Hawaii, he helped establish a threadfin (moi) farm off the island of Oahu in 1999 with early SeaStation cages.

In 2000, Chambers left Hawaii, where he had known Sims, to take the role of project manager at the University of New Hampshire's Open Ocean Aquaculture Project. In SeaStation cages off the Isle of Shoals, Chambers farmed cod, haddock, and halibut, all of which he found very difficult to raise. He eventually found a favorite. "Steelhead is more domesticated, it's easy to get the eggs to hatch and when we take them from freshwater to saltwater they explode."[19] In 2014, two lobstermen, Pete Flanagan and Vinnie Prien, used the University of New Hampshire permits to start Isle of Shoals Mariculture, farming blue mussels.

More recently, Chambers has been training fishermen on integrated multi-trophic aquaculture at the mouth of the Piscataqua River (the boundary near the coast between Maine and New Hampshire) with his nearshore AquaFort raft platform that supports steelhead, mussels, and kelp. It's a small but intensive ocean farm that produces food for local markets. "The AquaFort is for small-scale farming, not made for the open ocean," says Chambers. "The AquaFort could be a unique model for nearshore, small-scale, multi-trophic aquaculture."

The early 2000s seemed to be the dawning of a new era in mariculture, but the potential is yet to be unlocked. "I've typically been overly optimistic—until the last 10 years or so," says Chambers. "I'm now involved with six projects, most started in the last 4 years, and even with a track record in the open ocean off New Hampshire, I can't get permits. NGOs don't want anything to go into the water except sailboats."

When considering offshore-farm permits, regulators have a checklist of issues: potential impacts of bio-deposition of fish waste and uneaten food on the seafloor; potential increase in dissolved nutrients; seal attraction and predation; escapement of fish from cages; disruption of vessel navigation; and impact on endangered whales and turtles.

Most of these issues can largely be addressed with good spatial planning, but protection of the endangered North Atlantic right whale is the single biggest impediment to offshore farming in New England. As an example, even though Cat Cove completed an arduous academic study showing no interaction with whales or other mammals in three years, it has been denied a permit to expand from three ropes to 20 or 400.

The population of the North Atlantic right whale is roughly 350, with fewer than 100 breeding females. Right whales typically swim in the Gulf of Maine and Bay of Fundy in summer months but have begun to range into the Gulf of St. Lawrence, where until recently there were no protections for them.[20] Since 2017, "Unusual Mortality Events," a function of entanglement or vessel strikes, numbered at least forty-eight—thirty-three whale deaths and fifteen serious injuries (aka "swimming while dead")—and more than half occurred in Canada's Gulf of St. Lawrence.[21]

"The story of the North Atlantic right whale is complex, but it boils down to second-grade arithmetic," says Charles "Stormy" Mayo, founder and director of the Right Whale Ecology Program at the

Center for Coastal Studies in Provincetown, Massachusetts, where members of his family have lived since the 1600s. "The number of animals born minus the number that die gives us a trajectory. Right now, the arrow points to zero—extinction—and that's a very chilling finding."[22] He's been known to say that right whales are like neighborhood dogs to the people of Provincetown, "everyone knows them." In fact, many right whales are named by those who protect them.

A federal judge ruled in 2020 that the US government was violating the Endangered Species Act by failing to protect whales.[23] Thus, any offshore-farm project that has any possible hope of getting a permit has to persuade federal regulators that entanglement is not possible— and that's a high bar to clear.

Technological and policy solutions to the right-whale dilemma are clearly a necessary precondition for permitting offshore farms. Getting ropes out of the water, which lobstermen have been asked to do with "ropeless pots," is one solution; another is composite-culture lines that could reduce the risk of entanglement. "We're looking at lines with 1,000 pounds of tension that would snap like raw spaghetti if hit by a whale and not entangle it," says Chambers. "For mussels, we're looking at bottom planting in pots as opposed to long lines in the water column."

Blue Ocean Mariculture in Hawaii, the former Kona Blue Water Farms, has net pens in a humpback-whale sanctuary. "We've been farming here for 15 years, watching whales and dolphins swim around our cages without incident," says Blue Ocean Mariculture's Korte. "We have good, high-tension rigging designed and set with those animals in mind."

Given his experience with mariculture, Chambers is a valuable adviser to ocean-farm startups. He is now advising Blue Water Fisheries, which is looking to farm steelhead trout and blue mussels off the coast of New Hampshire, and Manna Fish Farms, looking to farm steelhead off the tip of Long Island, as well as red drum and striped bass in the Gulf of Mexico.

Donna Lanzetta, an attorney and entrepreneur, started Manna Fish Farms in Hampton Bays, New York, in 2013. She had her first permit "pre-application" meeting with regulators in 2015—and the second one 5 years later! Thus, she is now in year 8 of her business with no permits to farm. While waiting quasi patiently, Lanzetta has bought land for a hatchery and is opening the Manna Restaurant and Lobster Inn in Southampton, New York, which specializes in serving local, under-utilized fish species.

Manna has identified a site more than 8 miles off Shinnecock Bay, off the south fork of Long Island, which NOAA Fisheries, the National Ocean Service, and the National Center for Ocean Science have said is in the "least impactful location, with negligible conflict." The 70-acre site is in approximately 145 feet of water.

Lanzetta is leaning toward farming steelhead trout, which Mike Meeker, Manna Fish Farms' Chief Operating Officer, has raised for 30-plus years in Ontario at his Meeker Aquaculture. Black sea bass is a possible alternative or addition, the idea being to harvest in December when the wild fish are not plentiful. But steelhead fits the temperature profile, especially with the ability to lower nets into a colder thermo-cline, and it grows fast. "I think the best species for offshore farming in the northeast are steelhead and blue mussels," says Chambers.

Manna Fish Farms has also applied for permits in the Gulf of Mex-ico to raise striped bass, which Chambers's research shows will grow faster in Florida than New York, or red drum, which Chambers raised in the early 1990s for Occidental Petroleum. Manna Fish Farms' pre-ferred site is 23 miles south of Sarasota, 120 acres in water 150 feet deep—in the same general area as Sims' Oceans Era Farms site.

Another offshore-farm applicant is Blue Water Fisheries, a part-nership between Chambers, InnovaSea, and Scott Flood, an ocean engineer and lawyer. "I'm good at regulatory stuff, which is my focus," says Flood, whose career includes work with underwater remote sens-ing and side-scan sonar. "It's all in the permitting, as the technology is pretty well understood and much of it is off the shelf."

Blue Water Fisheries' plans call for forty SeaStations over 230 acres. Its species of choice is steelhead trout, along with a trial of lumpfish. The preferred site is roughly 10 miles off the coast of Seabrook, New Hampshire. The plan is to acquire rainbow-trout eggs from hatcheries on the West Coast (as Hudson Valley Farms does, see chapter 8) and spawn them in a land-based, freshwater hatchery in New Hampshire. After the eggs hatch and are reared for 6 to 8 months, they will be acclimatized to saltwater and transferred to offshore net pens for a 10–12 month grow out.

The best catalyst to jumpstart offshore farming in the United States may be the blue mussel. It likes ropes but can grow in cages or on the ocean floor. And wild mussels are naturally moving further offshore, indicating the conditions are conducive to growth. "As a wild resource, mussels are setting in deeper waters," says Bill Silkes, CEO of American Mussel Harvesters (see chapter 9), the largest processor of mussels in the country. "If we're going to farm mussels, we've got to go further north and further offshore. That's what's driving my interest in offshore farming."

A few years ago, Silkes tried farming mussels in Rhode Island Sound, about a mile off the coast of Newport, but the warm water resulted in a high mortality rate. Right now, oysters are his primary farm crop, with about 65 acres farmed. But he hasn't given up on offshore farming and recently ordered some floating baskets—"a unique design"—from New Zealand, which he thinks might be more efficient than the raft or bottom-plant techniques for high-energy offshore waters. Given the federal response to date he's not optimistic about the future. "When I got into 'sustainable' farming and fishing in the 1980s, I didn't expect the government would exclude us from federal waters. But I just got kicked out of waters around Nantucket, where I've been fishing since the 1980s, because I was in a 'critical habitat for codfish.' There hasn't been a codfish there for 5 years—the gray seals from nearby Monomoy Point [off Chatham] have eaten all the codfish," he says. In 2019, NOAA Fisheries created the Great Round Shoal Habitat Management Area, setting aside 990 square miles to restore codfish and other species. The clam-and-mussel fishery was excluded from the area.

Silkes is hoping that the recent permitting of offshore wind-energy farms off the New England and New York coasts might signal acceptance of an alternative use for the ocean. Already, there are signs that mussels are growing naturally and profusely on the five turbine towers of the Block Island Wind Farm in Rhode Island, the first offshore commercial wind farm in the US.

"The development of sustainable mariculture in federal waters should be a priority. Look at the Whakatōhea Mussels farm in New Zealand, run by the government and the Maoris. It's 6–10 miles off Ōpōtiki and the scale is enormous [9,000 acres]. The UK mussel farm, Offshore Shellfish, is another huge farm [4,000 acres]. That's the scale you need." Says Lindell of the Woods Hole Oceanographic Institution, "The UK's first offshore mussel farm is producing 4 million mussel meals per year, heading toward 20 million in 2 to 3 years. That's real food capacity." At least it was heading in that direction before the restaurant closures during COVID and access to EU markets was restricted in the wake of Brexit.

Both Silkes and Lindell lament the influence of NGOs and environmentalists that are opposed to mariculture. "If you want to know what drives fisheries policy, it's the environmental community and their attorneys," says Silkes. Lindell sees homeowners who romanticize lobster boats and buoys but fight tooth and nail against mariculture and see it as an intrusion into their waters. "It's unfair that people glorify land farms but vilify aquaculture. All this smashes entrepreneurial interest in ocean farming," says Lindell.[24]

Meanwhile, NOAA Fisheries itself is promoting offshore mussel farming, suggesting that the most promising locations for mussel mariculture in the Northeast are off New York's Long Island, north of Cape Ann in Massachusetts (where the Cat Cove mussel farm is located), and off the New Hampshire coast (where mussels are now being farmed off the Isle of Shoals). Gary Wikfors, director of NOAA's Milford Laboratory, and Darien Mizuta, a postdoc at the Milford lab, wrote in the *Journal of Marine Science and Engineering* about the potential for mussel farming: "Blue mussels have an established market, are commercially important to the region, and we know the culture technologies. We import 225 times as much as we are producing and American consumption is growing. Increasing national production would help our food security and lessen the seafood trade deficit."[25]

As the US tries to figure out the offshore problem, with basically no clear path forward, Norway and China are pushing the envelope. Norway's Salmar designed its huge Ocean Farm 1 like an ocean oil-and-gas rig, rising 200 feet out of the water and more than 100 yards wide. It was built in China and towed to Norway. With a volume of 250,000 cubic meters, it can grow up to 1.5 million fish in 14 months. About 20,000 sensors allow complete automation to monitor and feed the fish.[26]

"The first one's just a prototype. The next Ocean Farm will be designed to grow 3 million fish," says NOAA Fisheries' Michael Rubino. "The anchor cables appear to be several feet thick [hence not a risk to entangle marine life]. Along with other innovative ocean farming designs, Ocean Farm could be a gamechanger for offshore finfish if such designs were deployed in American waters—it wouldn't take too many of those to substantially increase production."

China—through the state-owned China State Shipbuilding Corporation—is building the world's largest "farm ship," more than 800 feet long, with 80,000 cubic meters worth of aquaculture tanks to produce 3,500 metric tons per year. "With deeper water, faster currents, and more suitable temperatures, the offshore farms can minimize their impact on the environment while ensuring the needs of the domestic market are met," said Chen Xiangmiao, an associate researcher at the National Institute for South China Sea Studies.[27]

Whether these technological marvels from Norway and China are cost-effective and environmentally friendly, or produce quality fish, are big unknowns. What is clear is that unless the US simplifies its Byzantine offshore-farming permit process, the seafood trade deficit is likely to continue rising. Rubino suggests that the solution is hiding in plain sight. "If you want to know how to manage offshore farming, look at how the state of Maine manages salmon farming just below the Bay of Fundy," says Rubino. "State, federal, and industry reports indicate that Maine salmon operations have barely used antibiotics in 10 years, have had virtually no escapes, net-pen sites lay fallow between harvests, underwater cameras monitor feeding, and managers collaborate with federal and state agencies to protect the genetics of wild and hatchery-raised-and-released salmon to maintain wild salmon runs in Maine rivers. These are examples of state-of-the-art operations."

PART 3

Global Challenges:
Criminals, Climate, Conservation

One of the most persistent threats to marine conservation is illegal, unregulated, and unreported fishing. Illegal fishing accounts for more than 20 percent of all fish caught and is a $23 billion business. Collectively, due to its indiscriminate nature and focus on high-value targets, like sharks, tunas, squid, octopus, and sea urchins, illegal fishing is a huge threat to the sustainability of global fishing. In addition to "stateless" vessels, sovereign-state vessels are also guilty of illegal fishing and supported by more than $35 billion in subsidies for an otherwise unprofitable business on the "high seas." Big data, machine learning, and artificial intelligence are now mapping fishing activity in real time on the oceans and have been instrumental in apprehending vessels fishing illegally and prosecuting white-collar owners.

Marine protected areas that prohibit fishing can increase conservation and biodiversity, and perhaps even mitigate some of the impacts of climate change, which is quickly becoming as big a risk to long-term sustainability as overfishing. Protected reserves now cover less than 8 percent of the world's oceans, with a goal of 30 percent by 2030 gaining international support. Meanwhile, nearshore coastal communities have shown that they can put traditional fisheries on a long-term sustainable path, as they leverage collective marine know-how to add mariculture initiatives and build a larger BlueTech economy.

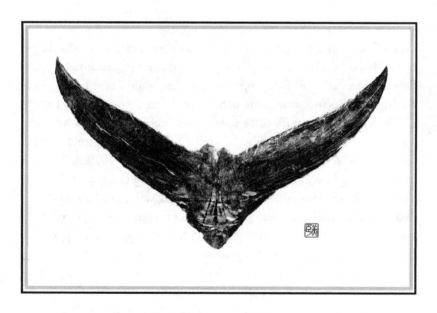

Tuna Tail

Chapter 12

Big Data versus Pirates
on the High Seas

*So, if you have a crew from Indonesia and you have your vessel
flagged in Mongolia and it's owned by Panama, and then you have
countries that don't have a Navy to go down to Patagonia to arrest
you, [the ships] don't really care. You have all these tax havens and
strange-flag states that will sell their sovereignty to vessels like this.*

—Kjetil Saeter, investigative journalist, *Norwegian Business Daily*

We are living in a postindustrial age—the Fourth Industrial
Revolution characterized by digital technologies, robotics,
big-data analytics, machine learning, and artificial intelligence—but that doesn't mean the last vestiges of industrial fishing
have disappeared. Even if every country in the world managed its fisheries like the United States does, there would still be a major problem
to confront: illegal, unreported, and unregulated fishing.

In the summer of 2020, a huge fleet of Chinese fishing vessels,
estimated at 350, plied the waters near Ecuador's Galapagos Islands,
a UNESCO World Heritage Site. The captains disabled tracking
systems, changed ship names, and left a trail of marine debris. The
vessels used stadium-style lighting to attract squid, almost certainly
overfishing the species. Yolanda Kakabadse, a former minister of the
environment in Ecuador, noted that the "fleet's size and aggressiveness

against marine species is a big threat to the balance of species in the Galapagos."[1]

The overwhelmed Ecuadorian Navy requested assistance from the United States Coast Guard, and the two nations jointly escorted the Chinese out of Ecuadorian waters. Undeterred, the Chinese fleet motored south and into Chile's exclusive economic zone, where it continued to fish until late 2020, despite an active response from the Chileans. Then secretary of state Mike Pompeo called out China for subsidizing "the world's largest commercial fishing fleet, which routinely violates the sovereign rights and jurisdiction of coastal states, fishes without permission, and overfishes licensing agreements."

At the time, Ecuador had a $5.3 billion debt with China, which Pompeo described as "debt-trap diplomacy"—a predatory tactic wherein a creditor nation intentionally allows a debtor to overextend and then demands excessive economic or diplomatic concessions (such as fishing rights). In Africa, governments have been mortgaging their natural resources to secure loans from China, which totaled $153 billion from 2002 to 2019. The International Monetary Fund notes that eleven Sub-Saharan African countries are at high risk of debt distress.[2]

One of the reasons the appearance of the large Chinese fleet caused so much alarm in Ecuador, aside from its steadfast protection of the Galapagos Islands, was the memory of *Fu Yuan Yu Leng 999*, a Chinese trawler interdicted in 2017 with 6,600 illegally caught sharks onboard.[3]

Argentina, Peru, and Chile have had their own confrontations in recent years with Chinese fishing fleets. In March 2016, the Argentinian Coast Guard caught three vessels illegally fishing. Two vessels fled but the third, *Lu Yan Yuan Yu 010*, was shot and sunk by Argentinian patrol boats. China fishes in territorial waters of other countries more than any other country, sometimes with a license, sometimes not. But it is not the only country guilty of stealing fish from other countries' "exclusive" territories.

In July 2021, on the other side of the world, Indonesian authorities chased a Vietnamese fishing vessel in their waters. In 2014, Indonesia had banned all foreign ships from its exclusive economic zone, due to a high incidence of illegal fishing that was negatively affecting domestic fisheries. The Vietnamese boat revved its engines, tossed a fishing net overboard to destroy evidence, and burned tires to obscure visibility as it zigzagged at high speeds. Indonesian Coast Guard officers eventually ordered the boat to stop; the Vietnamese boat instead tried to ram the Indonesian patrol boat. The Indonesians pumped gunfire into the vessel and the Vietnamese finally yielded to inspection—which uncovered two tons of fish.[4]

Illegal fishing is estimated to account for 20 percent or more of the global catch, worth $20–$30 billion.[5] Illegal fishing is essentially a large-scale, global, criminal enterprise, with boats flying under various "flags of convenience," turning off transponders, and using drift nets (outlawed by the United Nations in 1992) to scoop up every organism in their path. Vessels often transfer fish to larger refrigerated ships ("reefers") that bring the fish to port, obscuring the origin of the catch and allowing the pirates to remain at sea for months.

Illegal fishing takes place in national territories, on the "high seas" outside national territories, and sometimes in marine protected areas, like the Chinese fleet around the Galapagos Islands. Collectively, due to its indiscriminate nature and focus on high-value targets, like sharks, tunas, squid, octopus, and sea urchins, illegal fishing is a huge threat to the sustainability of global fishing.

Artisanal fishers, who make up more than 96 percent of the world's fishers and land 35 percent of fish in the world, according to the United Nations Conference on Trade and Development, are particularly harmed by illegal fishing. About half the fishers are women and 9 of 10 jobs in artisanal fisheries are held by women. In West Africa, for example, illegal fishing robs coastal communities of 300,000 jobs and $2 billion in revenues every year. From a food-security perspective, 50 to 90 percent of the protein consumed in vulnerable, coastal economies comes from fish caught by small-scale artisanal fishers, well above the global average of 17 percent.[6]

Global Fishing Watch: Eyes on the Ocean

The ocean is vast and opaque, a deep, dark, watery jungle. But big data and data analytics are bringing transparency to the opaque ocean with startling rapidity, providing a bull's-eye view of activity and producing a flood of actionable data. Machine learning and artificial intelligence translate this data into powerful new tools for governments and scientists to study, track, and manage ocean resources and habitats.

Global Fishing Watch is a big-data technology platform that analyzes signals emitted from ocean vessels to create a map of the world's trackable commercial-fishing activity—with a 72-hour delay (you can monitor global ship traffic at www.globalfishingwatch.org). Global Fishing Watch has been instrumental in apprehending illegal fishing boats and "trans-shippers"—large vessels that meet smaller vessels on the high seas to collect illegal catch like shark fins, Patagonian tooth fish, and octopus and deliver it to port. Global Fishing Watch data have also been instrumental in planning and studying marine protected areas that prohibit fishing in large reserves (see chapter 13).

Launched by Oceana, Google, and SkyTruth in 2016, Global Fishing Watch analyzes signals emitted from automatic identification systems (AIS) and vessel-monitoring systems (VMS). AIS is a tracking technology designed for collision avoidance—required on boats of 50 feet or more—that transmits a ship's location, identity, course, and speed. Satellites and terrestrial receivers pick up these transmissions, which are delivered to Global Fishing Watch.

Vessels with AIS account for more than half the fishing effort more than 100 nautical miles from shore and as much as 80 percent of the fishing on the high seas, where bigger vessels are the norm. AIS is not widely used on small boats or in some regions, such as the Indian Ocean, but the number of fishing vessels with AIS is increasing by 10 to 30 percent each year.

Sovereign nations use VMS to track their own fleets. Roughly twenty governments have agreed to voluntarily supply these data to Global Fishing Watch. In 2017, Indonesia became the first nation to make its proprietary data publicly available, instantly putting 5,000 smaller commercial fishing vessels that do not use AIS on the map. Peru shared its VMS data in 2018, followed by Chile and Panama in 2019.[7]

Global Fishing Watch now tracks roughly 65,000 fishing vessels and hopes to increase that to 300,000 this decade. Machine-learning algorithms can identify a fishing vessel (as opposed to a cargo or other type of ship), whether it is in transit or actively fishing, whether it is long-lining or purse seining, and whether it is offloading catch at sea. Global Fishing Watch is a game-changer for transparency on the ocean.

Vessel captains, of course, can and do turn off or smash their electronic-tracking systems, or squelch and distort signals, if they want to elude detection. But Global Fishing Watch has access to other layers of data. A Visible Infrared Imaging Radiometer Suite detects lights of brightly lit vessels that are not sharing their position with electronic signals. An "encounters layer" indicates boats gathering near each other to exchange fish, fuel, food, or people, which is almost always a sign of criminal behavior. Illegal fishing vessels are often wide-ranging criminal enterprises—relying on slave labor, and trafficking humans, weapons, and drugs. As Global Fishing Watch increases its collection of datasets and improves its algorithms, the platform has been increasingly effective as a partner to governments and enforcement agencies that are developing their own datasets to track and apprehend vessels fishing illegally.

"Transparency is crucial for responsible stewardship of our global ocean—to fight illegal fishing, to protect fish stocks and livelihoods, and to increase the safety and welfare of fishers," says Tony Long, a former surveillance expert in the British Royal Navy, who is CEO of Global Fishing Watch. "Governments that decide to publish their vessel data via our map add real momentum to the drive for more public information on fishing activity."[8]

Sovereign governments are becoming more proactive about their own data collection and efforts to resist illegal fishing. The Vietnamese fishing boat that was apprehended by Indonesian authorities was the result of the Indonesian Maritime Information Center, which had gone active just 2 days before the chase. Organized by the Indonesian Coast Guard (Bakamia), the new information center pools surveillance data from a variety of sources, including satellite imagery, aerial surveillance, and ships' AIS signals. Muhammad Arifuddin, program manager for Destructive Fishing Watch Indonesia, praised Bakamia as a pioneer for pinpointing fishing violations with "heat maps" drawn from geographic-information-systems technology. "I expect illegal fishing will decrease, especially in hotspots for foreign vessels, because they're aware we have stronger surveillance," says Wildan Ghiffary, program officer for Global Fishing Watch.[9]

Indonesia has become a major global player in the hunt for pirates; it has seized, destroyed, or sunk close to 400 illegal fishing vessels in the last 5 or so years.[10] Even before its new data-information center launched, Indonesia had seized one of the world's most wanted pirate fishing vessels after it had evaded capture in many countries. Called *ANDREY DOLGOV, STS-50, SEA BREEZ 1,* and many other names over a decade of lawlessness, the ship was suspected of transnational fisheries-related crime, including illegal fishing, document and identity fraud, manipulation of shipborne equipment, and illegal open-sea transshipments. The *STS-50,* a stateless vessel that had been illegally fishing for Patagonian toothfish (Chilean sea bass) in the Southern Ocean, had previously been detained by China but escaped and was then caught in Mozambique, where it once again escaped, leading to the chase.

The *STS-50* was a master of disguise, according to INTERPOL, the international criminal police organization. It changed its name six times, flew the flag of as many nations, and disguised its electronic-identification systems to confuse pursuers. For years it illegally fished across three oceans, misreporting the type of fish being offloaded to avoid sanctions and retreating to the relative safety of international waters whenever the risk of capture was high. It is believed to have pilfered $50 million worth of fish from the sea.[11]

INTERPOL had issued a Purple Notice against the vessel, which allows police worldwide to share information about vessels known or suspected of engaging in illegal fishing activities. In 2018, acting on a tip from INTERPOL, which was acting on a tip from New Zealand, the Indonesian Navy apprehended the *STS-50.*

The arrest was made after a 3-week chase across the Indian Ocean involving INTERPOL, FISH-i-Africa (a partnership of eight East African countries: Comoros, Kenya, Madagascar, Mauritius, Mozambique, Seychelles, Somalia, and the Republic of Tanzania), and Sea Shepherd Conservation Society, the antiwhaling and anti–illegal fishing advocacy organization. Sea Shepherd's *Bob Barker* vessel was named after the former host of *The Price Is Right,* a long-running TV game show, who chipped in $5 million to buy the boat in 2010. Other celebrity donors include Mick Jagger, Pierce Brosnan, Sean Penn, Uma Thurman, Ed Norton, and Martin Sheen.[12]

FISH-i-Africa is an enforcement model that has been tested under real-world conditions and designed to be replicated globally in resource-poor regions. Launched in December 2012 by Pew Charitable Trusts, FISH-i-Africa partner countries monitor and enforce fishing policies across exclusive economic zones that cover 1.9 million square miles. For comparison, the ocean territory of the "lower 48" states in the United States comprises about 3.1 million square miles.

There are several illegal-fishing hotspots—the Southern Indian Ocean, much of the Pacific, and both African coasts. Many African countries have reserved a nearshore zone for local, artisanal fishermen, who are particularly vulnerable to illegal incursions, in terms of losing catch and the risk of collisions and death. On top of that, corrupt African government leaders often make lucrative side deals with other countries (like China) to "legally" fish in African waters without public notice.

Sea Shepherd's mission is to partner with governments to assist with the detection and capture of criminal enterprises. Since 2016, Sea Shepherd has been fighting illegal fishing in the Gulf of Guinea in West Africa, in partnership with authorities in Gabon, and São Tomé and Príncipe. Sea Shepherd has been patrolling the Bouche du Roy Ecological Reserve, Africa's largest marine protected area, which has a mangrove swamp-and-lagoon ecosystem. The reserve is part of the UNESCO Ono Biosphere Reserve, a wildlife corridor rich in biodiversity, including migrating tuna and humpback whales. Since 2017, Sea Shepherd has also had a partnership, called Operation Sola Stella, with the Liberian Ministry of National Defense, and has arrested at least fifteen vessels. In 2018, Sea Shepherd joined Operation Jodari in partnership with Tanzania, with support from FISH-i-Africa, and joined forces with Benin. In 2019, Sea Shepherd launched a partnership with the Namibian Ministry of Fisheries and another with The Gambia.

The obvious problem with trying to police the global ocean is that it covers 70 percent of the planet. No country has the resources or will to effectively monitor and enforce their own waters, let alone the high seas—even with help from INTERPOL and Sea Shepherd (which has just three ships). Regional partnerships such as FISH-i-Africa are clearly needed to patrol vast tracts of the ocean. In South America, Uruguay, Brazil, and Argentina are talking about forming a similar regional ocean police force.

But even before Global Fishing Watch launched and before the robust regional partnerships, there were success stories. Protection of the Patagonian toothfish (aka Chilean sea bass) in the Southern Ocean stands out.

Patagonian toothfish became popular in high-end restaurants in the 1990s. Because they live in deep (up to 12,000 feet), cold waters around Antarctica, where there are few ships, the fish has been prize booty for pirates. The toothfish—it is not a sea bass and it is not really from Chile, although some are caught there—can grow to 7 feet or more and weigh up to 220 pounds. Toothfish are slow growing, don't reach sexual maturity until they are 8 to 10 years old, and have a low reproductive rate. The combination of poaching and slow population growth was pushing the toothfish toward extinction.

From 2014 to 2016, Sea Shepherd led Operation Icefish, a campaign to shut down the so-called Bandit Six, the last six vessels illegally fishing Patagonian toothfish in the Southern Ocean. Among other tools, Operation Icefish used $10,000 scanners to pick up buoy transmitters attached to illegal nets. The most notorious vessel was the *Thunder*, which Sea Shepherd vessels chased for 110 days over 11,550 nautical miles until the boat's captain abandoned and sank his ship to destroy evidence in the Gulf of Guinea, somewhere off the coast of Nigeria.[13]

The captain of the *Thunder* and two crew, who were rescued by Sea Shepherd, were sentenced to 3 years in prison and fined 15 million euros by a court in the island state of São Tomé and Príncipe in 2015. Owner González Corral (aka the "pirate fishing tycoon") went free until 2018, when he was fined 8.2 million euros, thanks to evidence seized by Sea Shepherd crew from the sinking vessel and the investigative journalism work of Kjetil Saeter and Eskil Engdal of the *Norwegian Business Daily*. Raids of properties belonging to Galician fishing syndicates by law enforcement agents working in Operation Sparrow—named after Johnny Depp's character in the movie *Pirates of the Caribbean*— had previously targeted other Spanish toothfish operators, including

Vidal Armadores, who was fined more than 17.8 million euros.[14] "One of Spain's poorer regions, Galicia is often described as the 'Sicily of Spain' because it is home to the country's most famous crime syndicates known for smuggling drugs, black-market tobacco, but most often illegal fish," says Ian Urbina, author of *Outlaw Ocean*.[15] The Patagonian toothfish fishery is now certified as sustainable by the Marine Stewardship Council.[16]

These white-collar pirates make Carlos Rafael, New Bedford's Codfather (see chapter 1), seem like an angel. An INTERPOL statement details the breadth of criminal behavior associated with illegal fishing—and its white-collar management structure:

> Money laundering, labor exploitation, corruption, and forgery are a small sample of serious crimes commonly committed during illegal, unreported and unregulated fishing today. Unlike a decade ago, it is not just fishing-vessel captains and owners who are responsible for present-day fisheries crime. It is largely down to business executives, public officials, lawyers, accountants, and other white-collar professionals. These executive criminals create shell companies in offshore financial havens. They conspire with accountants to launder money, nurture corrupt relationships with government officials, falsify regulatory documents, and consistently resort to forced labor on their ships.[17]

Illegal-fishing vessels generally target prized and rare fish, such as the Patagonian toothfish. Again, according to INTERPOL, "One kilo of Totoaba fish bladder [a rare and large porpoise found only in Mexico's Gulf of California] is worth more than 1 kilo of cocaine on illegal Asian markets—a low-risk, high reward alternative fetching up to $50,000 per bladder."[18]

But there is a soft spot in the illegal-fishing business model: Fishermen need to land and sell their fish, which gives international ports the ability to stop it cold. To that end, one of the most significant recent developments in curbing illegal fishing is the Port State Measures Agreement. This international agreement, signed in 2016, sets standards that ports need to apply when foreign vessels seek entry.

Any vessel suspected of illegal fishing can be inspected or denied access to port. To date, the port agreement has sixty-nine signatories, with China a notable exception.

Port inspections are less expensive and safer than monitoring, pursuing, and inspecting vessels at sea, but they require adequate investment in people, technology, and training to track information and share it across relevant agencies and countries. And, unlike cargo and passenger vessels that meet certain size requirements, fishing vessels are not required to adhere to the gold standard of unique vessel identifiers: the International Maritime Organization number. Given the importance to police worldwide of such identification numbers, there is no credible counterargument to requiring them on fishing vessels.[19]

A good example of how the Port State Measures Agreement can lead to the arrest of criminals is the case of the *MV NIKA*. In July 2019, Global Fishing Watch gave Panama a report on the 750-ton "cargo ship" flying a Panamanian flag that was suspected of illegally fishing in the Russian Arctic and as far south as the Georgia Islands east of Argentina. The *MV NIKA*, owned by the same Spanish outfit that owned the *STS-50*, was limping back to China (an 8,000 mile journey) after hitting an iceberg. When Panama was informed about the ship's activities, it alerted INTERPOL and Indonesia—aware that the *MV NIKA*'s route home might take it through Indonesian territory—and asked authorities that the vessel be intercepted and brought to port under the Port State Measures Agreement. The ship was picked up in the narrow Strait of Malacca, the main shipping route between China and India and one of the busiest waterways in the world. Ironically, the Strait has been a haven for pirates for centuries, given its lucrative cargo traffic, the lack of egress for large vessels, and the thousands of islets and many rivers that make it easy for small vessels to evade authorities. "We thank Global Fishing Watch for providing assistance to track *MV NIKA* until its apprehension in Indonesia," said Susi Pudjiastuti, Indonesian minister of Maritime Affairs and Fisheries.[20]

Another data-analysis tool is DETECT-IT, developed by the World Wildlife Fund, TRAFFIC (a wildlife trade–monitoring network), and Hewlett-Packard Enterprises. DETECT-IT analyzes

United Nations data tracking the movement of fish from port to port in more than 170 countries and flags suspicious activity.

Sovereign governments also have a role to play in choking illegal trade. The United States, for example, is the world's largest seafood importer. A 2014 study estimated that 20 to 32 percent of seafood imported into the United States was coming from illegal fishing.[21] In 2018, the US government officially activated the Seafood Import Monitoring Program to address the illegal seafood trade. The new rule sets up reporting and record-keeping requirements for certain seafood products, initially those fish and fish products identified as particularly vulnerable to illegal fishing and fraud.

Enforcement of laws, of course, is the "stick" in the fight against illegal fishing. But there is a "carrot": Fast-tracking compliant vessels so that they spend less time in port. Tony Long, CEO of Global Fishing Watch, has floated this idea:

> We could learn from "trusted-traveler," border-control programs, which operate in Canada, Germany, Japan, the United States and the United Kingdom, among others, and allow low-risk travelers expedited clearance upon arrival in a country. A similar process could apply to fishing vessels, with pre-screened, compliant ones being fast-tracked, while those with a record of infringements or missing paperwork face automatic scrutiny and a possible bar to entry. This is wholly in line with the principles of the Port State Measures Agreement but reverses the burden of proof: Operators must prove they are compliant."[22]

If there's a carrot for honest captains and fishermen, there's also a carrot for compliant countries: big rewards in sustaining their domestic fisheries and increasing profits. Countries whose exclusive economic zones are plundered by illegal fishing vessels could clamp down on illegal fishing in their territory and effectively put their own fisheries on the path to sustainability without the need for domestic reforms.

This has been the case in Indonesia, the world's leading producer of tuna and second largest producer of wild-capture fish. It had been losing $4 billion a year to illegal poachers and was ranked as the fifteenth and thirteenth nation most fished by foreign fleets in 2013 and 2014, respectively. Some illegal fishing comes from foreign boats that are authorized to fish but underreport the size of the boats, others disguise ownership under local names to take advantage of Indonesia's fuel subsidy, and others falsify permits to fish in water reserved for local artisanal fishers.

Starting around 2014, Indonesia banned foreign fleets within its territory and began to aggressively track down and destroy foreign vessels. The result, according to a paper in the journal *Nature: Ecology and Evolution*, is that total fishing effort has been reduced by 25–35 percent. Without banning foreign fleets, that outcome would have required a significant reduction in the domestic catch. Expanding beyond Indonesia, using levels of illegal fishing in other parts of the world, the authors project that this approach could significantly narrow the gap to achieving global sustainability, often without reducing catch or profit.[23]

These gains would not be remotely possible without the big-data tracking of vessels on the oceans in near real time. Global Fishing Watch data, for example, show that the top three flag states fishing in foreign economic zones between 2013 and 2016 were China, South Korea, and Taiwan—each illegally fishing in more than 50 foreign zones.

Using skipjack tuna as a model case study, the *Nature* authors found that the new Indonesian policies resulted in a 40 percent reduction in fishing effort. At the same time, Indonesia was increasing the capacity of its domestic fleet with more than 3,000 new boats. Because the boats are much smaller than the foreign vessels they replace, net fishing pressure will still be 25–35 percent lower than before the restrictions on foreign vessels.[24]

The Gambia, on the West coast of Africa, also banned all illegal fishing in its territory in 2015, targeting both foreign and domestic vessels. Using the high-value common octopus as the model species, the results in The Gambia were like those in Indonesia, in terms of catch and profits. The authors of the *Nature* paper conclude the following:

> Most regions of the world currently experience fishing pressure above the sustainable level [maximum sustainable yield]. If [illegal]

fishing was addressed in all regions, the gap to global fishery sustainability would narrow significantly and fisheries reform would become much more feasible. As was the case for Indonesia and The Gambia, addressing [illegal] fishing in many regions (that is, the northwest Pacific, eastern Indian, southwest Pacific and western-central Pacific oceans) could be sufficient to recover fisheries to sustainable exploitation levels while avoiding the dreaded "valley of death" [a loss in domestic catch and profits].[25]

That is one of the more optimistic statements in the recent annals of fisheries-management research. As the precision of big data accelerates, the cooperation between state and nonstate actors increases, and the world inches toward protection of 30 percent of the global ocean, it might even be prophetic.

FLOUNDER

Chapter 13

Conservation and Climate,
Adaptation and Resilience

*We are not doomed to do stupid things. We made the ivory trade
illegal, we made whaling illegal, we stopped smoking, we signed the
Montreal Protocol and the Paris Climate Change Agreement. We can
protect the high seas if we don't let laziness overtake us.*

—Daniel Pauly, University of British Columbia

When faced with data about overfishing, particularly in the
later decades of the twentieth century, it is reasonable to
ask: How many fish are left in the sea? How many species
have disappeared—or are on the verge of extinction?

A few years ago, *Science* magazine asked this question of Douglas
McCauley, an ecologist and director of the Benioff Ocean Initiative
at the University of California at Santa Barbara. His team responded
with good news and bad news.[1]

The good news: Marine fauna are generally in better condition than
terrestrial fauna. There have been far fewer extinctions, the ranges of
marine organisms have shrunk less, and marine ecosystems are much
more wild than terrestrial ecosystems. The International Union for
Conservation of Nature records only fifteen extinctions of marine-
animal species in the past 500-plus years and none in the last 50 years,
although many marine species are endangered (like the North Atlantic
right whale and the Atlantic salmon) and others are "data deficient."

Terrestrial extinctions began more than 10,000 years ago. Marine extinctions began several hundred years ago, even though humans have been harvesting marine organisms for 40,000 years. Compared to terrestrial animals, marine animals are effectively in the Pleistocene age, when humans started migrating from Africa and hunting land animals around the world. Consequently, rehabilitation of marine animals theoretically remains within the reach of managers and policy makers.

The bad news: "Complacency about the magnitude of contemporary marine extinctions is ill-advised," write McCauley et al. in *Science*. In the last four decades, marine fishes have declined in abundance by 38 percent, and some increasingly rare species—such as Pacific bluefin tuna and sea cucumbers—are being hunted and harvested with greater fervor as their value increases.[2] Individual Pacific bluefin tunas can sell for $100,000, and rare sea cucumbers and shark fins are worth hundreds of dollars per pound. As with elephant tusks, the value of some endangered organisms clearly makes it hard to curb humans' instinct for predation, although protection of the Patagonian toothfish gives a ray of hope (see chapter 12). "About a third of all corals are at threat of extinction, so are a third of sharks, a quarter of mammals, a fifth of all reptiles, and a sixth of all birds," David Wake and Vance Vredenburg suggest in their alarming paper, "Are We in the Midst of the Sixth Mass Extinction?"[3,4]

Terrestrial extinctions started after intense hunting and then continued as human population growth and development destroyed habitat. As marine hunting is more controlled, at least in certain parts of the world, the focus turns to habitat. McCauley et al. suggest that marine habitats may eventually join the ranks of once pristine terrestrial frontier areas, such as the American West, the Brazilian Amazon, and Alaska, that have been degraded by development. The authors conclude, "Comparing patterns of terrestrial and marine defaunation helps to place human impacts on marine fauna in context and to navigate toward recovery. Humans have caused few complete extinctions in the sea, but we are responsible for many ecological, commercial, and local extinctions. Despite our late start, humans have already powerfully changed virtually all major marine ecosystems."[5]

Much of the marine defaunation to date is a function of human predation and habitat destruction. But, as more controls are exerted by fisheries managers, climate change—another function of human behavior—is becoming an equally serious concern. At this point it is a lot easier to change predatory behavior (difficult as that is) than it is to slow climate change, the consequences of which are baked in for the next 50 or so years even if carbon emissions were to miraculously stop today.

The impacts of climate change—specifically warmer and more acidic ocean water—are changing the whole biogeochemistry of the ocean and threaten to accelerate marine defaunation over the next century. "Ocean animals are moving 10 times faster than animals fleeing climate change on land," says Malin Pinsky, a marine biologist at Rutgers University. "These range shifts are causing headaches for fishermen, who are forced to head farther out to sea or hundreds of miles further from home ports."[6]

Accelerated migration is not to be confused with adaptation. "Any more time we can buy for the rate of temperature and acidity to go up is going to buy more time for the ocean animals to adapt," says McCauley. "If the process doesn't totally swamp their physiology and knock them out it's possible they can adapt." Says Jon Hare, science and research director of NOAA Fisheries' Northeast Fisheries Science Center: "Marine organisms can certainly adapt, some better than others of course. But the unknown is whether they can adapt faster than the increasing pace of climate change."

Warming water and acidification are the two main impacts of climate change. For the moment, warming water is a more serious threat and one that has been much more widely studied. Warming waters will generally favor fish in the northern and southern latitudes, where the water is cooler, and adversely affect fish in tropical regions. Moreover, big fish will likely become smaller, as the energy and oxygen required by large animals to propel themselves through warm water will force physiological changes. As oceans heat up, hypoxic areas with low oxygen levels are expected to spread. Warmer ocean water holds less oxygen even as it increases animals' need for oxygen.[7]

"Metabolic rate increases with temperature, and big fish have less gill area per volume, which puts them in a squeeze as swimming in warmer temperatures requires more oxygen," says Daniel Pauly, director of the Sea Around Us project at the University of British Columbia. He, too, is quick to point out that a reduction in fish size is not adaptation. "Adaptation means you're doing fine. When fish respond to higher temperatures, they're being pushed and making the best of a bad situation."

Lisa Levin, a professor at Scripps Institution of Oceanography, says that when oxygen levels decrease, "it's effectively habitat loss."[8] In 2015, Curtis Deutsch, a professor of chemical oceanography at the University of Washington's School of Oceanography, and colleagues published a study in *Science* showing that the double bind of warm water and deoxygenation would change distributions for marine animals—and reduce their habitat by 14 to 26 percent. "Fish need more [oxygen], at the same time that they have less," said Deutsch.[9]

"Eventually, for every species, there comes a point where it can't actually get enough oxygen at very high temperatures to avoid being eaten or to catch enough to eat and survive itself," says Pinsky of Rutgers. "We're reshuffling the marine ecosystems like a deck of cards. We don't entirely know what will happen, but we know there will be surprises."[10]

Looking at the Northeast Continental Shelf, which stretches from Cape Hatteras in North Carolina up through the Gulf of Maine, black sea bass, butterfish, crabs, lobsters, striped bass, and bluefish are moving north. Other species are moving laterally into deeper waters and sometimes south and west into the deep canyons in the Gulf of Maine that were created by ancient glacial activity. In 2016, an analysis of eighty-two species by NOAA Fisheries scientists found that around half the fish and shellfish on the Northeast Continental Shelf were highly vulnerable to climate change. "Summer flounder [fluke], scup, black sea bass, longfin squid, and Jonah crab like it warm," says NOAA Fisheries' Hare, the lead author of the report. "Gone with the cold are cod, pollock, herring, cusk, and Northern shrimp."[11] "We're at a point, at least in the United States, where the fishing effort is well managed in most cases, but some species are recovering and others aren't. It's not just cod —yellowtail flounder, red hake, winter flounder, and other species are at historically low fishing rates and not rebuilding. That's because the environment is changing so dramatically that even a reduction is fishing is not going to help them recover. We long thought about fish stocks from the perspective of fishing pressure, but now it's from a perspective of climate, habitat degradation, *and* fishing pressure. Fishing effort is likely no longer the main driver of fish populations but a co-driver. For much of the last 20 years we were trying to rebuild cod without considering climate. Like most scientific questions, there are multiple hypotheses. Climate change is one of the prominent ones for why cod is not rebuilding."

In addition to its effects on high-trophic marine species, warming ocean water also affects phytoplankton at the bottom of the food chain. Like land plants, phytoplankton have chlorophyll to capture sunlight, and they use photosynthesis to turn it into chemical energy. They consume carbon dioxide and release oxygen—and are responsible for 50 percent of the oxygen humans breathe.

One mechanism that inhibits plankton growth is the stratification of water that keeps cold-water nutrients from "upwelling" to the top layer of warm water, where plankton bask in the sunlight. "A warming Arctic reduces the temperature differential between the Arctic and the tropics, which reduces the wind speed," says Pauly. "Yes, we will have bigger storms, but less ordinary wind, which means less ocean turbulence and less upwelling of nutrients."

A model developed by the Massachusetts Institute of Technology's Program in Atmospheres, Oceans and Climate suggests that if global temperature trends continue, by 2100 half the population of phytoplankton that existed in any given ocean at the beginning of the century will have disappeared.[12] If that happens, the marine food web will be altered in ways impossible to foresee.

Warming ocean water will clearly change the type, size, range, and lifespan of marine organisms. Ocean acidification, less well studied, will have known and unknown effects. The ocean is a great carbon sink, absorbing about one-third of the carbon dioxide from the atmosphere. Carbon dioxide sequestered in the ocean is called "blue carbon," to distinguish it from the "green carbon" that trees and plants sequester. Coastal habitats are important to this process even though they account for less than 2 percent of the ocean. Mangroves, sea grasses, and tidal mudflats and estuaries store more "blue carbon" per unit area than territorial forests, in some cases 400 percent or more, according to the Blue Carbon Initiative. Of course, these restorative coastal habitats are threatened by sea-level rise as well as development in many parts of the world (40 percent of the world's population lives within 60 miles of the coast).[13]

There is a limit to how much carbon dioxide the ocean can "buffer" and the result of excess carbon dioxide results in ocean acidification. Meanwhile, coastal acidification is more a function of nitrogen from agricultural waste and other chemical effluents from land. Ironically, phytoplankton need both carbon dioxide and nitrogen to grow, so the dynamic between promoting growth at the bottom of the food web and reducing acidification is complex. The acidity of the ocean today, on average, is about 25 percent higher than it was during preindustrial times.[14]

While more is known about the impacts of temperature than the impacts of ocean acidification, it is clear that acidification makes shell building more physiologically costly—mollusks or crustaceans need to exert energy on shell building to the detriment of the core organism. Eggs, larvae, and juveniles of some commercial shellfish are less likely to survive in more acidic waters. Meredith White, director of research and development at Mook Sea Farm in Walpole, Maine (see chapter 9) has conducted experiments to explore the vulnerability of juvenile oysters (between 1 to 3 years old) compared to larval oysters (0 to 1 year old) to acidic seawater. The results indicated that juvenile oysters aren't as sensitive to acidification as larval oysters are—in part because larval oyster shells are made of aragonite, a more soluble form of calcium carbonate than the shells of juvenile oysters. Other studies have shown that shellfish with thinner shells than oysters, such as mussels, tend to be more vulnerable to acidification, so each species must be assessed on a case-by-case basis.

Like larval oysters, coral skeletons are also made of aragonite. As acidity increases and carbonate ions decline in ambient seawater, corals can't produce as much aragonite to thicken the skeleton, according to research by the Woods Hole Oceanographic Institution. The corals continue to invest in upward growth, but "densification" or thickening suffers, making them more susceptible to damage from pounding waves or attacks by organisms.[15]

In New England, the effects of acidification are of critical importance because the Gulf of Maine's wild harvest is dominated (73 percent of value in 2017) by two species—lobsters and sea scallops—both susceptible to acidification.[16] Ironically, the Gulf of Maine, which is warming faster than the rest of the global ocean, is currently acidifying less quickly than other ocean regions. "Warm water holds less gas," says Samantha Siedlecki, an oceanographer at the University of Connecticut. "Because carbon dioxide is a gas, its absorption by the ocean is sensitive to those changes. But we should not get comfortable. By 2050, under the most severe emissions scenario, waters in this region will continue to absorb more carbon dioxide, and the impacts of acidification will ripple across the Gulf of Maine despite continued warming.[17]

Innovations in shellfish aquaculture could generate hatchery technologies to raise species like blue mussels and sea scallops that have proved difficult for marine biologists to spawn but may be more effectively raised in hatcheries moving forward. If and when that happens, hatchery broodstock programs will be able to select for offspring that are more tolerant of stressors like acidification.

Marine Protected Areas: Let the Ocean Heal

"We are not necessarily doomed to helplessly recapitulate the defaunation processes observed on land in the oceans," says the University of California's McCauley. "However, we must play catch-up in the realm of marine protected areas." Primarily created by governments in their exclusive economic zones, marine protected areas have the potential to increase conservation and biodiversity, and perhaps even mitigate the impacts of climate change.

Ocean reserves now cover about 7.6 percent of the world's oceans, although less than 3 percent are fully protected, no-take, no-use zones.[18] The United Nations General Assembly Sustainable Development Goal 14 was to protect 10 percent of the oceans by 2020, which did not happen; the current goal, which many nations support, is to set aside 30 percent of the global ocean to marine protected areas by 2030.

A dramatic example of how quickly nature can rebound when left alone is the restoration of Cabo Pulmo National Park in the Baha region of Mexico, a once vital fishing ground that turned barren after intense overfishing. In 1995, fishermen established a park with no-take restrictions. Between 1999 and 2009, a period when it was studied, the total amount of fish in the ecosystem (the "biomass") increased more than 460 percent. "In 1999, Cabo Pulmo was an underwater desert. Ten years later, it was a kaleidoscope of life and color," says Enric Sala, director of the National Geographic's Pristine Seas initiative. "I spent 20 years studying human impacts on the ocean. But when I saw firsthand the regeneration of places like Cabo Pulmo it gave me hope. I decided to quit my job as a university professor to dedicate my life to save more ocean places like this." Sala says humans have treated the oceans like a debit account with no deposits and eventually the account will run dry. Reserves, by contrast, are like a savings account that delivers compound interest to both fisheries and ocean conservation. Scientists say that recovery of marine life in Cabo Pulmo was at a level that made the reserve comparable to remote, pristine sites that have never been fished by humans.[19]

While there is an unofficial goal to put 30 percent of the global ocean into reserves by 2030, only one country has done so to date. Seychelles, an archipelago of 1,115 islands in the Indian Ocean, created thirteen protected reserves covering 158,000 square miles, an area larger than Germany. The multi-island nation is much more economically dependent on the ocean and more susceptible to the effects of coastal climate change than nations with a relatively larger land mass. But Seychelles also had an immediate economic incentive, thanks to a debt-financing enticement designed by The Nature Conservancy.

Blue Bonds for Conservation—a "debt for conservation deal"—allows nations that put 30 percent of their oceans in conservation to refinance sovereign debt at a lower interest rate and with a longer payback period. In the Blue Bonds program, The Nature Conservancy helps buy back sovereign debt at a discount using loans from investment banks. The lower interest rate and longer repayment term provide savings compared to the original loan. Seychelles signed the deal with The Nature Conservancy in February 2016 and met its conservation goals in early 2020. The Seychelles government bought back $21.6 million of its sovereign debt at a discount; the loan restructuring frees up $430,000 a year to fund management of the protected marine reserves.

"The genesis of the debt-restructuring idea was built on work we had done in rain forests, although we were using debt forgiveness there," says Melissa Garvey, global director, Ocean Protection, at The

Nature Conservancy. "The series of storms in recent years that caused damage in the Caribbean and left countries with high debt for the rebuilding loans led us to think about ways to restructure the debt."

The Nature Conservancy is scaling up its Blue Bonds program, working with stable governments that have a high debt-to-GDP ratio, weak credit ratings, and have ocean areas with opportunities to make significant conservation gains, such as coral reefs, mangrove swamps, or fisheries—what Garvey calls "enabling conditions."

With the Seychelles pilot as a proof of concept, Garvey is looking to engage China, which holds a vast amount of debt for developing countries, about the possibility of debt forgiveness in exchange for a commitment to conservation, either terrestrial or marine. "Given the scale and scope of China's fishing effort, it could be a face-saving and reputational benefit for them," says Garvey. "But it's a bit of a pipe dream."

So is the idea of closing the "high seas" to fishing. In 2014, Christopher Costello, a colleague of McCauley at UC Santa Barbara, and Crow White, of the California Polytechnic State University, published a paper in the *PLOS Biology* journal suggesting just that: entirely closing the high seas to fishing.[20]

The "high seas" encompass all the oceans that are not part of sovereign economic zones and comprise 59 percent of the global ocean. This was a thunderbolt of an idea. Currently, the only part of the high seas that is protected by a marine-protected area is the Ross Sea in Antarctica. The Weddell Sea, along the Antarctic Peninsula and one of the most pristine marine ecosystems in the world, has been proposed as a marine protected area but that is not yet agreed to by the twenty-nine "consultative parties" of the forty-eight countries that have signed the Antarctic Treaty.

White and Costello posit that completely closing the high seas to fishing would simultaneously give rise to large gains in fisheries profit (> 100 percent), fishery yields (> 30 percent), and fish-stock conservation (> 150 percent). "Smaller marine protected areas, increasingly common and well studied in coastal waters, are too small to produce significant benefits for most migratory stocks. Also, closing only a portion of the high seas may simply displace fishing effort to other open-access areas, thereby leaving the problem unsolved," White and Costello wrote.[21]

How can their projected gains be possible? How can fisheries' profits and yields increase while stocks rebuild? Pauly's answer is that the high seas yield just 6 percent of the world's catch (and 8 percent of catch value), and many of those fish would migrate into sovereign economic zones as stocks rebuild, so the net loss of catch would be minimal. Most fish in the high seas, like tuna, are hypermigratory. The theory is that if they are left alone in the high seas to rebuild they will be more plentiful and migrate in and out of sovereign-state economic zones.

A high-seas fishing ban might also result in more equitable global distribution of fish, with more fish migrating into sovereign economic zones on both African coasts, Southeast Asia, and the Caribbean, regions where larger percentages of artisanal fishers and people are dependent on fish for livelihoods and protein. Countries most adversely affected by such a high-seas fishing ban would be China, Taiwan, Japan, Indonesia, Spain, and South Korea, which accounted for 77 percent of the global high-seas fishing fleet in 2014 and a significant majority of the global high-seas fishing revenue.[22]

Closing off all the high seas may seem to be an ambitious and idealistic goal, given some of the voracious fishing nations that would need to sign off on a United Nations resolution. "The idea is not idealistic," Pauly insists. "The 400-mile exclusive economic zones were laughed at when countries such as Peru and Costa Rica proclaimed them, but today we have 200-mile economic zones, so it wasn't a crazy idea. The high seas are exploited for tuna and sharks by a handful of countries that heavily subsidize their fleets. If the World Trade Organization were to forbid subsidies, which came close to happening in the Doha round [the last round of international trade negotiations], the high-seas fisheries would go bankrupt." That's because, between fuel and labor costs, high seas fishing is expensive. Researchers estimate that as much as 54 percent of high seas fishing would be unprofitable were it not for government subsidies, estimated at $35 billion a year.[23] "If it costs so much, provides so little food, and reaps such ecological damage, the glaring question is, why trawl for fish in the deep at all?" asks Helen Scales in her book, *The Brilliant Abyss*.[24]

Pauly suggests that the current approach to expansive fishing is essentially a Ponzi scheme—when humans fish out one area they move on to another and another. At some point there will be no more territory to exploit, and the scheme will collapse:

> A few decades ago, when global catches were higher (yes, higher!), we were exploiting a smaller fraction of the ocean. However, in most of the world, rather than rebuilding stocks that were overexploited, fisheries expanded, and catch was maintained through expansion. Marine-protected areas contribute to reversing the trend: rather than obtaining our seafood from far away, we should obtain it from our rebuilt stocks. Otherwise, our footprint will keep expanding even if catches do not grow, just as the impact of mining grows even when production does not. Here again, the United States took a very positive stance, with the first large no-take marine reserve in the northwestern Hawaiian Islands and the first scientifically designed network of marine-protected areas in California.[25]

Since passage of California's Marine Life Protection Act in 1999, approximately 16 percent of state waters have been protected by 124 marine reserves that represent most marine and estuarine habitats, which are designed to be ecologically connected. The public–private planning effort, which took almost 7 years and was not without controversy, was backed by $19.5 million in private charitable foundation funds and $18.5 million in public funds.[26]

To date, the roughly 8 percent of the global ocean protected by reserves has been a quasi-random effort by certain countries. The vast majority of the 16,500-plus reserves are quite small, less than 4 square miles; only sixty are more than 38,000 square miles. The four biggest are Weddell Sea (proposed), Ross Sea, the National Park of the Coral Sea, and the US Pacific Remote Islands. Thanks in large part to the Pacific Remote Islands, along with the Papahānaumokuākea (pronounced Papa-ha-now-moh-koo-ah-kay-ah)[27] Marine National Monument in the Northwestern Hawaiian Islands, the United States has 26 percent of its ocean territory protected to various degrees.

While the idea of closing off all the high seas is appealing to many biologists and economists, doing so would require agreement by all the world's fishing nations, a big political lift. The last major international treaty governing the ocean was the 1982 ratification of the

United Nations Convention on the Law of the Sea, which established the 200-mile exclusive economic zones and remains the foundation for international discussion. Some international treaties on whaling and highly migratory species predate the 1982 UN treaty. The International Convention for the Conservation of Atlantic Tuna, for example, was adopted in 1966. But such treaties can take decades to ratify.

A 2021 paper published in *Nature*—"Protecting the Global Ocean for Biodiversity, Food, and Climate"—suggests a more methodical and targeted "conservation-planning framework." The authors (*National Geographic's* Enric Sala was the lead) analyze the most effective way for marine protected areas to provide three inter-related benefits: protecting biodiversity, boosting the yield of fisheries, and securing marine carbon.[28]

Identifying where ocean reserves would be most effective at achieving these goals, the authors found that 90 percent of the top 10 percent priority areas lay within national ocean territories—that is, they are not part of the high seas. The remaining effective areas on the high seas were in seamount clusters, offshore plateaus, and biogeographically unique areas, like the Antarctic Peninsula.[29]

After trialing different approaches to determine the best planning framework—the one that provided the maximum potential benefits across all three areas—the authors chose to focus on the highest benefits to biodiversity and fishing yield.

"If society were to value biodiversity benefits as much as food-provision benefits, the optimal conservation strategy would protect 45 percent of the global ocean and would deliver 72 percent of the maximum potential biodiversity benefits, 92 percent of food-provisioning benefits, and 29 percent of carbon benefits.

The authors also suggest that if 71 percent of the ocean were put into a reserve, 91 percent of the biodiversity and 48 percent of the carbon benefits would accrue with no change in the future yields of fisheries. If, on the contrary, we placed no value on biodiversity, the optimal strategy would call for the protection of 28 percent of the ocean, providing a net gain of 5.9 million metric tons of seafood and incidentally securing 35 percent of biodiversity benefits.

"This framework is clearly flexible and can be used in different ways by different governments and international bodies," write the authors.

Applying this conservation-planning and climate-mitigation framework in a globally coordinated fashion would prove Pauly's point: "We are not necessarily doomed to do stupid things."

New Bedford 4.0 and Coastal Resilience

Ocean-use planning is about preserving wild habitats and marine animals—and trying to make sure people aren't doomed to do "stupid things." Planning for resilience in coastal communities is more about people, their livelihoods and economic security. It acknowledges that both are dependent on the health of the ocean and tries to make sure people do "smart things."

In the 400-plus years that New Englanders have been harvesting seafood from the ocean, there have been many eras of resilience after economic declines. New Bedford, the top-value port in the United States, has had three overlapping eras of industrial economic dominance and is now methodically planning for a fourth. After 20 years during which fish have generally done better than the fishermen, what is happening in New Bedford is a microcosm of what is happening all along the New England coast: communities are tactically leveraging valuable marine know-how and assets to build a new BlueTech economy in the postindustrial age.

Starting in the early 1800s, New Bedford was the top whaling port in the United States. At the height of the industry in 1857, the harbor hosted 329 vessels, and New Bedford was the richest city in the world, per capita. For its whale-derived lamp oil, New Bedford was known as the "City That Lit the World."[30] Alas, 2 years later, in 1859, petroleum was discovered in Titusville, Pennsylvania, and the value of whale oil began to diminish (as did the whale population). By 1880, the year after Thomas Edison invented the light bulb, San Francisco was the largest whaling port in the United States. That was New Bedford 1.0.

New Bedford 2.0—textile manufacturing—started before the peak of whaling with a mill to manufacture cotton cloth in 1846. By the turn of the nineteenth century, New Bedford was one of the largest producers of cotton yarns and textiles in the United States. In 1875 alone, the Wamsutta Mills produced 20 million yards of cloth, which had a wholesale value comparable to that of the entire whaling catch. By

1920, New Bedford had twenty-eight cotton establishments and seventy cotton mills employing more than 41,000 workers.[31] Once again a rich city, New Bedford's wealth would evaporate with the Depression, World War II, and the southerly migration of textile companies fleeing the unionized North.

New Bedford 3.0—commercial fishing—started in the early 1890s before the peak of the textile industry, with sloops and catboats fishing for mackerel, swordfish, groundfish, and bay scallops. By the 1930s, seven out of ten scallop draggers fishing on Georges Bank were from New Bedford. By the 1960s, 95 percent of all scallops were landed in New Bedford. By the early 1990s, New Bedford was the top grossing port in the United States.[32] It lost that perch due to severe declines in cod and scallops but regained it in 2000 and has maintained it for the last 20 years.

Now, New Bedford 4.0 is unfolding—building on the port's infrastructure and commercial fishing expertise but expanding into renewable offshore energy, mariculture, and marine innovation and ocean technology. In the same way, Maine is leveraging its marine know-how to build a vibrant mariculture industry while protecting its traditional fisheries.

In 2021, the New Bedford Economic Development Council forged an alliance between the New Bedford Port Authority, a public nonprofit, and the New Bedford Ocean Cluster, a private nonprofit (see chapter 5). "It's our goal to ensure that the vast number of enterprises that support America's number 1 fishing port also play a role in wind, aquaculture, and technology-based industries into the future," says Ed Anthes-Washburn, former director of the Port, now director of business development at Crowley Maritime, a marine-logistics company, and vice-chair and cofounder of the New Bedford Ocean Cluster. "The port is the nexus for people and services for a 6-mile band, extending 3 miles to sea and 3 miles inland, which is crucial to ocean health, economic health, and community health," says Chris Rezendes, a cofounder (with Washburn) of the Cluster.

The city is looking to designate 8,400 ocean acres as eligible for mariculture. (Dale Leavitt of Blue Stream Shellfish has the first permit for a pilot in New Bedford's outer harbor for a bottom-cage [25 feet deep] oyster farm.) "As the leading seafood hub on the East Coast,

New Bedford's industrial waterfront contains an astounding resource of seafood infrastructure—a labor force, fuel, ice, packaging, cold storage, vessel repair and equipment supplies—that certainly could be integrated into a burgeoning aquaculture industry," according to a 2018 study on aquaculture opportunity.[33]

The city is also looking to add and upgrade fish-processing facilities, along with dredging the inner harbor and adding pier facilities for bigger vessels, more of which are coming from distant ports between Maine and Florida. But it first wants to cement its role in offshore-wind energy. The National Offshore Wind Institute, under the auspices of the Bristol Community College, is part of the New Bedford Ocean Cluster, as is Xodus Group, a leading global-energy consultancy.

After a long permitting process, Vineyard Wind is now building the first large-scale, offshore wind-energy system in the United States, 35 miles from New Bedford Harbor and 15 miles south of Martha's Vineyard. Vineyard Wind and Mayflower Wind, which has also won a lease from the state as the second of three wind developers, have signed leases worth over $30 million to utilize the New Bedford Marine Commerce Terminal, which the Commonwealth invested $113 million, primarily in state bonds, to fortify for heavy industrial use.[34] In addition, in 2021 private investors bought a 29-acre power station that had been decommissioned in 1992 with a plan to develop more staging infrastructure for the wind industry. Vineyard Wind plans to erect sixty-two 850-foot wind turbines, each separated by a nautical mile, to generate 800 megawatts of electricity, enough to power 400,000 homes each year. Another 1,600 megawatts are planned.

This massive project gives New Bedford the *potential* to be the national leader in another industry, which is exciting from an economic-development and clean-energy perspective. But fishermen don't see it that way. They see the project as another case of the government infringing on their unfettered access to the ocean. Rhode Island and Massachusetts fisheries have vociferously opposed the project from the beginning, saying that the turbines create navigational hazards en route to Georges Bank and the mid-Atlantic Bight, and may disturb habitat when cables are buried to deliver power to substations on land. From the fishermen's perspective, the wind project is a new front in the ongoing battle over catch quotas and closing of fishing grounds.

To allay concerns, Vineyard Wind is providing fishermen in Massachusetts and Rhode Island with an estimated $16 million in each state to mitigate any loss of fishing opportunities or for investment in new fishing gear.

Welcoming the nascent wind industry while supporting the historic fishing industry has clearly required some political jujitsu. The battle lines are similar in many ways to the "social-license" wars in Maine over siting of both land-based and ocean-based salmon farms. In both cases, two very different industries are sharing the same waters, and in New Bedford, the same harbor.

"The mayor convinced enough supporters of the fishing industry that offshore wind wouldn't take over the port," says Anthony Sapienza, president of the New Bedford Economic Development Council. New Bedford mayor Jon Mitchell says that the wind-energy siting area—which was identified as the windiest portion of the ocean off the continental United States—has historically not been as heavily fished as other areas and presents one of the lowest potential conflicts with commercial fishing. "I believe that both industries can successfully coexist, but there has to be an honest dialogue about which areas pose the greatest conflict and which ones don't," Mitchell said. "In New Bedford, we want to continue to be America's leader in fishing and we want to eventually be America's leader in offshore wind."[35]

This is "new think" you wouldn't have heard 5 years ago—the idea that traditional fisheries aren't doomed but can take a new path to sustainable, long-term success, and that centuries of accumulated wisdom and experience can be the springboard to vibrant, new marine industries.

As Chris Rezendes of the New Bedford Ocean Cluster, says, "No one wants to be the one to catch the last fish!"

Acknowledgments

I started thinking about and researching this book in January 2017, more than 5 years ago. After my preliminary research, one of the first people I spoke to was John Bullard. A former mayor of New Bedford, John was then NOAA Fisheries' Greater Atlantic Regional Administrator. John was generous with his time and gave me a great overview of fishery-management issues on the East Coast. He introduced me to several people at NOAA Fisheries, including Jon Hare, science and research director of the Northeast Fisheries Science Center, and Michael Rubino, NOAA Fisheries' senior adviser for Seafood Strategy (and formerly director of the Office of Aquaculture). Michael has a keen sense of what US fisheries need to do to compete with the rest of the world. Jon described in detail the complexity of fisheries management, given the number of species and ecosystems, and a shifting climate. He introduced me to others at NOAA Fisheries, including Gary Wikfors, chief of aquaculture sustainability at NOAA Fisheries' Milford Laboratory. Thanks to Fred Whoriskey, director of the Ocean Tracking Network managed by Dalhousie University, I would later talk with NOAA Fisheries scientists John Kocik at the University of Maine and Tim Sheehan, in Woods Hole, Massachusetts, about dam removals and the upriver return of spawning fish. I did the same with Mark Rasmussen and Brendan Annett of the Buzzards Bay Coalition.

In New Bedford, I talked many times with Ed Anthes-Washburn, then director of the New Bedford Port Authority. Despite Ed's heavy workload managing and expanding the nation's top fishing port, he was happy to talk about larger trends and specific New Bedford issues as the fleet was reshaping after 25 tough years. I thank Eli Powell, who was then working with Ed to help develop aquaculture in New Bedford, for his reporting on new port developments. Cassie Canastra, director of operations at the Buyers and Sellers Exchange (BASE) auction, kindly let me visit an (electronic) auction during the

COVID lockdown. Ralph Pope, a veteran fish dealer who exported dogfish to France and monkfish livers to Japan, among other transactions, knew all the players. Scalloper Danny Eilertsen allowed me on board the *Liberty* to see his QR-system for freshly packed bags of shucked scallops. Chris Rezendes, chief business officer at Spherical Analytics, preached the power and value of "immutable data in a cyber-physical world." Brian Rothschild, the founding dean of the School for Marine Science & Technology at the UMass Dartmouth, and Professor Kevin Stokesbury, shared their long-term perspectives on surveying Atlantic fish stocks. Laura Orleans, executive director of the New Bedford Fishing Heritage Center, a folklorist and ethnographer preserving the history of the waterfront, was a font of ideas and leads.

One of my early supporters was Rockford ("Rocky") Weitz, director of The Fletcher School's Maritime Studies Program. At one of Rocky's many Fletcher Arctic Conferences I met Thor Sigfusson, founder of the Iceland Ocean Cluster; 2 years later I joined Rocky and a group of Fletcher students at the Arctic Circle Assembly in Iceland and stayed on for a few days to meet with Thor and tour the Iceland Ocean Cluster. I credit Crocker Snow, who was director of the Edward R. Murrow Center at Fletcher, for initiating the Arctic conference, and I thank Robert Barber, a friend and former Ambassador to Iceland, for facilitating meetings in Iceland—and for bringing Thor Sigfusson to New Bedford to inspire the launch the New Bedford Ocean Cluster. I also met several times with Patrick Arnold, founder of the New England Ocean Cluster, another spinoff of the Iceland cluster. I attended many cluster events in Portland, Maine, which connected me with dynamic entrepreneurs, fishers, and farmers, many quoted in the book. Bhaskar Chakravorti, dean of global business at The Fletcher School, produced the Ocean's Turn conference in 2019 and included me as an adviser, which gave me a chance to dig into many of the fishing-related issues covered in this book. Dorothy Orszulak, in charge of corporate engagement at The Fletcher School, was also a driver of that conference and has been a support to me in various projects for more than 20 years. I invited Paul Greenberg, author of *Four Fish* and writer-in-residence at the Safina Center, to keynote Ocean's Turn, and later met Carl Safina, founder of the center. Both are leaders in blending "science, art, and literature" to promote action on sustainable fishing and ocean restoration. Andy and Amy Burnes, and Dan Noyes, first introduced me to the wonders and vastness of the open ocean.

Alissa Peterson, cofounder and executive director of SeaAhead, a BlueTech-innovation incubator in Boston and Providence, connected me to her global network through "brown-bag" lunches, both real and virtual. Alissa also published some of my early stories on fishing. Through SeaAhead I met Luke Sawitsky, a former fish buyer turned fisheries advocate (at Catch Invest) who gave me multiple names and leads in the early days of my research; and Taylor Witkin, program manager at SeaAhead, who had worked with the Local Catch Network and introduced me to Josh Stoll, the founder. I enjoyed several seafood lunches with Kate Masury, director of Eating with the Ecosystem, a nonprofit that promotes "underutilized" fish, and local fishermen and coastal communities. She introduced me to Kelly Harrell of Sitka (Alaska) Salmon Shares and Stuart Melzer, owner of Fearless Fish Market in Providence. Peter Neill, founder and director of the World Ocean Observatory, published an early essay called "Imagining a Post-Industrial Future for Fishing" in the World Ocean Forum. Sarah Kelley, then a senior program officer at the Island Foundation near New Bedford, was an early fan of the book's topic and a steady supporter.

Doing research is fun—but figuring out what to do with gobs of information is work. Consultation with a variety of accomplished writers and editors helped. Victoria Pope, a writer and former editor at *U.S. News & World Report* and *National Geographic* magazines, urged me to beware of an overly academic approach to a visceral topic. Fen Montaigne, an author and senior editor at *Yale Environment 360*, encouraged me to find experts and tell their stories. To that end, he introduced me to Daniel Pauly, director of the *Sea Around Us* project at the University of British Columbia, one of the country's most cited scientists (and *I* cite him often) and Douglas McCauley, an ecologist who teaches at the University of California at Santa Barbara. When I told Tom Peters, author of the best-selling *In Search of Excellence* books, that I had been awarded a writing residency and wondered if I should use it to write a book proposal, he quickly squashed that idea:

Just write the book! Two gifted science writers, Alan Poole (former editor of the *Birds of North America* series and author of several books on birds) and Ann Parson (a prolific writer on science and medicine), encouraged me with periodic check-ins on progress. Sadia Shepard, who teaches documentary film at Wesleyan University, got me excited about doing a podcast but thought the book should come first. The Zoom H6 tape recorder she suggested was invaluable. Tom Swift, a lawyer with experience in the music and movie business, got me excited about translating my seafood story into film. Maybe some day.

Mentors from a previous era include Claudia Cohl, a legendary editor at Scholastic, who taught me to "write for the reader, not yourself." Adrian Slywotzky, a renowned consultant at Oliver Wyman, with whom I worked, modeled for me the practice of diving deeper and deeper into a topic until you can connect and make sense of all the dots.

Most of the final manuscript was written during the COVID lockdown so I thank the farmers and processors that invited me to visit their operations (not all of which happened): American Mussel Harvesters, Bangs Island Mussels, Blue Stream Aquaculture, Cuttyhunk Shellfish Farms, Foley Fish, Great Falls Aquaculture, Gulf of Maine Sashimi, Hudson Valley Farms, Ideal Fish, Island Creek Oysters, Mook Sea Farm, and New Hampshire Sea Grant's AquaFort.

I thank The Rockefeller Foundation for the opportunity to develop my rough idea at the Bellagio Residence Center in Italy. In particular, I thank Pilar Palacia, director of the Bellagio Center, for providing such a collaborative, productive, and inspirational work environment. I got a great start on this book at Bellagio in May 2019, and that positive experience pulled me through some bumps and roadblocks until I submitted the manuscript 2 years later.

Island Press took my proposal and helped shape it into a book. I thank the Island Press team, led by president David Miller, for its support of this book and David Ter-Avaneyan for a beautiful cover design. Erin Johnson, my editor, was an ally from the proposal stage onward, a wonderful navigational guide with a light and persuasive touch throughout the process of producing a book.

The map of the Northeast Fishing Grounds at the front of the book was created by Michelle Bachman, a fisheries analyst at the New

England Fisheries Management Council, who undertook the project on her own time. Artist Stephanie Mason, whose fish prints I describe in the preface, worked tirelessly to convert her color images to black-and-white, and to photograph and scan them in high resolution (600 dots-per-inch). Phil Mello, a plant manager at Bergie's Seafood in New Bedford and a long-time photographer of the working water-front, whose work is on display at the Library of Congress, took my author photo on the working waterfront.

My sister, Suzanne, introduced me to *The Book of Eels*, which I have referenced. My brother, Tim, introduced me to several of his for-mer colleagues at The Nature Conservancy, including Sally McGee (Shellfish Growers Climate Coalition) and Melissa Garvey (Ocean Protection), who in turn introduced me to Robert Jones (Global Lead for Aquaculture). My daughters, Sarah J. and Lucy, gave me constant encouragement about the book and were a test foil for my fish factoids and stories. I have dedicated this book to my wife, Deborah Kovacs, an author and editor of young-adult fiction—for her love, encouragement, and canny editorial advice. She was the first to read through tens of thousands of words. I used her comments to revise, but neither she nor any of the others mentioned here are responsible for any content, or errors of omission or commission!

Nicholas P. Sullivan, June 2021

Notes

1. Sacred Cod, Sustainable Scallops

Epigraph: Jeffrey Bolster, *The Mortal Sea: Fishing the Atlantic in the Age of Sail.* (Cambridge, Harvard University Press, 2012): 220.

1. Brendan Borrell, "The Last Trial of the Codfather," *Hakai Magazine*, January 10, 2017.

2. Jesse Bidgood, "A Famed Fishing Port Shudders as Its Codfather Goes to Jail," *New York Times*, February 11, 2018.

3. Ben Goldfarb, "The Deliciously Fishy Case of the 'Codfather,'" *Mother Jones*, March 15, 2017.

4. Jason Hoffman, "Codfather Gets Early Release from Prison Amid COVID-19 Concerns," *Undercurrent News*, June 29, 2020.

5. Borrell, "Last Trial."

6. Bidgood, "A Famed Fishing Port Shudders."

7. Kathleen McKiernan and Andy Tomolonis, "Fishing Mogul Carlos Rafael Arrested on Federal Conspiracy Charges," *Standard-Times*, March 1, 2016.

8. Borrell, "Last Trial."

9. Doug Fraser, "Petition to NOAA Calls for Prohibition on Cod Fishing," *Standard-Times*, February 13, 2020.

10. Richard Volkomir, review of *Cod: A Biography of the Fish That Changed the World*, by Mark Kurlansky, *Smithsonian Magazine*, May 1998.

11. A. A. Rosenberg et al., "The History of Ocean Resources: Modeling Cod Biomass Using Historical Records," *Frontiers in Ecology and the Environment*, 3 (2005): 84–90.

12. Daniel Pauly and Ashley McCrea Strub, "Atlantic Cod: Past and Present," Sea Around Us, University of British Columbia, June 6, 2011.

13. Katy Donoghue, "Maya Lin Asks: What Is Missing?" *Art & Innovation Talks by Whitewall*, August 22, 2016.

14. Daniel Pauly, *Vanishing Fish* (Washington, DC: Island Press, 2019), 92.

15. "Northern Cod Failure Continues after Last Year's Harmful Decision to Hike Up Quota," *Oceana Canada*, July 9, 2020.

16. Fishing Heritage Center, "The Overfishing Metaphor: Conversation with Brian Rothschild," in *Working Waterfront Festival Program Guide* (New Bedford Fishing Heritage Center, 2012), https://fishingheritagecenter.org/wp-content/uploads/2016/03/Overfishing-Metaphor-by-Dr.-Brian-Rothschild-2012.pdf.

17. Andrew J. Pershing et al., "Slow Adaptation in the Face of Rapid Warming

Leads to Collapse of the Gulf of Maine Cod Fishery," *Science* 350, no. 6262 (November 13, 2015): 809–812.

18. Sam Walker, "Georges Bank Closes, Ending an Era," *Christian Science Monitor*, December 12, 1994.

19. James J. Corbett, "An Overview of Cod Fishing Regulations: Implications for the New England Fishing Industry," *Journal of Food Distribution Research* 35, no. 1 (March 2004): 51–52.

20. Jay Lindsay, "New Data on Cod Could Have Dire Impact on Industry," *Boston Globe*, November 26, 2011.

21. Mark Kurlansky, *Cod: A Biography of the Fish That Changed the World* (New York: Penquin/Random House, July 1998).

22. Wikipedia, https://en.wikipedia.org/wiki/Allee_effect.

23. Charles Darwin, *On the Origin of Species* (New York: Signet, 2003).

24. "New Bedford Worries about What Happens to the Codfather's Fishing Permits," WBUR Radio, Boston, April 11, 2017.

25. Michael Liddel and Melissa Yencho, eds., "Fisheries of the United States 2019," National Marine Fisheries Service Office of Science and Technology, May 2021.

26. "Scallopers See a Livelihood Imperiled," *New York Times*, April 19, 1993.

27. Rory Nugent, *Down at the Docks* (New York: Anchor Books/Random House, 2010): 89–91.

28. Nugent, *Down at the Docks*, 108–110.

29. Carol Lee Costa-Crowell, "Recalling the Drug Boats," *Standard-Times*, February 15, 1996.

30. Allison Guy, "How Science and a Bit of Luck Brought Atlantic Sea Scallops Back from the Brink," *Oceana*, June 6, 2006.

31. Guy.

32. Brock B. Bernstein and Suzanne Iudicello, "National Evaluation of Cooperative Data Gathering Efforts in Fisheries," National Fisheries Conservation Center, November 21, 2000.

33. American Scallop Association, "America's Most Valuable Fishery—Atlantic Scallops—Is Certified 'Sustainable' by Marine Stewardship Council," *Saving Seafood*, December 19, 2013.

34. Jennette Barnes, "SouthCoast Man of the Year: Kevin Stokesbury Continues to Seek Solutions to Fishing Industry Challenges," *Standard-Times*, January 3, 2019.

35. Guy, "How Science and a Bit of Luck."

36. Scott Allen, "Regulators Ease Fishing Ban on Georges Bank," *Boston Globe*, April 15, 1999.

37. American Scallop Association, "America's Most Valuable Fishery."

38. Bernstein and Iudicello, "National Evaluation of Cooperative Data Gathering."

39. Bernstein and Iudicello.

40. Kevin D. E. Stokesbury, "The New Bedford Fishery Now and Onward," *New Bedford Harbor in a New Light*, UMASS Art Gallery catalog.

41. Kevin D. E. Stokesbury and N. David Bethoney, "How Many Sea Scallops

Are There and Why Does It Matter?" *Frontiers in Ecology and the Environment* 18, no. 9 (November 2020), https://doi.org/10.1002/fee.2244.

42. Bernstein and Iudicello, "National Evaluation of Cooperative Data Gathering."

43. The latest School for Marine Science and Technology pyramidical camera rig (2019) has hi-res video that is six times sharper than TV resolution and can identify scallops merely 10 mm in diameter (less than the size of a dime). These data are publicly available on a Google-Earth website that allows viewers to click on grids from Carolina to Canada and see the density and size of the scallops (see BIT.LY/scallopsurvey).

44. Stokesbury and Bethoney, "How Many Sea Scallops Are There?"

45. 65th Northeast Regional Stock Assessment Workshop (65th SAW) Assessment Summary Report, Northeast Fisheries Science Center, August 2018.

46. American Scallop Association, "America's Most Valuable Fishery."

47. American Scallop Association.

48. Steve Urbon, "SMAST Founding Dean, Chancellor Medal Recipient Brian Rothschild, Reflects on State of Fisheries Science," *Standard-Times*, May 16, 2016.

2. Changing Rules for a Changing Ecosystem

Epigraph: Daniel Pauly, *Vanishing Fish* (Washington, DC: Island Press, 2019), 64.

1. "Disaster Declaration Issued for NE Groundfish Industry," *Martha's Vineyard Times*, September 13, 2012.

2. "Daniel Pauly Amongst the World's Most Cited Scientists," Sea Around Us, University of British Columbia, November 21, 2019.

3. Trevor Branch et al., "The Trophic Fingerprint of Marine Fisheries," *Nature* 468 (2010): 431–435.

4. Chris Costello et al., "The Future of Food from the Sea," *Nature* 588 (2020): 95–100.

5. Pauly, *Vanishing Fish*.

6. Michael Liddel and Melissa Yencho, eds., "Fisheries of the United States 2019," National Marine Fisheries Service Office of Science and Technology, May 2021.

7. Virginia Gewin, "Time to Flip the Ocean Script—from Victim to Solution," Society of Environmental Journalists, October 14, 2020, https://www.sej.org/publications/sej-news/time-flip-ocean-script-victim-solution.

8. Slow Fish, "Swordfish," http://www.slowfood.com/slowfish/pagine/eng/pagina--id_pg=110.lasso.html.

9. "Swordfish—a Sustainable Seafood Choice," NOAA Fisheries, November 8, 2012, https://www.fisheries.noaa.gov/feature-story/swordfish-sustainable-seafood-choice.

10. William Warner, *Distant Water* (New York: Penguin, 1984).

11. Ray Hilborn and Ulrike Hilborn, *Overfishing* (New York: Oxford University Press, 2012).

12. Hilborn and Hilborn, *Overfishing*.

13. Michael Conathan, "Waking from the Gluttony," Center for American Progress, March 11, 2011.

14. Jim Leape, "Harnessing the Fourth Industrial Revolution for Oceans," *World Economic Forum Agenda*, November 2017.

15. Andrew J. Pershing et al., "Slow Adaptation in the Face of Rapid Warming Leads to Collapse of the Gulf of Maine Cod Fishery," *Science* 350, no. 6262 (November 13, 2015): 809–812.

16. Laura Poppick, "Why Is the Gulf of Maine Warming Faster than 99% of the Ocean?" *EOS*, November 12, 2018.

17. "Will the Fish Return? The Sorry State of Georges Bank," American Museum of Natural History, February, 2002, https://www.amnh.org/explore/videos/bio diversity/will-the-fish-return/the-sorry-story-of-georges-bank.

18. Pershing et al., "Slow Adaptation."

19. Christopher Burns, "Witnesses to Harpswell Shark Attack Heard Laughter, Then Screams," *Bangor Daily News*, July 28, 2020.

20. Deepa Shivaram, "Heat Waves Killed an Estimated 1 Billion Sea Creatures, and Scientists Fear Even More," National Public Radio, July 9, 2021, https://www .npr.org/2021/07/09/1014564664/billion-sea-creatures-mussels-dead-canada-british -columbia-vancouver.

21. "Commerce Department Declares West Coast Salmon Disaster," *Columbia Basin Bulletin*, December 20, 2018.

22. Steven A. Murawski, "A Brief History of the Groundfishing Industry in New England," Northeast Fisheries Science Center, mid-1990s, https://www.fisheries .noaa.gov/new-england-mid-atlantic/commercial-fishing/brief-history-ground fishing-industry-new-england.

23. Gewin, "Flip the Script."

24. Steve Urbon, "40 Years of Change: For Fishing Industry, the Spring of 1976 Was the Start of a New Era," *Standard-Times*, June 18, 2016.

25. Hilborn and Hilborn, *Overfishing*.

26. Mary Whitfill, "Can Scituate's Last Four Fishermen Stay Afloat?" *Patriot Ledger*, October 29, 2018.

27. Whitfill.

28. Bidgood, "A Famed Fishing Port Shudders As Its Codfather Goes to Jail," *New York Times*, February 11, 2018.

29. Magnuson-Stevens Fishery Conservation and Management Act Provisions; Fisheries of the Northeastern United States; Northeast Groundfish Fishery; Amendment 18, *Federal Register*, April 21, 2017.

3. As the Cowboys of the Sea Fade Away, a Postindustrial Fishery Emerges

Epigraph: Claire Martin, "Is That Real Tuna in Your Sushi? Now, a Way to Track That Fish," *New York Times*, August 13, 2016.

1. Don Cuddy, "Blue Harvest a Major New Presence Among City Houses," *Standard-Times*, August 19, 2017.

2. "Quinn Fisheries Buys Six of Carlos Rafael's Scallop Boats," *Standard-Times*, September 24, 2019.

3. Kiernan Dunlop, "Old 'Revere Copper and Brass' Will Get New Life as Shipyard," *Standard-Times*, July 27, 2019.

4. Martin, "Is That Real Tuna?"

5. Cuddy, "Blue Harvest."

6. Anastasla E. Lennon, "Former Workers Allege BASE Involved in Fraud," *Dartmouth Chronicle*, February 17, 2021.

7. Jason Huffman, "Blue Harvest CEO Says So Far, So Good for Voluntary Monitors," *Undercurrent News*, August 4, 2020.

8. Mary Whitfill, "Can Scituate's Last Four Fishermen Stay Afloat?" *Patriot Ledger*, October 29, 2018.

9. Martin, "Is That Real Tuna?"

4. Eating with the Ecosystem

Epigraph: "Growing a Values-Based Seafood Movement," Sitka Salmon Shares, https://sitkasalmonshares.com/pages/community-supported-fisheries

1. Critical Sustainabilities Project, UC Santa Cruz, UC Berkeley, UC Davis, U. of San Francisco, supported by the University of California Humanities Research Institute, 2012–2013, https://critical-sustainabilities.ucsc.edu/locavore/.

2. "Paul Greenberg: Uniting the Fishies and Foodies," *Oceana* (blog), February 15, 2011, https://usa.oceana.org/blog/paul-greenberg-uniting-fishies-and-foodies.

3. "Building the Massachusetts Seafood System: Innovation, Infrastructure, and Systems Change," Urban Harbors Institute conference, University of Massachusetts Boston, December 2017.

4. Claire Martin, "Is That Real Tuna in Your Sushi? Now, a Way to Track That Fish," *New York Times*, August 13, 2016.

5. Laine Welch," Community-Supported Fishery Programs Are Catching On," *Capital City Weekly*, September 16, 2009.

6. Robin McDowell, Margie Mason, and Martha Mendoza, "AP Investigation: Fish Billed as Local Isn't Always Local," Associated Press, June 14, 2018, https://apnews.com/article/north-america-us-news-ap-top-news-international-news-nc-state-wire-73646ad2aaac4666a7124806b2e6a5bc?-It-may-not-be-true.

7. "3rd Local Seafood Summit," Local Catch Network, Portland, Oregon, October 2019, https://localcatch.org/wp-content/uploads/2020/01/3rd-Local-Catch-Summit-Report.pdf.

8. "Eat Like a Fish," Eating with the Ecosystem, 2019, https://www.eatingwiththeecosystem.org/eat-like-a-fish.

9. "The Ecosystems in New England's Seafood-Shed," Eating with the Ecosystem, https://www.eatingwiththeecosystem.org/new-englands-seafood-shed.

10. John Mariani, "Blue Ridge's Barton Seaver: Chef of the Year," *Esquire*, October 12, 2009.

11. Madelyn Kearns, "Selling Aquaculture to Americans: Chef Barton Seaver Advocates for the 'Only Protein That Is Guilty Until Proven Innocent,' *Seafood Source*, December 7, 2018.

12. Barton Seaver, "Sustainable Seafood? Let's Get Smart," TED Talk, October 27, 2010, https://www.ted.com/speakers/barton_seaver.

13. Terry Gross, "'American Seafood' Author Recommends Putting 'Underloved' Fish on the Plate," *Fresh Air*, National Public Radio, December 18, 2017.

14. Barton Seaver, *The Joy of Seafood* (New York: Sterling Epicure, 2019), viii.

15. Jamie Coelho, "Fearless Fish Market Makes Local Seafood Species More Accessible," *Rhode Island Monthly*, August 16, 2020.

16. Harvard University Dining Services, https://dining.harvard.edu/about-huds /menus-change/reds-best-catch-week-program-harvard.

17. "Food Forward: The Sea, Dunn Vision," September 2020, https://dunnvision. ca/app/watch/series/3ad4ed30-ef8f-11ea-abb3-1b2d0b88b9de/cfecc420-ef91-11ea-ab3d -bf6f84b33453.

18. Taylor Witkin and Scott Nuzum, "Seafood Systems of the (Future) Present," *SeaAhead Newsletter*, May 11, 2020.

19. Joshua S. Stoll et al., "Alternative Seafood Networks during COVID-19: Implications for Resilience and Sustainability," Frontiers in Sustainable Food Systems, March 31, 2021, https://doi.org/10.3389/fsufs.2021.614368.

20. Witkin and Nuzum, "Seafood Systems."

21. Noah Asimow, "Statewide Ban on Lobstering Approved, with Exemption for Vineyard," *Vineyard Gazette*, January 29, 2021.

22. Stoll et al., "Alternative Seafood Networks."

23. Burt Helm, "Coffee Fuels a Lobster Empire," *New York Times*, March 3, 2019.

24. Ben Coniff, "Luke's Flash Frozen 101," Luke's Lobster (blog), https://www .lukeslobster.com/news-item/lukes-frozen-seafood-101/.

25. Coniff.

26. Coniff.

5. The Silicon Valley of Cod (and Other Innovation Clusters)

Epigraph: Thor Sigfusson, *The New Fish Wave: How to Ignite the Seafood Industry* (Sedgwick, ME: Leete's Island Books, 2020), 16.

1. What Are the Benefits of Cod Liver Oil?, *Medical News Today*, https://www .medicalnewstoday.com/articles/270071.

2. Robert S. Kirsner et al., "Fish Skin Grafts Compared to Human Amnion/ Chorion Membrane Allografts: A Double-Blind, Prospective, Randomized Clinical Trial of Acute Wound Healing," *Wound Repair and Regeneration*, 28 (September 11, 2019): 75–80, https://doi.org/10.1111/wrr.12761.

3. "Gudmundur Fertram Sigurjonsson: Entrepreneur, CEO, Biotech Evangelist & Oceans Advocate," LinkedIn, https://www.linkedin.com/in/fertram/.

4. Jared Gilmour, "Fish Skin Grafts Are Doctors' New Way to Heal Wounds on Burn Victims and Diabetics," *Miami Herald*, January 4, 2019.

5. Stephanie Ujhelyi, "ELCH Doctor Gives Glowing Review of New Wound Treatment," The Review, March 28, 2019.

6. Michael E. Porter, "Clusters and the New Economics of Competition," *Harvard Business Review*, November–December, 1998.

7. Thor Sigfusson, *The New Fish Wave: How to Ignite the Seafood Industry* (Sedgwick, ME: Leete's Island Books, 2020), 13.

8. "Ocean Cluster Analysis, Twice the Value for 40% of the Catch," Iceland Ocean Cluster, November 25, 2014, http://www.sjavarklasinn.is/en/portfolio/ioc -analysis-double-value-for-40-of-the-catch/.

9. In 1981, cod generated 0.75 SDR (an international currency value based on a basket of major currencies); in 2013, it generated 2.3 SDR (a bit more than a 300 percent gain), according to Matís, an Icelandic research firm specializing in food production, biotech, and food safety.

10. "Icelandic Spawning Cod Stock Largest in 40 Years, Thanks to Responsible Fisheries Management," *Iceland Magazine*, June 10, 2016. (The cod catch in 2017 was 253,000 tons, on par with the long-term (1955–2015) average, according to Iceland's Marine Research Institute.)

11. "Icelandic Spawning Cod Stock Largest."

12. "Sonardyne Suite for Dive Technologies' AUV," *Offshore Engineer*, January 12, 2021.

13. Global Fishing Watch–Ecuador, https://globalfishingwatch.org/press-release /ecuador-to-publish-data/.

14. Rachel Pichette, "Student Spotlight: Nicholas Calabrese," UMASS Dartmouth, October 27, 2020, https://gss.umassd.edu/2020/10/27/graduate-spotlight -series-student-spotlight-nicholas-calabrese/.

15. Don Cuddy, "SMAST Codfish Counting Innovation Looks Promising," *Standard-Times*, February 17, 2018.

16. Mika Higurashi, "Making the Grade: Leading the Way to Sashimi Grade Fish," Sea State Lecture Series, Gulf of Maine Research Institute, January 1, 2018.

17. Susan Axelrod, "Turning the Tide," *Maine Magazine*, March 2020.

18. Axelrod.

6. Run, Herring, Run: Restoring the Marine Food Web

Epigraph: St. Croix River and Alewife Resolution, "Joint Tribal Council of the Passamaquoddy Tribe," September 2013, https://www.nrcm.org/wp-content/uploads /2013/09/PassamaquoddyAlewivesResolution.pdf.

1. See John Banks, "Celebrating Progress in the Penobscot River," YouTube, November 10, 2020 (minute 18:18), https://www.youtube.com/watch?v=F6SQ7HNeHYE

2. Colin Woodward, "4 Dams, the Future of Kennebec Fish Runs and Salmon's Survival at Stake in Federal Licensing Battle," *Portland Press Herald*, January 3, 2021.

3. Tara R. Trinko Lake, Kyle R. Ravana, and Rory Saunders, "Evaluating Changes in Diadromous Species Distributions and Habitat Accessibility following the Penobscot River Restoration Project," *Marine and Coastal Fisheries*, 4 (2021): 284–293.

4. Byron Anderson, "Biographical Portrait: Spencer Fullerton Baird," *Forest History Today* (Fall 2002): 31–33.

5. Spencer Baird, *Report of the Commissioner for 1883* (US Fish and Fisheries Commission, 1883), https://penbay.org/cof/cof_1883.html.

6. Tara Lohan, "How Removing One Dam 20 Years Ago Changed Everything," *The Revelator*, February 11, 2019.

7. Bruce Babbitt, "Dams Are Not Forever," Ecological Society of America Annual Meeting, August 4, 1998.

8. Lohan, "Removing One Dam."

9. Lohan.

10. Lohan.

11. Peter Taylor, *From the Mountains to the Sea* (Yarmouth, ME: Islandport Press, 2020).

12. Henry David Thoreau, *The Maine Woods* (University of Virginia, Electronic Text Center, 2000), https://onlinereadfreenovel.com/henry-david-thoreau/34786 -the_maine_woods_writings_of_henry_d_thoreau.html.

13. In 2020, 9,190 shad were counted by mid-June, breaking the previous full-season season record of 8,231 set in 2016. In a single day, 3,844 shad were counted, more than the entire 2019 run, according to the *Bangor Daily News* (see note 14).

14. John Holyoke, "Fish Are Thriving in the Penobscot as Shad Returns Shatter Record," *Bangor Daily News*, June 19, 2020.

15. Herman Melville (1851). "Wheelbarrow," chap. 13 in *Moby Dick* (Lit2Go Edition), retrieved April 10, 2021, https://etc.usf.edu/lit2go/42/moby-dick/640 /chapter-13-wheelbarrow/.

16. Tony Chamberlain, "Famed Penobscot Gets Clean, Fresh Start," *Chicago Tribune*, June 30, 1991.

17. "What 25 Years of River Herring Data Tell Us about Restoring These 'Foundation' Fish in Buzzards Bay," Buzzards Bay Coalition, April 12, 2017, https:// www.savebuzzardsbay.org/news/25-years-of-river-herring-data/.

18. Julia Werth, "Old Dams and New Problems for Connecticut Homeowners," *CT Examiner*, September 30, 2019.

19. Werth.

20. Peter A. Smith, ed., "Fisherman, Lobsterman, Scientist, Historical Ecologist, Blooming Optimist," *Maine Mag*, October 2009.

21. Edward P. Ames, "Atlantic Cod Stock Structure in the Gulf of Maine," *Fisheries* 29, no. 1 (January 2004): 10–28.

22. Alec Wilkinson, "The Lobsterman," *New Yorker*, July 23, 2006.

23. Smith, "Fisherman, Lobsterman."

24. Lohan, "Removing One Dam."

25. Woodward, "4 Dams."

26. Justin R. Stevens, John F. Kocik, and Timothy F. Sheehan, "Modeling the Impacts of Dams and Stocking Practices on an Endangered Atlantic Salmon Population in the Penobscot River, Maine, USA," *Canadian Journal of Fisheries and Aquatic Sciences* 76, no. 10 (December 19, 2018): 1795–1807.

7. The Blue Revolution and Atlantic Salmon

Epigraph: Mark Kurlansky, *Salmon: A Fish, the Earth, and the History of Their Common* Fate (Ventura, CA: Patagonia, 2020), 294.

1. Kenneth W. Thompson, "The Green Revolution, Leadership and Partnership in Agriculture," *Review of Politics*, Vol. 34 No.2 (April 1972): 174–189.

2. Rick Boychuk, "The Blue Revolution," *New Internationalist*, no. 234, August 5, 1992.

3. G. Chaput et al., "Provision of Catch Advice Taking Account of Non-stationarity in Productivity of Atlantic Salmon (*Salmo salar L.*) in the Northwest Atlantic," *ICES Journal of Marine Science*, 62 (2005): 131–143.

4. Katherine Mills, Andrew Pershing, Timothy Sheehan, "Climate and Ecosystem Linkages Explain the Widespread Decline in North American Atlantic Salmon Populations, *Global Change Biology* 19 (2013): 3046–3061.

5. Mark Renkawitz et al., "Changing Trophic Structure and Energy Dynamics in the Northwest Atlantic: Implications for Atlantic Salmon Feeding at West Greenland," *Marine Ecology Progress Series*, 538 (October 2015), 10.3354/meps11470.

6. "Atlantic Salmon," Maine Aquaculture Innovation Center, https://www.maine aquaculture.org/atlantic-salmon/.

7. "Imports and Exports of Fishery Products Annual Summary, 2018," NOAA Fisheries, July 16, 2019.

8. Stian Olsen, "The Salmon License Auction Completed," *Salmon Business*, June 22, 2018.

9. Amy Nordum, "U.S. Consumers Might Get Their First Taste of Transgenic Salmon This Year," *IEEE Spectrum*, January 5, 2020.

10. "Whole Oceans, LLC, Bucksport," Maine Department of Environmental Protection, https://www.maine.gov/dep/projects/wholeoceans/index.html.

11. Michael Grunwald, "Will Your Next Salmon Come from a Massive Land Tank in Florida?" *Politico Magazine*, July 14, 2020.

12. "Atlantic Sapphire Blames RAS 'Design Weakness' for US Fish Die-Off," *Fish Farming Expert*, March 24, 2021.

13. Grunwald, "Will Your Next Salmon?"

14. Nancy Harmon Jenkins, "Salmon Farming Has Come a Long Way from the Early Days," MaineBoats.com, *Special Report on Aquaculture in Maine*, https://maineboats.com/harbors/reports/aquaculture/salmon-farming-has-come-a-long-way-from-the-early-days.

15. Nick Sambides, Jr., "This Company Is the Only One Raising Salmon in Maine So Far, As More Look to Join It," *Bangor Daily News*, July 29, 2019.

16. "Whole Oceans Signs 15-year Lease with Kuterra," *Aquaculture North America*, December 20, 2019.

17. Lynda Clancy, "State Approval of Belfast Salmon Farm Is Appealed; City Planning Board OKs Project," *Penobscot Bay Pilot*, December 27, 2020.

18. Abigail Curtis, "Don't Believe Everything You Hear about Belfast's Proposed Salmon Farm. Here's What You Need to Know," *Bangor Daily News*, September 16, 2019.

19. Rachel Sapin, "US Land-Based Salmon Farm Targets 2021 Launch," *Intrafish*, February 12, 2020.

20. Fred Bever, "Closed-Pen Salmon Farms Proposed for Frenchman Bay," *Maine Public*, March 10, 2021.

21. Cliff White, "Kingfish Zeeland Details Plans for New US RAS Yellowtail Farm in Jonesport, Maine," *SeafoodSource*, November 21, 2019.

22. Arieta Simke, "Black Soldier Flies Are the New Superstars of Sustainable Aquaculture," *Forbes*, December 1, 2019.

23. Salmon's Fish In–Fish Out ratio (FIFO)—calculated by the Marine Ingredients Organization using data from the UN's Food and Agriculture Organization—dropped from 2.57 in 2000 to 1.38 in 2010 to 0.82 in 2015. According to this metric,

the salmonid feed industry supports the production of more pounds of farmed fish than it uses as feed fish.

24. "Feeds for Aquaculture," NOAA Fisheries, https://www.fisheries.noaa.gov /insight/feeds-aquaculture.

25. Jeff Bercovici, "How Sea-Monkeys, NovoNutrients, and Synthetic Biology Will Save the World," *Inc.*, May 2019.

26. Nicki Holmyard, "Tilapia Players Debate Industry Future," *SeafoodSource*, April 25, 2018.

27. Ikram Belghit et al., "Black Soldier Fly Larvae Meal Can Replace Fish Meal in Diets of Sea-Water Phase Atlantic Salmon (*Salmo salar*)," *Aquaculture*, 503 (2019): 609–619.

28. Katie Serena, "Unbelievable but True: The Maine Coastline Is Longer Than California's Coastline," November 14, 2017.

29. Grunwald, "Will Your Next Salmon?"

8. Fish for a Small Planet

Epigraph: Charles. P. Pierce, "The Next Big Fish," *Boston Globe*, November 26, 2006.

1. "New Model for Aquaculture Takes Hold Far from the Sea," *Yale Environment-360*, June 21, 2011.

2. Pierce, "Next Big Fish."

3. Josh Goldman, "So, You Want to Be a Fish Farmer?" *World Aquaculture*, June 2016: 24–27.

4. Pierce, "Next Big Fish."

5. Pierce.

6. Australian Barramundi Farmers Association, Queensland, Australia, http:// www.abfa.org.au/barramundi_name.html.

7. Australian Barramundi Farmers Association.

8. Australian Barramundi Farmers Association.

9. "St. Croix River and Alewife Resolution," Joint Tribal Council of the Passamaquoddy Tribe, September 29, 2012, https://www.nrcm.org/wp-content /uploads/2013/09/PassamaquoddyAlewivesResolution.pdf.

10. *Yale Environment 360*, "New Model for Aquaculture."

11. Jessie Johnson, "Josh Goldman on the Future of Sustainable Aquaculture," *At the Table* podcast, November 10, 2017, https://www.atthetablepodcast.com/episode-03 -josh-goldman-future-sustainable-aquaculture/.

12. Josh Goldman, "So You Want to Be a Fish Farmer?"

13. Stephen Singer, "From Brass to Bass: Prized Mediterranean Fish Raised in One-Time Waterbury Factory," *Hartford Courant*, January 2, 2019.

14. Ann Loynd Burton, "A Waterbury Company Is Raising and Distributing Fish That Never Swim in the Sound," *Connecticut Magazine*, October 20, 2020.

15. Greg Bordonaro, "Ideal Fish Reels in New Customer Base Amid Restaurant Closures," *Hartford Business*, June 15, 2020.

16. "Market Needs Drive Blue Stream's Evolution," *Aquaculture North America*, September 18, 2019.

17. Patrik Svensson, *The Book of Eels: Our Enduring Fascination with the Most Mysterious Creature in the Natural World* (New York: Ecco/HarperCollins, 2019): 2

18. Svensson, 24, 50, 51.

19. Nestor Arellano, "Bangkok Shrimp Producer Builds RAS Facility in Florida," *RASTECH*, May 5, 2020, https://www.rastechmagazine.com/bangkok-shrimp -producer-builds-ras-facility-in-florida/.

9. The Beauty of Filter-Feeding Bivalves

Epigraph: Rachel Carson, *The Sea Around Us* (New York: Oxford University Press, 2018), p. 155.

1. Lela Nargi, "An Uptick in Industrial Aquaculture in Maine Has Lobster- and Fishermen Hot Under the Collar," *The Counter*, August 8, 2021, https://thecounter .org/uptick-industrial-aquaculture-maine-lobster-fishermen/.

2. Jason Smith, "Anti-aquaculture Groups Form Coalitions, Try Novel Tacks to Stop Permits," *Undercurrent News*, August 19, 2021.

3. John G. Ruge, "Florida Oysters," *Fishing Gazette*, March 26, 1898, 193–194.

4. Clyde L. MacKenzie Jr., "History of Oystering in the United States and Canada, Featuring the Eight Greatest Oyster Estuaries," *Marine Fisheries Review*, NOAA Scientific Publications Office.

5. Doe Boyle, "Oystering in Connecticut, from Colonial Times to the 21st century," Connecticut History, a CT Humanities Project, https://connecticuthistory .org/oystering-in-connecticut-from-colonial-times-to-today.

6. Ruge, "Florida Oysters."

7. Carmen Nigro, "History on the Half Shell: The Story of New York City and Its Oysters," New York Public Library, Milstein Division of U.S. History, Local History & Genealogy, June 2, 2011.

8. MacKenzie, "History of Oystering."

9. Tom Seaman, "Oyster Bars Are Like Cigars in the '90s. They are Hot," *Undercurrent News*, January 16, 2014.

10. Ed Myers, "The Maine Guide to Mussel Raft Culture," Island Institute, September 1999, https://cpb-us-w2.wpmucdn.com/wpsites.maine.edu/dist/1/43/files /2015/05/mussel-raft-guide-1ykcca2.pdf.

11. Fred Ferretti, "Farming the Sea Bottom to Fill Mussel Demand," *New York Times*, August 24, 1983.

12. Ferretti.

13. Eider ducks are the primary predator of blue mussels. "I had an interesting conversation with an ornithologist this week," Silkes said in 2021. "His favorite animal is the eider duck and mine is the blue mussel, so we didn't agree there, but we were in agreement that something is going on with wild mussels. Eider ducks are at low levels because the wild mussels aren't there."

14. Myers, "The Maine Guide."

15. "SOAR: Supporting Oyster Aquaculture and Reproduction," The Nature Conservancy, https://www.nature.org/en-us/what-we-do/our-priorities/provide-food-and-water-sustainably/food-and-water-stories/oyster-covid-relief-restoration/.

During the COVID lockdown and restaurant closures that hurt shellfish (and other) farmers, The Nature Conservancy in partnership with Pew Charitable Trusts created the Supporting Oyster Aquaculture and Restoration (SOAR) program, spending $2 million to buy more than 5 million oysters in New England, the Mid-Atlantic and Washington state to restore shellfish reefs at 20 locations. Robert Jones, Global Lead for The Nature Conservancy's Aquaculture Program, coordinated with NOAA and the US Department of Agriculture, which offered similar but smaller programs in several states.

10. Kelp—for Food, Fuel, Pharma

Epigraph: Bren Smith, *Eat Like a Fish: My Adventures Farming the Ocean to Fight Climate Change* (New York: Vintage Books, 2020): 131.

1. Tom Breen, "From the Lab to the Dinner Table: Seaweed," *UCONN Today*, August 19, 2013.

2. Dana Goodyear, "A New Leaf," *New Yorker*, November 2, 2015.

3. Melissa Godin, "The Ocean Farmers Trying to Save the World with Seaweed," *Time*, September 4, 2020.

4. Charles Yarish, "Developing the US Seaweed Industry," Lecture at the Darien Men's Association, October 14, 2020, https://youtu.be/jFnVv3aXD3s.

5. Alyse Whitney, "15 Spice Blends We Can't Live Without," *Bon Appetit*, January 30, 2017.

6. Godin, "The Ocean Farmers."

7. Godin.

8. Scott Lindell, "Farming the Ocean to Feed the World," TEDx Cambridge, October 5, 2020, https://www.tedxcambridge.com/talk/farming-the-ocean-to-feed-the-world/.

9. "Milford Lab Takes on Sugar Kelp Cultivation," NOAA Fisheries, October 13, 2017.

10. Susie Arnold, "When Kelp Met Mussel . . . ," Island Institute, *The Working Waterfront*, October 26, 2018.

11. Alexis Benveniste, "This Startup Grows Kelp Then Sinks It to Pull Carbon from the Air," CNN Business, May 3, 2021.

12. Ann Trieger Kurland, "Kelp from Off the Maine Coast Is Turned into Seaweed Salad, Kimchi, Kraut, and Cubes," *Boston Globe*, February 9, 2021.

13. Amelia Nielson-Stowell, "Q&A with CEO of Atlantic Sea Farms," Fermentation Society, December 7, 2020.

14. Bren Smith, "Frontlines of the Blue-Green Economic Revolution," *In These Times*, February 26, 2016.

15. Smith, "Frontlines."

16. *Aquaculture Environment Interactions*, 8 (April 19, 2016): 201–205.

17. "A Culinary Celebration of IMTA Products," The Seaweed and Integrated Multi-Trophic Research Laboratory of Thierry Chopin, University of New Brunswick, November 2013, https://www2.unb.ca/chopinlab/imta/news/IMTA%20 Dinner/index.html/.

18. "Culinary Celebration."

19. Lesley Evans Ogden, "Aquaculture's Turquoise Revolution: Multitrophic Methods Bring Recycling to the Seas," *BioScience* 63, no. 9 (September 2013): 697–704.

20. Kezia Parkins, "Bren Smith: The Fisherman Pioneering 3D Ocean Farming," *Global Shakers*, August 28, 2019.

21. Andrea Miller, "Food, Fertilizer, Fuel: Why the World's Demand for Seaweed Is Growing," *CNBC.com*, September 19, 2020.

22. "Fuller Challenge Archive," Buckminster Fuller Institute, https://www.bfi.org /challenge.

23. "Commercial Seaweed Market Size to Exceed $95bn by 2027," *Global Market Insights*, July 28, 2021, https://www.gminsights.com/pressrelease/commercial-seaweed -market.

24. Yarish, "Developing the US Seaweed Industry."

25. "Fucoidan," Memorial Sloan Kettering Cancer Center, https://www.mskcc.org /cancer-care/integrative-medicine/herbs/fucoidan.

26. Sarah Mizes-Tan, "Kelp Farming Sees a Rise in Interest on the Cape," CAI: Local NPR for the Cape, Coast & Islands, May 10, 2018.

27. Lindell, "Farming the Ocean to Feed the World."

11. The Holy Grail: Farming the Open Ocean

Epigraph: Interview, 1971, wikiquote.org, https://en.wikiquote.org/wiki/Jacques -Yves_Cousteau.

1. "New Study Measures Nations' SeafoodPrint," *Oceana*, September 9, 2010.

2. Steve Newborn, "Nation's First Deepwater Fish Farm Proposed for Gulf Off Sarasota," WUSF Public Media, September 27, 2019.

3. Allessandra Bianchi, "The Next Seafood Frontier: The Ocean," *Fortune Small Business*, April 28, 2009

4. Josh Schonwald, "A Fish Farmer's Tale," *Miami Times*, January 19, 2006.

5. Whit Richardson, "Open Blue Sea Farms," *SeafoodSource*, November 16, 2009.

6. Richardson.

7. Richardson.

8. Bianchi, "The Next Seafood Frontier."

9. Bianchi.

10. Jeffrey Kofman, "Farming the Fish of the Future," ABC News, February 27, 2008.

11. Aaron W. Welch et al., "The Nutrient Footprint of a Submerged-Cage Offshore Aquaculture Facility Located in the Tropical Caribbean," *Journal of World Aquaculture Society* 50, no. 5–6 (February 2019).

12. Daniel Stone, "The Other White Meat," *National Geographic*, April 30, 2014.

13. James Wright, "Kona Blue Dissolved, Kampachi Farms Launched," *SeafoodSource*, September 18, 2011.

14. Wikipedia, https://en.wikipedia.org/wiki/Velella.

15. "*Time* Hails 'Drifting Fish Farm' One of Best Inventions of Year," *Undercurrent News*, November 5, 2012.

16. Patrik Jonsson, "Deep-Water Fish Farming in the Gulf: Who Benefits?" *Christian Science Monitor*, August 31, 2020.

17. Julie Cart, "Did Sea Farm Debacle Sink California Aquaculture?" *Cal Matters*, May 13, 2020.

18. Deborah Sullivan Brennan, "Open-Ocean Fish Farm Proposed Off San Diego Coast Could Be First in Federal Waters," *Los Angeles Times*, September 20, 2020.

19. Catherine Smart, "When a Chef and a Marine Biologist Team Up, Everyone Wins," *Boston Globe*, December 18, 2017.

20. Renee Ebersol, "At Sea and in Court, the Fight to Save Right Whales Intensifies," *Yale Environment 360*, November 17, 2020.

21. David Abel, "New U.S. Plan to Aid Right Whales Faces Wide-Ranging Wrath," *Boston Globe*, March 8, 2021.

22. Ebersol, "At Sea and in Court."

23. Abel, "Plan to Aid Right Whales."

24. Scott Lindell, "Farming the Ocean to Feed the World," TEDx Cambridge, Massachusetts, October 5, 2020, https://www.tedxcambridge.com/talk/farming-the-ocean-to-feed-the-world/.

25. "Deep Water Sites Off the U.S. Northeast Coast Are Suitable for Offshore Blue Mussel Farms," NOAA Fisheries, October 16, 2019, https://www.fisheries.noaa.gov/feature-story/deep-water-sites-us-northeast-coast-are-suitable-offshore-blue-mussel-farms.

26. Andrew Hoyle, "World's First Offshore Fish Farm Arrives in Norway," *Fish Farming Expert*, May 8, 2017.

27. "China Plans Huge Mobile Fish Farm Vessel for Early 2022," *Undercurrent News*, June 10, 2020.

12. Big Data versus Pirates on the High Seas

Epigraph: Monique Ross and Ann Arnol, "*Thunder* versus Sea Shepherd: The True Story of the World's Longest Ship Chase," ABC Radio National, August 18, 2018.

1. Lisa McKinnon Munde, "The Great Fishing Competition," *War on the Rocks*," August 17, 2020.

2. Njiraini Muhira, "Limited Sovereignty as African Countries Mortgage Resources to China," *Maritime Executive*, April 4, 2021.

3. Munde, "The Great Fishing Competition."

4. Julia John, "Indonesia's New Intelligence Hub Wields Data in the War on Illegal Fishing," *Mongabay*, September 29, 2020.

5. Mansi Konar and U. Rashid Sumalia, "Illicit Trade in Marine Resources

Keeps Billions Out of Pacific Economies Every Year," World Resources Institute, December 16, 2019.

6. "Artisanal Fishers Are on the Frontline of the Overfishing Crisis," United Nations Conference on Trade and Development (UNCTAD), April 5, 2017, https://unctad.org/news/artisanal-fishers-are-frontline-overfishing-crisis.

7. Global Fishing Watch–Ecuador, https://globalfishingwatch.org/press-release/ecuador-to-publish-data/.

8. Global Fishing Watch–Costa Rica, https://globalfishingwatch.org/press-release/costa-rica-mou/.

9. John, "Indonesia's New Intelligence Hub."

10. "Escaped Fishing Vessel Recaptured in Indonesia," *Maritime Executive*, April 9, 2018.

11. "Fighting Illegal, Unreported, and Unregulated Fishing," *Interpol News*, June 5, 2019.

12. Ian Urbina, *Outlaw Ocean: Journeys across the Last Untamed Frontier* (New York: Vintage Books/Penguin Random House, September 2020), 9.

13. Urbina, *Outlaw Ocean*, 7, 9.

14. "Pirate Fishing Tycoon Hit with 8.2 Million Euro Fine in Spain," *Sea Shepherd News*, April 17, 2018.

15. Urbina, *Outlaw Ocean*, 7.

16. "Overfishing, Illegal, and Destructive Fishing," Marine Stewardship Council, https://www.msc.org/what-we-are-doing/oceans-at-risk/overfishing-illegal-and-destructive-fishing.

17. "Fighting Illegal, Unreported, and Unregulated Fishing," *Interpol News*, December 7, 2020.

18. Christopher Joyce, "Chinese Taste for Fish Bladder Threatens Rare Porpoise in Mexico," National Public Radio, *All Things Considered*, February 9, 2016.

19. "How to End Illegal Fishing," The Pew Charitable Trusts, December 2013.

20. Sarah Bladen, "The Capture of the NV NIKA: A Case of Illicit Fishing and a Showcase for How to Beat It," *Global Fishing Watch*, July 23, 2019.

21. Ganapathiraju Pramod et al., "Estimates of Illegal and Unreported Fish in Seafood Imports to the USA, *Marine Policy*, 48 (2014): 102–113, https://doi.org/10.1016/j.marpol.2014.03.019.

22. Tony Long, "Fast-Tracking Law-Abiding Ships at Ports Could Help End Illegal Fishing, *Global Fishing Watch*, February 8, 2020.

23. Reniel B. Cabral et al., "Rapid and Lasting Gains from Solving Illegal Fishing," *Nature Ecology Evolution*, 2 (2018): 650–658, https://doi.org/10.1038/s41559-018-0499-1.

24. An analysis of Global Fishing Watch data showed a 90 percent reduction in fishing hours of foreign vessels, with most of the reduction from China, Thailand, Taiwan, and South Korea. Consequently, Indonesia dropped from fifteenth and thirteenth in the world in 2013 and 2014 to below eightieth in 2015 and 2016. To put that into economic terms, if Indonesia had not implemented its illegal-fishing reductions, it would be looking at a 59 percent decrease in catch and a 64 percent decrease in profit by 2035. However, with the reduction and assuming sustainable management

to achieve maximum sustainable yield, skipjack-tuna landings and profit could increase by 14 and 12 percent, respectively.

25. Cabral et al., "Rapid and Lasting Gains."

13. Conservation and Climate, Adaptation and Resilience

Epigraph: Daniel Pauly, interview with author, June 2019.

1. Douglas J. McCauley et al., "Marine Defaunation: Animal Loss in the Global Ocean, *Science* 347, no. 6219 (January 16, 2015): 247–253, DOI: 10.1126/science.1255641.

2. Douglas J. McCauley et al. In last four decades, marine vertebrates (fish, seabirds, sea turtles, and marine mammals) collectively have declined in abundance by an average 22 percent.

3. David B. Wake and Vance T. Vredenburg, "Are We in the Midst of the Sixth Mass Extinction? A View from the World of Amphibians," Proceedings of the National Academy of Sciences, August 2008, 105 (Supplement 1) 11466-11473, DOI: 10.1073/pnas.0801921105.

4. A mass extinction is defined as a loss of ~75 percent of all species on the planet over a geologically short period of time. Corey J.S. Bradshoe et al., "Underestimating the Challenges of Avoiding a Ghastly Future," *Frontiers in Conservation Science*, 13, Article 615419, January 13, 2021, doi: 10.3389/fcosc.2020.615419.

5. McCauley et al., 247.

6. Kathleen M. Wong, "In Hot Water Due to Climate Change, Many Ocean Fish Are Moving to Higher Latitudes or Deeper Waters to Find the Conditions They Need to Survive," *San Francisco Estuary Magazine*, https://www.sfestuary.org/estuary-news-pearls-hot-water/.

7. "Ocean Deoxygenation," International Union for Conservation of Nature, https://www.iucn.org/resources/issues-briefs/ocean-deoxygenation.

8. Ben Goldfarb, "Feeling the Heat: How Fish Are Migrating from Warming Waters," *Yale Environment 360*, June 15, 2017.

9. Curtis Deutsch et al., "Climate Change Tightens a Metabolic Constraint on Marine Habitats," *Science* 348, no. 6239 (June 5, 2015): 1132–1135, DOI: 10.1126/science.aaa1605.

10. Jan Ellen Spiegel, "Beneath the Waves, Climate Change Puts Marine Life on the Move," *CT Mirror*, August 8, 2016.

11. Jonathan A. Hare et al., "A Vulnerability Assessment of Fish and Invertebrates to Climate Change on the Northeast U.S. Continental Shelf," *PLOS ONE* 11, no. 2 (February 3, 2016), https://doi.org/10.1371/journal.pone.0146756.

12. Gavin MacRae, "Will Climate Change Threaten Earth's Other 'Lung'?'" *The Revelator*, Center for Biological Diversity, April 16, 2020.

13. "Percentage of Total Population Living in Coastal Areas," United Nations, https://www.un.org/esa/sustdev/natlinfo/indicators/methodology_sheets/oceans_seas_coasts/pop_coastal_areas.pdf.

14. "Ocean Acidification," NOAA.gov, https://www.noaa.gov/education/resource-collections/ocean-coasts/ocean-acidification. "When the ocean absorbs carbon

dioxide, it reacts with seawater and the resultant carbonic acid releases hydrogen ions that increase the acidity of the ocean, measured as pH—on a scale from 0 (highly acidic) to 14 (alkaline). Prior to the Industrial Revolution, average ocean pH was about 8.2. Today, the average ocean pH is about 8.1. This is a seemingly minor shift, but the scale is logarithmic meaning that each decrease of one pH integer is a tenfold increase in acidity. Acid rain, by contrast, which includes nitrous oxides and sulphur dioxide, is much more acidic than ocean water with a pH of 4.2–4.4."

15. "Scientists Pinpoint How Ocean Acidification Weakens Coral Skeletons," Woods Hole Oceanographic Institution, January 29, 2018.

16. Jennie E. Rheuban et al., "Projected Impacts of Future Climate Change, Ocean Acidification, and Management on the US Atlantic Sea Scallop (*Placopecten magellanicus*) fishery," *PLOS ONE* 13, no. 9 (September 21, 2018), https://doi.org/10.1371/journal.pone.0203536.

17. "Gulf of Maine 2050 International Symposium Report: Ocean Acidification," Gulf of Maine Research Institute, 2020.

18. Chris Arsenault, "Countries Fall Short of UN Pledge to Protect 10% of World's Oceans by 2020," *Mongabay*, December 2, 2020.

19. Enric Sala, "Let's Turn the High Seas into the World's Largest Nature Reserve," TED Talk, June 6, 2018, https://www.ted.com/talks/enric_sala_let_s_turn_the_high_seas_into_the_world_s_largest_nature_reserve?language=en.

20. Crow White and Christopher Costello, "Close the High Seas to Fishing?" *PLOS Biol* 12, no. 3 (March 25, 2014), https://doi.org/10.1371/journal.pbio.1001826.

21. White and Costello.

22. Enric Sala et al., "The Economics of Fishing the High Seas," *Science Advances* 4, no. 6 (June 6, 2018), DOI: 10.1126/sciadv.aat2504.

23. U. Rashid Sumaila et al., "Updated Estimates and Analysis of Global Fisheries Subsidies," *Marine Policy*, 109 (2019), https://doi.org/10.1016/j.marpol.2019.103695.

24. Helen Scales, *The Brilliant Abyss: Exploring the Majestic, Hidden Life of the Deep Ocean, and the Looming Threat That Imperils It* (New York: Atlantic Monthly Press, July 6, 2021).

25. "Interview with Daniel Pauly: The Present and the Future of the World and U.S. Fisheries," American Fisheries Society, *Fisheries News and Science*, November 9, 2015.

26. Mary Gleason et al., "Designing a Network of Marine Protected Areas in California: Achievements, Costs, Lessons Learned, and Challenges Ahead," *Ocean & Coastal Management*, 74 (2013): 90–101, https://doi.org/10.1016/j.ocecoaman.2012.08.013.

27. Juliet Eilperin, "Obama Creates the Largest Protected Place on the Planet, in Hawaii," *Washington Post*, August 26, 2016.

28. Enric Sala et al., "Protecting the Global Ocean for Biodiversity, Food and Climate," *Nature* 592 (2021): 397–402, https://doi.org/10.1038/s41586-021-03371-z.

29. Sala et al.: Focusing exclusively on *biodiversity*, protecting 90 percent of the maximum potential benefits could be accomplished by closing off 21 percent of the ocean—43 percent in EEZs and 6 percent in the high seas. That would increase

protection of endangered species from 1.5 percent of their current range to 87 percent. Focusing exclusively on *fishing yield*, protecting 28 percent of the ocean could increase yield by 5.9 million metric tons—assuming fisheries that were closed moved into new areas—and even more if they did not. Future fishing yields would improve even outside MPAs due to adult and larval spillover. This study looked at 1,150 commercial species, comprising 71 percent of global maximum sustainable yield. Focusing exclusively on *carbon sequestration*, protecting just 3.6 percent of the world's ocean would lead to a huge reduction in the release of carbon dioxide. Marine sediments hold the world's largest pool of organic carbon. When "disturbed" by bottom trawlers, sedimentary carbon turns into carbon dioxide and "reduces the buffering capacity of the ocean." The first trawl releases the most carbon dioxide but continued trawling still releases millions of metric tons per year. "Only 1.3 percent of the ocean is trawled every year. The global benefit of protection for sedimentary carbon accrues quickly—because the footprint of trawling is small," write the authors. Priority areas where anthropogenic threats and carbon stocks are highest include China's EEZ, Europe's Atlantic Coast, and other productive upwelling areas, some in Russia.

30. Mike MacEacheran, "The City That Lit the World," http://www.bbc.com/travel/story/20180719-the-city-that-lit-the-world.

31. Henry Beetle Hough, *Wamsutta of New Bedford, 1846–1946: A Story of New England Enterprise* (Ann Arbor: University of Michigan, 1946, digitized August 14, 2006).

32. "A Century of Progress and Innovation: The New Bedford Fishing Fleet," New Bedford Fishing Heritage Center, https://fishingheritagecenter.org/exhibits/industry-timeline/.

33. Ruby Gonzalez, "New Bedford Top Bet for Aquaculture Development," *Aquaculture North America*, March 26, 2019.

34. Jon Chesto, "$113m New Bedford Marine Terminal Sits Largely Idle," *Boston Globe*, August 30, 2015.

35. Anastasia E. Lennon, "America's Leader in Offshore Wind: What Vineyard Wind Approval Means for New Bedford," *Standard-Times*, May 12, 2021.

About the Author

Photo by Phil Mello, Big Fish Studio

As a writer and editor, Nicholas P. Sullivan has focused on how technology and entrepreneurship affect international development. *The Blue Revolution* is his fourth book. It follows *Money, Real Quick: Kenya's Disruptive Mobile Money Innovation*; *You Can Hear Me Now: How Microloans and Cell Phones Are Connecting the World's Poor to the Global Economy*; and *Computer Power for Your Small Business*. He has been codirector of The Fletcher School's Leadership Program for Financial Inclusion (Tufts University), a consultant to central banks in developing countries, and a visiting scholar at MIT's Legatum Center for International Development. In the publishing world, he was publisher of *Innovations: Technology/Governance/Globalization* (MIT Press); editor-in-chief of *Inc.com* (Goldhirsh Group); and editor-in-chief of *Home Office Computing* (Scholastic Corp.), where he wrote the long-running column *Workstyles* about remote work in the information age. Sullivan is currently a writer for Oliver Wyman, a global consulting firm; a senior fellow at The Fletcher School's Council on Emerging Market Enterprises; and a senior research fellow at Fletcher's Maritime Studies Program. He has twice been a resident fellow at the Rockefeller Foundation's Bellagio Center. A graduate of Harvard University and The Fletcher School of Law & Diplomacy, he lives in Dartmouth, Massachusetts.

Index